More praise for *The Ecstatic Journey*

"Absorbing reading . . . Destined to become a classic . . . A splendid book on a subject which is, at best, a difficult one on which to speak. The nature of mysticism, with its emphasis on the interior territory of spirituality, is usually expressed best in silence. Yet Burnham has managed to capture this territory for us with amazing clarity and depth, through personal anecry of mysticism and stories of tra- ditions. This book is a en- gaged in the study and this postmodern era. . . . A and the agony of the spiritu eeply comforting and a valuable companion to her/his journey. . . . I heartily recommend it!"

— *Convergence* magazine

"Spiritual seekers are less interested in old-style religion than they are in exotic journeys that promise direct encounters with the transcendent. . . . [Burnham] blends historic research with down-home spirituality in ways that should broaden her book's appeal."

— *Los Angeles Times*

"Amazing . . . A deeply moving personal account . . . Readers who have enjoyed her previous books (*A Book of Angels, Angel Letters, Revelations*) will be intrigued by the 'story behind' the author's work. . . . This book will speak to those who are struggling to reconcile the sublimity and the insecurity that accompany the radical life changes of attempting to live 'spiritually.' "

— *NAPRA ReView*

"Provocative . . . *The Ecstatic Journey* offers some landmarks along the way. . . .[A] sprightly, sometimes humorous volume."

— *The Taos News*

T·H·E
ECSTATIC
JOURNEY

WALKING THE MYSTICAL PATH
IN EVERYDAY LIFE

SOPHY
BURNHAM

BALLANTINE BOOKS
NEW YORK

A Ballantine Book
Published by The Ballantine Publishing Group

Copyright © 1997 by Sophy Burnham

Grateful acknowledgment is made to the following for permission to reprint previously published material:

Beacon Press: Excerpts from poems from *The Kabir Book*, versions by Robert Bly. Copyright © 1971, 1977 by Robert Bly. Reprinted by permission of Beacon Press, Boston. Based on *The Poems of Kabir* by Rabindranath Tagore, published by Macmillan General Books, London.

Harcourt Brace & Company and Faber and Faber Ltd.: Excerpt from "The Waste Land" from *Collected Poems 1909–1962* by T. S. Eliot. Copyright © 1936 by Harcourt Brace & Company, copyright © 1964, 1963 by T. S. Eliot. Reprinted by permission of the publishers, Harcourt Brace & Company and Faber and Faber Ltd.

Harvard University Press: Poem #388 from *The Poems of Emily Dickinson*, Thomas H. Johnson, ed., Cambridge, Mass.: The Belknap Press of Harvard University Press. Copyright © 1951, 1955, 1979, 1983 by the President and Fellows of Harvard College. Reprinted by permission of the publishers and the Trustees of Amherst College.

Houghton Mifflin Company and Sterling Lord Literistic, Inc.: Excerpt from "Rowing" from *The Awful Rowing Toward God* by Anne Sexton. Copyright © 1975 by Loring Conant, Jr., executor of the Estate of Anne Sexton. Reprinted by permission of Houghton Mifflin Company and Sterling Lord Literistic, Inc. All rights reserved.

Alfred A. Knopf, Inc., and Gower Publishing Limited: Excerpts from *Tao Te Ching* by Lao Tsu, translated by Gia-fu Feng and Jane English. Reprinted by permission of Alfred A. Knopf, Inc., and Gower Publishing Limited.

New Directions Publishing Corp.: Excerpts from *Poems from the Book of Hours* by Rainer Maria Rilke, translated by Babette Deutch. Copyright © 1941 by New Directions Publishing Corp. Reprinted by permission of New Directions Publishing Corp.

Sheed & Ward: Excerpts from *The Life of Teresa of Jesus: The Autobiography of St. Teresa of Avila*, translated by E. Allison Peers. Reprinted by permission of Sheed & Ward, 115 E. Armour Blvd., Kansas City, MO 64111. (800) 333-7373.

The University of Chicago Press: Excerpts from *Poems of St. John of the Cross*, translated by John Frederick Nims. Copyright © 1959, 1968, 1979 by John Frederick Nims. Reprinted by permission of The University of Chicago Press.

University of Pittsburgh Press: Excerpts from *The World Was Flooded with Light: A Mystical Experience Remembered* by Genevieve W. Foster. Copyright © 1985 by University of Pittsburgh Press. Reprinted by permission of University of Pittsburgh Press.

www.randomhouse.com/BB/

Library of Congress Catalog Card Number: 98-96982

ISBN 0-345-42479-4

Cover design by Barbara Leff
Cover painting: Joachim Patinir, *The Penitence of St. Jerome*. The Metropolitan Museum of Art, Fletcher Fund, 1936 (36.14). Photograph © 1980 The Metropolitan Museum of Art

Manufactured in the United States of America

First Hardcover Edition: November 1997
First Trade Paperback Edition: April 1999

10 9 8 7 6 5 4 3 2 1

Awake! For Morning in the Bowl of Night
Has flung the Stone that puts the Stars to Flight
—*RUBÁIYÁT OF OMAR KHAYYÁM*

CONTENTS

ACKNOWLEDGMENTS

It is customary for an author to acknowledge all those who have helped with the creation and production of a book, and in this vein I gratefully thank Joëlle Delbourgo, who first encouraged this work; my editor, Joanne Wyckoff, who has shepherded it to maturity; and my friend and agent, Anne Edelstein.

In addition I thank all those who have helped with their prayers, their letters, and their recommendations, searching and finding; all those who have brought little treasures to this work, and you know who you are. I thank all those who have written your beautiful stories to me over the past years, my only regret being that we could not print them all.

Finally and most humbly, I thank all spiritual forces that aided in the construction of this work, which is offered to the glory of God and in praise to all Holy Names.

Sing praises to God, sing praises: sing praises unto our King, sing praises.

—PSALMS 47:6

Make a joyful noise unto God, all ye lands: Sing forth the honour of his name: make his praise glorious.

—PSALMS 66:1–2

Know this Atman,
Unborn, undying,
Never ceasing,
Never beginning,
Deathless, birthless,
Unchanging for ever.

—BHAGAVAD GITA

INTRODUCTION

When *A Book of Angels* was published in 1990, I was astonished at its reception. People bought ten and twelve copies at a time to give to their friends, who in turn bought ten and fifteen copies to give away to others. I was swept off my feet by the sudden change from the quiet obscurity of an unknown writer to being called the "angel lady" or "angel expert," and my surprise was matched only by that of my publisher.

Yet even while working on that book I'd had an intuition—a psychic glimmering—that it would comprise the first of three books; that the second, taken from letters received, would describe other people's experiences with angels; and the third would be about a subtler and possibly more difficult subject, the mystical experience itself, which I define as the direct encounter with God (however that word is understood).

A Book of Angels was followed by *Angel Letters*. Together, these works have been translated into twenty languages. Now the third and last in this series appears, the volume you are holding in your hands. It has been a frightening project, for in working on it I realize my own inadequacy and realize, too, that almost everything of importance ever spoken or written relates in some way to this subject: the Psalms, the Torah, the Qur'an, the Holy

1

Bible, all our prayer books and shamanistic literature, the poetry and sacred books of every culture and every religion, from Sikhism to Baha'i. To make the topic more difficult to grapple with is the fact that no one can speak of these things easily, for what we know is best communicated in silence or in music and metaphor, in poetry, in parable and paradox; and yet one moment of this connection with the Divine, one taste of that honey, and we are never again the same. The Spanish monk Saint John of the Cross wrote in one of his ecstatic poems about how you know nothing when struck by these moments of grace yet transcend all knowledge.

> I entered—yes but where,
> knew nothing being there,
> burst the mind's barrier.
>
> I entered—where, who knows?—
> but being where I would
> (where, who dare suppose?)
> great things understood
> no telling if I could.
> Knew nothing being there,
> burst the mind's barrier.[1]

We can read books. We can go to church or synagogue or mosque, study the Scriptures; but we forget that the formation of a religion (from the Latin *religare*, to tie back) always comes *after* the revelation. The mystic sees, then tries to explain, hold on to what was shown, tries to freeze the transport by creating a formal worship that will recapture that moment with the Divine. Then comes fear. Because we cannot reclaim the ecstasy, we think we must be doing something wrong. We work at it harder. Now the religion tightens around itself; it grows into an institution, and often tips into a bureaucracy, with its hierophants using their position to control the followers through guilt or fear—always in the vain attempt to re-create that magic moment of grace. In fact what the mystic saw was that nothing exists but love: there is no wrong so long as we love. Christ, guru, rabbi, priest, teacher, lama, master all come carrying the same message. "Keep my sheep," said Christ on his last night. "Love one another as I have loved you. Keep my sheep."

Saint Ignatius of Loyola confessed that "a single hour of meditation . . . had taught him more truths about heavenly things than all the teachings of all the doctors put together." His Jesuit biographer, Daniello Bartoli, offers this account:

> One day in orison, on the steps of the choir of the Dominican church, he saw in a distinct manner the plan of divine wisdom in the creation of the world. On another occasion, during a procession, his spirit was ravished in God, and it was given him to contemplate, in a form and images fitted to the weak understanding of a dweller on the earth, the deep mystery of the holy Trinity. This

last vision flooded his heart with such sweetness, that the mere memory of it in after times made him shed abundant tears.[2]

Near the end of his life, Saint Thomas Aquinas experienced a similar moment of "infused contemplation," after which he said that everything he had written, thought, argued, and defined during his brilliant theological life "was no better than straw or chaff." Afterward he refused to continue working on his unfinished book.

And Saint Teresa of Avila wrote that one day

it was granted me to perceive in one instant how all things are seen and contained in God. I did not perceive them in their proper form, and nevertheless the view I had of them was of a sovereign clearness, and has remained vividly impressed upon my soul. . . . The view was so subtle and delicate that the understanding cannot grasp it.[3]

In this book, you will find mixed the sayings and wisdom of the mystics of numerous faiths. We know so little about this phenomenon: that many people have such experiences, that there are various levels of mystical encounter, that afterward the person may undergo a profound emotional and psychological transformation. What we don't know is greater by far than what we do. We know the encounter creates turmoil. A tornado has passed through and it leaves havoc in its wake. The cleanup may take time. But why does the encounter come to one person and not another, at one moment and not another? We do not know. It is my belief that the experience comes to almost everyone and that these moments of grace are increasing now. More people are having them, although this may only be an impression, apparent because people seem more willing than earlier to reveal these sacred entries to the heart. Some people claim that mystical visions are occurring more frequently because we, as a species, are evolving, so that what was once the province of a few saints is now our common heritage.

This book is motivated by certain raptures and epiphanies granted me, and especially by some that happened to me nearly twenty years ago. I have already written two novels—*Revelations* and *The President's Angel*—about what happens when you have a mystical experience. Now I struggle to capture in the clumsier nonfiction form a story that is unconventional, erotic, creative, confusing. . . . I write in case others have had such experiences and want to know they are not alone. I write to note some landmarks on the path, point out the avalanche slopes, the food caches, and the cairns left by others long before. Twenty years ago, I felt alone, blindly groping on the path. Yet looking back I see that guides, both human and spiritual, remained always at my side, and that, yes, in the words of Psalm 91,

. . . he will give his angels charge of you,
   to guard you in all your ways.
On their hands they will bear you up,
   lest you dash your foot against a stone.

Nonetheless the journey itself is hard. It always begins, it seems, with a sick and longing soul, but always
ends—if we do not get sidetracked by shortcuts into
drugs or drink or material things—with the embrace of
the Divine.

You will find no angels in this book, not because they
were not present, pouring out their grace, but because we
speak here of *That* to which even the angels point: the
That toward which they guide, lead, nudge us along on
our lives. "Look," they are singing. "Listen to *That*.
Taste the music of I AM." We are rewarded with knowings, visions, and love beyond belief; and yet these ecstasies themselves, as you shall see, are no more than
little chocolates tossed out to encourage us on the Way.
Just when we think we've learned something, we find—
there's always more.

CHAPTER 1

ROWING
TOWARD GOD

*Wouldst thou know my meaning? Lie down in
the Fire.
See and taste the flowing godhead through thy
being.*

—MECHTILD OF MAGDEBURG

*Who is there to sing the music of my songs to
men, express the joys of my passion . . . ?*

—RICHARD ROLLE

*To the extent that my hands grew accustomed to
labor, that my eyes and ears learned to see and
hear and my heart to understand what is in it, my
soul too learned to skip upon the hills, to rise, to
soar . . . to embrace all the land round about, the
world and all that is in it, and to see itself embraced in the arms of the whole universe.*

—AARON DAVID GORDON

When I was a child of three or four I ran outside with my sister into the arms of a summer storm. Two naked little girls. The trees raked and swayed with the wind that stripped the green leaves and sent them tumbling over the grass. We danced in the wind. We flung out our arms and whirled with the electric leaves, and I *knew* that if I lifted my arms, my wings, I would rise up and soar like the hawks on the wind. I would sail across the skies, for nothing separated me from the elements. I *was* the wind, the blowing, bending trees, the green wild grass. I was the storm, the earth, the acorns that bruised my tiny bare feet. I was my sister and my own naked little body leaping and turning round and round in the summer storm.

Then my mother called us indoors. I don't remember anything else, but probably she toweled us dry while we pranced laughing around the kitchen, and then she gave us some dinner and read us to sleep.

At five I went to school and then I lost this sense of unity. Connectedness. All my life I have been trying to return to that innocent state of the child of three.

As a child I sat in church, the Episcopal church, confused and bored by the sermons and readings, uncomprehending. It was an eighteenth-century country church, with brick floors and high-backed pews with doors. I counted the stars on the dusty battle flags that hung above the nave, and I tried not to squirm or stir my mother's reproof by accidentally kicking the pew in front of me and sending a hollow echo through the church.

Later, as a teenager, I struggled to make sense of the sermons and readings. Much of what happened seemed dry ritual. I liked the music and the pageantry, but I found there was no *time* during the service to ponder or pray. I felt rushed from one duty to the next, kneeling, standing, singing, responding.

What I wanted to know was what mysteries Christ taught the disciples—not the fragments recorded in the Gospels, often without context, often contradictory. I wanted to know the secrets he passed on to them, one on one, the "whispered transmission" that was never written down in books. What did he tell them that permitted him to promise, "This and more shall you do in my name"?

And why did the disciples stay with him? He just walked up to a group of fishermen, who were pulling in their nets on the shore of the lake, and said, "Hi Peter, want to come with me?" And this grown, responsible, married man, the father of children (though we hear little of that), handed his nets to his brothers and friends and, without a backward look, followed the Master.

What did Jesus do to him? What unnamed longings did Jesus satisfy?

And once Our Lord had gathered the twelve around him, his best friends, once they ate and drank together and rolled up in their cloaks to sleep on the ground, side by side, once they had walked a hundred miles as a gang with Christ, bathing—no, wallowing—in the bliss of his light, did they become enlightened too? All of them? Except Judas, I guess—but that's another mystery.

None of the secrets were taught in church, nor how to reach the Light.

So I would kneel in Episcopalian reverence—which means I propped one elbow on my knee and rested my forehead devoutly on my fist. I bowed my head in prayer or peered around the congregation, wondering if the woman two pews ahead had dyed her hair or admiring the buttons on another's dress.

I was not a pious girl.

Yet I loved the mystery of the Communion, the Great Thanksgiving.

At fifteen I wanted to be a nun. (The thought may have lasted ten minutes.)

At sixteen I discovered boys.

At seventeen, in college, I lost my faith. The loss surprised me. Suddenly the idea of God meant nothing. I made an appointment with the minister at the Episcopal church that served Smith College.

"I've lost faith," I confessed guiltily. "What do I do?"

"You must have faith," he intoned.

I stared at him, stunned at the fatuous response, swallowed my sarcastic retort—that, hey, if I hadn't lost faith, I'd still have it, thank you—and walked out, freed of all misery, guilt, and doubts. Looking back I wonder if perhaps he'd lost his faith too, and found himself locked in his own misery. He had helped, but not the way he probably wished.

At twenty-five, under the influence of my brilliant husband, I converted to atheism. Yet I failed as an atheist too. For one thing I couldn't stop praying. Whenever I was scared or in trouble, "Help, help!" I'd whisper, and then scold myself, ashamed of my hypocrisy.

Sometimes I bargained with God. "If you give me this," I promised, "I'll never do such and such again." Usually I was quite specific with my deals, and usually God came through on His end of the bargain, though I mostly failed on mine.

Soon I had two children and was living in New York, writing articles. I published a bestselling book. I loved my family and garden and friends, was having a wonderful time, when suddenly, in 1973, we were moved back to Washington, D.C.

And all the while I did not know that I was "rowing toward God," as the poet Anne Sexton put it.

> I am rowing, I am rowing
> though the oarlocks stick and are rusty
> and the sea blinks and rolls
> like a worried eyeball,
> but I am rowing, I am rowing,
> though the wind pushes me back
> and I know that that island will not be perfect,
>
> . . . .
>
> but there will be a door
> and I will open it. . . .[1]

Once, a few years earlier, I'd had a kind of vision. I was working at my desk. I sat at my rickety manual typewriter, utterly absorbed in the article I was writing. At a certain moment I lifted my eyes from the page, glanced out the window at a maple tree—and for an instant I became the tree. No separation. I was the bark, the wood, the fleshy summer leaves. Time stopped.

Satori, came the ponderous thought, and with that word, arriving like an endless, slow, wavelike movement of my mind, with the naming of the moment, everything fragmented again back into its different parts—myself, the typewriter, the tree now safely separated from me by the windowpane.

Satori, the thought repeated. But I was back in my isolated body. That's how holy people see, I marveled, though I had only the dimmest idea of the meaning of the word I'd used, or of its sister word, *nirvana.*

The experience lasted hardly a second. But I have never forgotten that restful state of perfect peace. Time stopped, all feeling, analysis, all consciousness of self, all sense of being "I."

I knew that something precious had been given me. I didn't know it was a state that you could cultivate, or that it had anything to do with this word called "God."

I did not want to return to Washington. I loved New York, our life, our friends. For four years I had opposed my husband's wish to move, until one day a knowledge fell across my skin, like the shudder of a horse's skin when brushing off a fly: the move was decreed, inevitable. I remember I was walking from one room to another when this understanding hit. I stopped dead in my tracks. Later I came to trust these intuitions, but at the time the strength of this "knowing" frightened me. It was one of the first times I recognized an inner, silent voice and knew I was powerless to fight it.

Moreover, the move made sense. My father in Baltimore had had a stroke, my family needed me, and Washington was less expensive to live in, a more benevolent climate for children than New York. Finally, my journalist husband wanted with all his heart to be at the nerve center of politics, covering a particular beat, and of course I wanted his happiness.

We moved.

Yet something in me died.

I missed my friends, my work, my sense of place. Every morning the sun came up, a ball of fire flinging itself out of the tangle of tree limbs and up into the sky. I watched, surprised that it could dawn each day when my heart felt so heavy.

I cried. I felt abandoned.

Each morning, out of sheer willpower, I got out of bed to care for my house and children or try—without heart—to write. One morning, after the children had left for school, I found the opening lines of Dante's *Inferno* running through my mind. I had studied the poem in college. I went to the bookcase, pulled down my dog-eared copy, and read aloud to the empty room.

> *Nel mezzo del cammin di nostra vita*
> *mi retrovai per una selva oscura*
> *chè la diritta via era smarrita.*

In the middle of the journey of our life
  I found myself in a dark wood
  for the straight path had been lost.

The words struck me to the core.

*Ah quanto a dir qual era è cosa dura
esta selva selvaggia e aspra e forte
che nel pensier rinova la poura!*

Ah, how to describe how hard it was,
  this savage bitter wilderness,
  even to think of which strikes fear in me again!

I fell to my knees, the tears streaming down my
cheeks. "Help me, help me, help!"

The fit passed. After a few moments I dried my tears
and rose to my feet and went on about my day. It did not
occur to me that my cry constituted a prayer or that my
prayer had instantly been answered—my pain washed
mercifully away—for this was long before I noticed such
events. I only knew my deplorable weakness had passed.
I'd regained control. But in that moment of surrender I
shifted from agnostic—not knowing—to some flimsy ac-
ceptance that something spiritual existed beyond myself.
It was not done, however, without a quiver of shame at
having failed once more, this time the test of self-
reliance. I respected my husband all the more, for he had
no trouble with his disbelief.

They say that when the student is ready the teacher appears. They say that it is not the soul that struggles first toward God, but this Universe of Love which is fishing for us. God puts the longing in our hearts so that we will leap upstream, like a spawning salmon that throws itself against the river current, leaping up waterfalls in its passionate urge to reach the source, its birthplace, spawning ground, and death.

Just before leaving New York I had met, by the most striking accident, the first American woman to study in a Buddhist *wat*, or monastery, in Thailand. (Who was it who said coincidence is God's way of performing a miracle anonymously?) She taught me how to meditate, using the *vipassana* method of Theravada Buddhism— the Southern school, as practiced in Burma, Thailand, and Sri Lanka.

I loved it. For the next three years I practiced this form of meditation for twenty or thirty minutes every day. Gradually, almost imperceptibly, changes occurred. Later I would meet a Hindu guru (more about that later) who gave me a mantra (somewhat easier perhaps) and afterward I practiced that.

We should digress at this point to talk a little about meditation, though I'd suggest that anyone who knows these basics should skip ahead. There are many saints and holy masters, more learned than I, and they have written so gracefully about God and about meditation, which is the path to the spiritual dimension, that to read their works is to touch a point of peace. Go to these. There are Tibetan Buddhists like the Dalai Lama or Sogyal Rinpoche or the Vietnamese monk Thich Nhat Hanh. There are the Japanese Zen masters, like Shunryu Suzuki, and the Americans, such as Joseph Goldstein, Jack Kornfield, or, in the Christian tradition, Thomas Merton and Father Thomas Keating. There are the medieval mystics such as Julian of Norwich or Mechtild of Magdeburg, or, in Spain, Saint John of the Cross, Saint Ignatius, Saint Teresa of Avila. There are hundreds of wiser and more learned works than mine. But if you are reading about transcendent moments for the first time and know nothing of meditation, then perhaps this section may be of use.

Today, Christian meditation is having a rebirth; but in the 1970s, when I was beginning my search, that art had been lost since medieval times. Certainly it was not taught to ordinary people. In the tradition of seekers from Ralph Waldo Emerson to Aldous Huxley, I took a long journey through Buddhism, then Hinduism, before returning with new insights to my Christian roots. Therefore I describe the Eastern methods of meditation, with their long, unbroken history. In an appendix you will find a Christian path toward meditation; but keep in mind that all types of meditation are similar and all lead to the same golden center, for at the mystical level all religions have more in common than they differ, and all derive from the same source and long for the same goal.

Something happens in meditation, something so subtle and elegant that the great teachers and Zen masters and rabbis, the true Masters, are too clever to try to describe it. Was it this that Christ was teaching to his twelve?

Plato called the mystery of meditation *theoria*. Early Christians called it *contemplatio*.

Once the Buddha was asked, "Is there God?"

"I will not tell you," he answered. "But, if you wish, I can show you how to find out for yourself." Then he taught the gift of meditation.

The Buddha, the Compassionate One, understood how easily we become dependent on others, asking them to do the work for us. Unlike Christ, he refused to heal the sick.

"I will not make you well," he would say to the leper, the blind man, "but I can show you how to heal yourself." Then he would teach the seeker how to meditate.

Some learned. Others went away irritated that the Compassionate One would not hand them healing or wisdom or love the easy way.

Sages tell us that meditation confers three gifts. First, it brings deep peace and tranquility of mind. Second, it brings clear intuition, wisdom, and insight. Third, if it is pursued with constancy and devotion, it leads to the direct experience of God. Some people claim meditation does no more than transport us to our own interior and highest self, and others that it opens a doorway through which the Beloved comes. All we know is the love and power it confers.

There are various ways to meditate. Each system is designed to break sense-contact with the outer world and especially to stop the shrieking voices in our heads, the constant, taunting inner chatter. Whatever the system in whatever religion, meditation is always done by total concentration on one repetitive act. Perhaps you place your attention on your nostrils, watching your breath pass in and out, each breath as unique as a snowflake. Or perhaps you repeat a mantra, of which the best known is the Tibetan Buddhist *Om mani padme hum*, the mantra of compassion. Or the mantra is a Christian prayer. Saying the rosary becomes a meditation, or repeating over and over with absolute attention the Pilgrims' Prayer: "Lord Jesus Christ, Son of God, have mercy on me." Weeding the garden may become a meditation, or knitting, cooking, eating, walking, painting—doing whatever you are doing, so long as you do it alertly, with absolute attention, watching each movement of your hands or feet or breath.

Ram Dass tells how once he was giving a talk about his experiences in India. An old lady in the first row kept nodding and smiling in assent, the wooden cherries on her hat bobbing up and down. His vanity was pricked. How did *she* know about the esoteric things he'd spent years studying? At the end of the lecture, she went up to him.

"I enjoyed your talk."

"How do you know so much about meditation?" he asked.

"Oh," she confided, "I crochet."

I am told that in Thailand and Burma every adult man is encouraged to spend six or eight months in meditation at some time in his life. He is not considered educated without this entry into the spiritual journey, for this is the path by which you discover who you are.

From the beginning I loved meditating. Even my family found it helped my moods. Once my husband said to me, "You're out of sorts. Why don't you go upstairs and meditate. I'll feed the children."

But listen: The meditation I do is nothing compared to the practice of those who are truly serious.

The Dalai Lama meditates for four hours a day, and he is only just *beginning*, he told me, to sense accomplishment, "like a seed just starting to sprout. . . ."[2]

The Buddha spent two hours a day practicing one particular Forgiveness exercise—two hours a day, sending forgiveness to the world. Mother Teresa insists that her Missionaries of Charity carve out time every day for meditation, and she says that she herself could not do her draining and difficult work without this sweet and daily communion with God. For hours at a time, continuously, a Sufi master, practicing the Muslim mystical tradition, repeats the *dhikr*, the remembrance of God: *La ilaha ill-Allah,* he silently cries. "There is no God but God, *al-Lah*"—until slowly the words seep into his soul, like running water, excluding all other thoughts. His heartbeat slows. So quiet does the Sufi master become that they say he can repeat twenty-one *dhikr* on one long breath.

Years after I first learned to meditate, I spent several weeks at a Buddhist retreat in Massachusetts. There you go into silence. You do not speak. You avoid all eye contact. Certain orders of Christian monks maintain similar rules. And after being there for a time, I understood why. It's because you become so open, so sensitive, your antennae stretch so far, that if your eyes were to meet those of another person—man or woman—you would instantly fall in love!

We rose at four-thirty in the morning and meditated, alternately sitting or walking, until ten at night. Never was I so happy! By the end of two weeks, I was meditating twenty-two out of twenty-four hours a day, utterly absorbed and joyous in the discipline.

Many books describe how to meditate. You sit quietly with your back straight, either on the floor or in a chair. You close your eyes, scan your body, and relax, then set your attention on your nostrils and watch your breath pass in and out through this gateway, the portal to your life. At each inhalation, you take note: *In*, you say silently to yourself; on the exhalation, you say *out*.

The Tibetan monk Sogyal Rinpoche advises that you let your mouth drop slightly open, as if saying "Ahhh." He teaches that rather than express "in . . . out," you simply watch.

The Vietnamese monk Thich Nhat Hanh, on the other hand, who teaches crowds of disciples at Plum Village in France, counsels that you repeat an entire sentence to yourself.

Breathing in, I calm my body.
Breathing out I smile.
Dwelling in the present moment,
I know this is a wonderful moment.[3]

Now your thoughts leap like wild horses on a lead, crashing through the underbrush in fear and untamed rage. *Thinking,* you interrupt, naming the concept rather than being swept away by the horses of thought. Then quietly you return to your breath: *In . . . out . . .*

For the breath is the only true, factual, indisputable reality we know. Everything else is happening within our minds, planning, remembering, daydreaming, teaching, criticizing, judging; all things are reflections or projections of our minds.

In addition to noticing when you are *thinking,* you begin to name emotions—mind-states, as the Buddhists call them: anger, fear, jealousy, boredom, irritation, happiness, desire, longing, rapture, joy. They rise up, move like clouds across the limitless, blank, empty sky of your being, and pass away. You watch and return to your breathing. *In . . . out . . .*

It requires attention. Saint Teresa of Avila called this practice mental prayer and deplored her leaping thoughts. "This intellect is so wild," she wrote in her *Life,* "that it doesn't seem to be anything else than a frantic madman no one can tie down."[4]

Finally you grow so quiet that you differentiate the varying physical sensations in your body: a pain in your knee, a twinge in the neck, an itch or throbbing, a pulsing or tingling; and slowly, as you do this day by day, you become so still that soon you hear your own heartbeat, sense the blood pulsing through your veins. *In . . . out . . .*

You have visions. In the early days, violent, psychedelic

thunderstorms assailed me with swirling colors—red, black, purple, green—or else sequential waves of light moved in toward me or flowed outward in waves that reached to the farthest stars. These would be followed by periods of deep calm, the quiet of a mirror-sea on a windless summer day. Then I watched my thoughts lift in a gentle swell and imperceptibly subside.

One of the common early phenomena is the "eye of God." It appears as a luminous bright disk, a golden "eye" with its black pupil watching you. It is similar to the blinding spot that assails you when you step from a brilliant white snowfield into a dark room. In meditation, however, you cannot attribute this effect to the adjustment of the retina, for you are only sitting, eyes closed. What is it?

In . . . out . . . and soon the image of an eye fades, to be replaced by the sound of a birdsong or a numbness in your foot, or by the desire for a cup of tea; still you watch attentively, attaching no importance to any of these visions or events, sensations or ideas.

Later still, you grow so quiet that your body disappears. Then you find that you *are* the mind, and this mind that you are watching is a serene, deep, beautiful, blank sky, an empty space, elegant in its purity. It is what the Tibetans call *rigpa*, the beginning of the understanding of the richness of Emptiness. Across it slowly floats the cloud of a thought, which vanishes, and after a while there appears another cloud—an emotion perhaps, a memory, or else the high *ping* of the radiator—a sound which hits your ears and enters your body in observable waves . . . and these thoughts too, rise up, diminish, and disappear.

Who is the observing "I"?

Once, when I was just beginning, I saw to my horror a pack of small, wild, sharp-toothed, snarling, furry animals come pouring from my navel—badgers and wolverines—out into the air. I watched appalled as they spewed out of me, snapping and clawing the air. *(In . . . out . . .)* But when the meditation ended, I walked with a lighter step.

What had happened? I had no one to ask, and I think if I'd had a teacher, I would have been ashamed to admit my vision. I held my secret, vicious violence to myself.

Almost ten years later I read *The Last Temptation of Christ*, the novel by Nikos Kazantzakis. In one scene Our Lord is a young novice meditating at an Essene monastery, when suddenly two writhing black snakes appear outside the walls, whipping their tails. Hissing, they slither into the desert, the snakes of ancient sins.

I suspect that Kazantzakis knew what he was talking about. Born in Crete, he ricocheted between his spiritual longings and passionate, politically revolutionary ideals. He served as minister of education in Greece; worked for UNESCO; translated Dante, Homer, Bergson, Darwin, William James, Nietzsche, and other writers into modern Greek, and still found time to write plays, poetry, essays, and novels, including *Zorba the Greek*. As a young man he withdrew for a time to Mount Athos (where no female of any kind including hens and cows has set foot for ten centuries) and there he meditated with the monks so long that he developed what's called the meditator's rash. This is a real phenomenon. Apparently it heralds the energy shifts that consume one's body as vibrations rise—burning karma, as the Hindus call it. When I read Kazantzakis's description of those two black writhing snakes, I recalled my own disturbing vision and wondered if he was writing of what he himself had seen on Mount Athos, the physical manifestation of the cleansing of a soul.

For six years, then, I meditated, using either the Buddhist breathing meditation just described, or the mantra given later by my guru. In this second form of meditation, you concentrate on the sound of one of the names of God. It is not, however, the meaning of the word that assists the awakening, but rather the vibration, the frequency, resonating with your soul. (This is different from the Christian *lectio*, a discipline in which you take a Scriptural verse and read it over and over, concentrating, until its deepest meaning seeps into your heart.)

Studies of meditation show that precise changes occur in the meditator's brain waves and hypothalamus, as well as in the nervous, metabolic, and acupuncture meridian systems. I knew nothing of these studies, but I found my sharp mood-swings flattening out into a quiet steadiness. And periodically I would experience a fleeting moment of transcendence, a light-encapsulated epiphany, in which the world would be flooded with light, and I, too, momentarily. These came as little breakthroughs like the static an astrophysicist might hear when listening to the silence of space—a brief splutter of sound and gone. A blessing of light, and then darkness.

Looking back, I can see now that all this time that I was meditating, my prayers were also shifting, but so gradually, so imperceptibly I didn't notice at first. I wanted God.

"I want to understand," I prayed fervently, as indeed I had prayed since I was twenty. Understand what? I didn't know: all of it! Now I remembered those moments as a child, isolated flashes of memory, like a shaft of sunlight in the forest, when everything seemed pure. I remembered that instant of *satori* when, as a young married woman, I'd been typing my article and melted into the tree. I wanted that.

"Help me to serve you." I was struck by my own inconsequence and failings, including my sarcastic tongue, my flashy and uncompassionate retorts, my abiding vanity that took the form of showing off, often at the expense of others. It came of insecurity. I knew how poorly I stacked up to my own ideals. At one point the *Desiderata* fell into my hands—that famous paper found in the mid-1900s in old St. Paul's Church of Baltimore. I read and reread it, wondering if it were true that

> You are a child of God.
> You have as much right to be here as the stars and
> trees.

In those days, I had no sense of privilege. "Let me serve," I prayed, in part out of love for this pretty world of which I had no understanding and in part out of a

25

guilty wish to earn the right to live on this planet, instead of uselessly creating garbage, taking up space.

Passionately I worried questions like: Is God inside or outside of me? Is God a separate entity or a figment of my imagination? And these questions tormented me until one day they burst out, in a flood of tears, addressed to a monk. He listened. "Why couldn't He be both?" he asked.

"Oh."

Instantly the questions disappeared. How obvious the answer was.

What happened next may have had nothing to do with these events. The human brain struggles to make connections. It is especially fond of cause and effect. We say that B happened because of A: *post hoc propter hoc.* Perhaps we deceive ourselves and create imaginary connections to unrelated happenings. But in my mind, because my longings and prayers preceded the event, I claim connection; I believe in answered prayer.

I may have been thirty-eight or thirty-nine.

One evening I was taking a bath before bed, reclining in the warm and soothing water and praying in my usual fevered, longing way—as indeed I had been praying for months with increasing fervor. "Let me serve You; take me. Help me that I may be of service to You." I prayed without knowing who or what was meant by "God."

Suddenly I burst into tears. My whole body began to shake. Tears rained down my cheeks, falling as big drops into the bathwater, and in that moment I felt with pure and holy, teeth-chattering knowledge that my prayer had just been accepted. My soul dropped to its knees in humility and joy. I don't want to romanticize this moment, which has its humor. We like to think of the *mysterium tremendum*, the touch of angels, coming at an appropriate moment, when you're clad in glorious robes, not as you crouch naked in the bathwater, knees projecting like two ludicrous islands in the air. Nonetheless, I trembled, transported. I was shaking all over.

I didn't know what was happening, but it filled me—this Holy Presence—with passionate gratitude and joy.

Later I rose from my bath and crept to bed. I curled beside my husband, silently. I said nothing to him, for we did not talk of such matters, and I would not have known how to speak of this moment even if we did. There was so much I did not understand. At the time I did not know that one of the signs by which the Holy Spirit comes to me is as a gush of joyous tears.

After this, a new desire took shape: to see the face of God. "Show me," I prayed without an ounce of humility. "Let me know God."

CHAPTER 2

ECSTATIC VISIONS: FAIRY TALES

I know that He exists.
Somewhere—in Silence—
He has hid his rare life
From our gross eyes.

—EMILY DICKINSON

I stood with the warriors in the cause, but I did
not progress a single step with them. I stood with
those who pray excessively and those who fast
excessively, but I did not progress a footstep.
Then I said, "Oh God, what is the way to You?"
and God said, "Leave yourself and come."

—BAYAZID

Here is the myth. Everyone believes it. You are in trouble, in crisis, weeping, your heart twisting on its choke collar, your soul lunging out in prayer, perhaps even against your will—and, Lo! an angel appears in person or in disguise. You are filled with suitable emotions of awe, reverence, joy, warmth, light. The angel solves the problem. "Fear not!" it cries. It acts with slashing sword or perhaps with the gathering of all pain into its loving arms, and then it fades.

It is gone. Everything is as it was. You pick up your life and go on.

That is the story.

It is born of fact, of course, for the story comes from somewhere, happened once to you or to your relative or friend. But you don't live happily ever after. What happens then is more, is bouts of tears, distress, the next chapter in the novel. The girl leaves her husband or boyfriend (or mother, or father) blinded by that Light, and goes in search of the lost image—the journey of a lifetime. She straps on her iron sandals and picks up her iron staff, a loaf of bread, an oatcake baked perhaps by her mother, or perhaps by a kind and supportive older aunt, the wisdom-woman; off she goes in search of the angel again, in search of that moment when she felt washed by such unfathomable and unconditional love. The loss is insupportable. She will wear through nine pairs of iron sandals and wear down nine iron staves, walking nine or ninety years to find her lover again.

We tell this story again and again in literature, in fairy tales, in films and songs and poems, in country music: the fate of the soul, restless and in anguish, struggling through bog and swamp to find her missing half. It is the story of Psyche and Eros, of Orpheus and Eurydice.

There is this story too: The wicked stepsister, who is shown this same fairy-magic, the light of the Divine, turns her back on it in selfishness and fear, demanding her own satisfaction, denying love, denying mystery, denying the Divine, which is to say her Self.

What is a mystical encounter? The word itself connotes an intense consciousness of the beyond, of what cannot be uttered or discussed—not because we do not want to but because we lack the skill. The mystical journey is experiential, utterly. The word *mystical* is related to *mystery*, which is derived from the ancient Greek word for "close-mouthed," as of lips that are sealed. For the Greeks the mysteries were initiation ceremonies which brought the initiates (the mystics) through the doorway into what was holy. The seekers were not allowed to speak of what they'd seen.

By the time of Christ the word *mystical* had already come to encompass a reality beyond the ordinary human senses, the sense of the approaching Beloved. The mystery comes as the shadow that hovers at the corner of our eye, and when we turn to look—it has vanished, though beckoning to our hearts. It is the wisp, the elfin king, the Light of Light, calling to us silently. All artists know this muse—philosophers, musicians, dancers, poets. All feel at some level that they are inspired by something greater than themselves. I therefore define the mystical as the direct experience of the Divine, however we comprehend that word.

How is it seen? Sometimes it comes like a clap of thunder, as to Saint Paul, blinded by the light. Sometimes it enters slowly into consciousness like mist, seeping into you over the course of a lifetime. Or perhaps it comes as an angel's touch: invisible hands pulling you from a burning car, a voice, a vision, a series of miraculous small coincidences that cannot be ignored; to some few it comes as the angel herself, gloriously revealed. Afterward you cannot forget. But often it is almost too fragile to describe.

Not long ago I asked a woman to tell me the most important moment in her life, something she could not forget. Her face lit up. She said that once she had walked out on the deck of her house at sunset, and there before her was spread a glorious sky, all orange and purple and blue. She'd seen a thousand sunsets before, but this time, she said, eyes glowing with the memory, it was so stunning that she knew she was meeting God. She could not forget it. But what had happened? Almost nothing to the outside eye.

It is difficult to write about my personal journey. How to do it without sounding narcissistic? Or pretentious, or even boastful? There are things we think and do not like to put in words, even to our closest friends. But obviously by the time I asked in my prayer to *see*, to understand, I already believed there was a Force of the Universe, and it was on my side.

Once Einstein was asked what he thought the most

important question was. "Is the universe a friendly place?" he answered.

Originally, all those years ago, I had a more primitive question: Is there really something Out There? Or is the mystical a figment of my imagination? The question could be asked in other ways: Who am I? Why am I here? Is there life after death? And what are we to make of this strange planet on which we live, this world of happiness and sorrows, polarities and paradox?

The only way I knew to approach the answers was through those who gone before. This is not a stupid approach. "If one is not oneself a sage or saint," wrote Aldous Huxley, "the best thing one can do in the field of metaphysics, is to study the works of those who were...."[1]

All holy scripture tries to describe the mysteries. They are best approached only indirectly, through metaphor, music, poetry. They comprised the first songs chanted around the caveman's fires, and when people learned to write down words on clay tablets, or papyrus or calfskin, what did they record but first their financial accounts (cattle, armies, women, food) and then their sacred ecstasies. Here is an example from the Old Testament's Song of Songs, written down sometime after the mid-sixth century B.C.

Let him kiss me with the kisses of his mouth: for thy love is better than wine.... The voice of my beloved! Behold, he cometh leaping upon the mountains, skipping upon the hills. My beloved is like a roe or a young hart. . . . By night on my bed I sought him whom my soul loveth: I sought him, but I found him not. I will rise now, and go about the city in the streets, and in the broad ways I will seek him whom my soul loveth. . . .[2]

A millennium later the Spanish mystic known as Saint John of the Cross wrote in prison the famous poem *"Noche obscura del alma,"* "The Dark Night of the Soul."

> Once in the dark of night
> when love burned bright with yearning, I arose
> (O windfall of delight!)
> and how I left none knows—
> dead to the world my house, in dull repose;
> . . . .
> There in the lucky dark,
> in secret, with all sleepers heavy-eyed;
> no sign for me to mark,
> no other light, no guide
> except for my heart—the fire, the fire inside![3]

Preserved in all languages lie thousands of years of the spiritual mysteries. I didn't know the answer lay right at hand. Like a homesick child I was looking for the transcendent in every place but in my ordinary world. In fact, I don't think I really thought this question out—what I'd see if God showed up. I didn't yet know that all I had to do was drop "the shutters of the mind," as Jean Houston puts it in her book *A Mythic Life*, and God would be seen playing in every blade of grass, each movement of our thought, in (as Dante wrote) *il riso del universo*, the joy that spins the universe.

But at a more literal level, you'd think I'd have been cautious of my request. Not even Moses saw God straight on, but only the back of his head, so to speak. "To see me would blind you," says God, thoughtfully turning His back. The same danger is described in early Greek myth, when the mortal girl Semele falls in love with Zeus (and is there more than a rhyming relationship between the word Zeus and the Latin *deus,* meaning God?). Semele asks to see Zeus face to face. The god refuses. It would destroy her, he says, which is why he comes only in secret, at night, in the dark. But his mistress waits and one night when she has especially pleased him, the deity relaxes. "Ask anything," he says, "and I will give it to you."

"Let me see your face."

"No." He is upset. He tries to bargain, plead, wriggle out of his rash promise. She will not be dissuaded.

What can he do? He reveals himself—and Semele bursts into flames, consumed by the light of God.

Neither is it an accident that in Greek cosmology the son of Semele's union with the divine is Dionysus, the god of wine and hallucinogens, of altered, bacchanalian states, of god-madness, who together with Apollo and

Hermes is associated with creativity, the arts, music, sacred dance.

This urge to see God must run deep in us. "What I have been striving and pining to achieve these thirty years," wrote Mahatma Gandhi, "is to see God face to face."

So what reports have we of those who have?

In the early 1300s, Dante Alighieri wrote his magnificent three-part narrative poem, *The Divine Comedy*. At the very end of the poem Dante asks to see God's face. And then he describes his vision in what are perhaps the most beautiful lines ever written, though you have to read the entire work to understand them.

First Dante finds himself wandering in a spiritual morass, depressed, in despair. He is led by his beloved mentor Virgil, the Roman poet, down into Hell. Through nine concentric circles of the Inferno he takes us, until he meets the archfiend Lucifer, locked in a lake of ice—for hate is cold, not hot. The demon's huge bat wings fan the icy air chilling everything. He has three heads, and with three jaws, he chews for eternity on the heads of three traitors, the worst of whom is Judas Iscariot.

Shuddering, Dante clings to Virgil, his guide, who, catching hold of the shaggy hair of Satan, descends from tuft to tuft to the demon's ass, takes one turn so that his head is where his feet had been, and climbs hand over hand out of Hell, into the clear night, "to see the stars again."

From there, the two travelers move on to dim Purgatory, and finally they reach the gates of Paradise. And now his beloved Virgil, being a pre-Christian pagan, can go no farther. He hands Dante over to Beatrice, the poet's idealized perfect woman.

Dante Alighieri was nine years old when he first saw the child Beatrice Portinari on the Ponte Vecchio in Florence. He nearly fainted with love. He didn't speak to her until nine years later, at a wedding. Her own? We do not know. But we do know that to his distress she made fun of his embarrassment. She died seven years later, perhaps in childbirth. He lived on, however, first as a famous poet, metaphysician, philosopher, and politician, and later—banished from Florence—as an angry and embittered man.

Now in Paradise, Beatrice, the embodiment of beauty, carries Dante up through the heavenly ranks of angels until even she can move no higher; she gives him to the care of Saint Bernard, who leads the poet to the feet of the Blessed Virgin herself. This is as high as he can go—to the feminine principle, the goddess, the Mother of God.

I hated this poem when I studied it in college. The pride, the insuperable arrogance of this man who placed himself higher than the saints! What I didn't understand is that the mystical journey is one we all may take. Moving up from hell into the Light. The Buddhists call it Enlightenment. The Muslims call it *enour*.

Dante, standing at the side of the Madonna, is

overwhelmed by love. Yet still he wants more. He asks to see "the Primal Love." The goddess, the Virgin, the holy Mother pleads for the gift, and out of love it is granted him.

Dante looks. Words fail him. What he sees in the complexity and beauty of the Trinity . . . is his own image, "and the Love that moves the sun and stars."

But this is not the only view of the Divine.

Almost two thousand years earlier, the Hindu epic, the Mahabharata, described the encounter of Arjuna, the young prince who represents the soul, with God. This poem was composed sometime between the fifth and second centuries B.C. It originally consisted of twenty-four thousand verses, grew over time to one hundred thousand, and is said to be the longest poem in the world. One long segment, the Bhagavad Gita, the "Song of God," tells of the hero Arjuna, who is about to go to war against his own blood-relatives. Driving him into battle, serving as his charioteer, is Lord Krishna himself, the god of love.

As the two armies line up face-to-face, waiting for the conch to sound the opening of the fray, Arjuna pulls his horses between the lines to view the battlefield, and suddenly he is struck by dismay. How can he kill his own family—fathers, grandfathers, teachers, sons, brothers, uncles, cousins, and friends with whom he played as a child? His limbs grow weak. The bow drops from his hands.

In the rest of this exquisite poem Lord Krishna explains the meaning of the physical and spiritual realities and the path by which we escape our suffering. Arjuna knows the identity of his driver. He knows that Krishna is a god, indeed, that he is the incarnation of an even greater god, Vishnu; but so kind is Krishna that he causes Arjuna to forget his identity all the time, for no ordinary man can bear to consort with God for long. Arjuna refers to Lord Krishna, therefore, sometimes as a servant—his inferior—sometimes as his friend and equal, sometimes as his master or teacher.

Yet at a certain moment, Arjuna asks to behold the face of Krishna, to see him in his transcendent glory. Then "the son of Pandu [Arjuna] beheld the entire universe in all its multitudinous diversity, lodged as one being within the body of the God of gods."[4] The deity is adorned with countless divine ornaments, carries all kinds of heavenly weapons, is garbed in celestial garlands and the raiment of paradise. The forms continue to change.

Arjuna sees all gods in Krishna, forms without limit, speaking from innumerable mouths, seeing with thousands of eyes: infinite arms, eyes, mouths, bellies, all shining, so that Arjuna cannot look at the splendor which fills the four corners of the earth and around which all creation sings in praise. At the same time the vision strikes terror in his heart. He sees the God of Death—the terrible eyes, feet, thighs, bellies, fangs, the gnashing mouths, flaring like the fires of a doomsday morning, and all of creation is being sucked into these hideous jaws. Demons scatter in terror before the lord of fire and death, wind and moon and waters. Moreover,

Swift as many rivers streaming to the ocean,
Rush the heroes to your fiery gullets:
Mothlike, to feed the flame of their destruction,
Headlong these plunge into you. . . .[5]

Krishna appears also as Time, and what Arjuna sees is that it does not matter whether he kills his kinfolk in battle or not. All creatures die. And yet simultaneously he understands there is no such thing as death, but only God-ness, with all creation streaming back into the glory that is God. Overcome, Arjuna bows in awe, humility, adoration, and horror before the author of the world, whom he had dared to call his comrade. He is paralyzed with fear.

I have seen what no man ever saw before me:
Deep is my delight, but still my dread is greater.
Show me now your other Form, O Lord, be
    gracious.
. . . .
Show me now the Shape I knew of old. . . .[6]

In a flash Krishna changes back into his familiar friendly human form.

"Be glad, take courage," he says, calming Arjuna's fear. "Look, here I am transformed." We are reminded of the Transfiguration of Christ when his three closest friends, Peter, John, and James, fall down before him in awe, and Jesus returns to his own form.

Lord Krishna revealed his Form of Fire, he says, out

of love for Arjuna, and what Arjuna saw no one ever sees by his own efforts—not through sacrifice, or study, or good works, not through austerity, disciplines, or rituals, but only through one's single-minded, continuous devotion, and through freedom from hatred toward any creature, and freedom from attachment to results. (This detachment is not to be confused with indifference, carelessness, or an irresponsible or lazy attitude. It is detachment from the *fruits* of one's action—fear of failure or desire for success.)

Instantly Arjuna forgets both his awe and his dread. He sees only his friend and servant, his charioteer, who will drive his horses and stand at his shoulder as he fights. Thus it is with the mystical: we remember only as much as we can bear.

The conch shell sounds. The battle is joined. Arjuna must fight because it is his duty as a warrior to fight; it is God's will that he recover his kingdom, even at the risk of causing death. But first comes the understanding that there is no death, and secondly Arjuna fights with detachment, without hatred for the so-called enemy or obsession about the outcome.

Here is another Hindu story of seeing the face of God. This time Krishna was just a toddler. He was a very mischievous and much-loved little boy. Everyone who saw him was filled with love. Everyone adored him, though he always made laughing trouble, overturned pots, let out the animals, played practical jokes, created joyful disturbances. One day, the little baby playfully stuffed a handful of clay in his mouth, and his mother ran over, scolding. She forced open his jaws to pull out the clay. As she bent down to look inside her infant's open mouth, she suddenly saw, between the baby teeth . . . swarms of people, and spirits and *devas*, gods and demons, loving and warring, living and dying. Everything in all known and unknown worlds inhabited her baby's mouth. She staggered backward, faint. The baby, laughing, closed his lips.

Instantly, she recovered, and instantly forgot. Then she snatched up her baby and hugged and kissed him passionately, as an adoring mother does, overcome with delight in her enchanting child.

I read stories like these and pondered the various views—Greek, Hindu, Christian. Of the three stories just recounted, two begin in suffering. Arjuna must kill those whom he loves, his cousins and brothers, who are also aspects of himself. Dante is wrapped in depression, lost in an emotional wilderness. Only Krishna's mother is caught by surprise with a flash of insight—but notice that though she sees, she is not changed by what she saw. She was already happy with her baby; she didn't ask for anything more divine. Apparently the transformative spiritual experience always begins as a journey into despair, into the Garden of Gethsemane, into hell, into the Night of God.

This Night is also a gift of God. It is the Creative Potential moving us toward light. In Hindu cosmology, the ultimate godhead is Brahman experienced as wordless

Existence, Knowledge, Bliss. Brahman cannot be known by the conscious mind, but only experienced in *samadhi*— the state of blissful union with God—and that is found through the discipline of meditation and the inward journey to the heart. It is this mysterious practice that the Bhagavad Gita reveals.

Brahman is so great that it manifests on earth only through three other godheads: the attributes of creation (Brahma), preservation (Vishnu), and dissolution (Shiva). But Shiva's dissolution is not the same as destruction, for nothing can be destroyed in the universe but only shifts in a constant oscillation between possibility and expression. Potential is called the Night of Brahma, and expression the Day of Brahma.

In Christianity this moment of spiritual potential is sometimes mistaken for the Dark Night of the Soul, which also foreshadows great shifts. But the Dark Night marks a particular, intense period on the mystic's path, dividing the early, ecstatic moments of the Illuminative Way from the quieter Unitive Way. The Dark Night of the Soul, as defined by Saint John of the Cross, is a time of blankness, misery, a stagnation unlit by any of the voices, visions, and raptures that defined and made glorious the earlier stages of this joyous inward journey toward self-discovery. It will be followed by quieter intensity.

However, at present we are concerned with a different yearning, the sighing Night of God that precedes a spiritual transformation.

Does conversion always require that depression? Or

can the spiritual just come out of the blue, for no reason, when you're trotting about your day contentedly, minding your own business, so to speak? That's what happened to Saul of Tarsus, or so we're led to believe.

In the first century A.D., Saul of Tarsus, scourge of the new cult called Christianity, was going about his sullen work. Did he first experience this long, searching hopelessness, before he was thrown to the ground by Christ? We do not know. The story is silent about his state of mind. But a smoldering resentment sometimes masks depression, a gnawing at the heart.

Saul was a Roman citizen, a Jew adhering to the strict orthodoxy of the fundamentalist Pharisees. He found repugnant the extravagance of the messianic Christians and made it his righteous duty to hunt down these deviant Jews. One day, on the road to Damascus, he fell from his horse, blinded by the Light.

"Saul, Saul, why do you persecute me?" came a voice. Not only did Saul hear the voice, but so did the men with him. They all heard the disembodied voice direct Saul to go to Damascus and wait for further instructions. What could he do? He was blind. He went. Later another voice spoke to an old Christian Jew, Ananias, and told him to go find Saul. Ananias laid his healing hands on the blind man, prayed to Christ, and instantly Saul's sight was restored. Darkness into Light.

In that moment his life changed. He took another name. He was no longer Saul, from the Hebrew for "asked for," but Paul, from the Latin for "little." Little Paul. Small in proportion to Christ. From that moment he was no longer the hunter of Christians but the indefatigable convert, traveling the length and breadth of the Mediterranean by foot, horse, cart, ship, to found the Christian church.

Six hundred years later, in A.D. 620, Muhammad was carried on the back of a Buruq (a camel-headed, winged mount) to within two bow-shots of God. Like Moses, he did not see God, but only the signs of God, both seeing and not seeing the essence of Divinity. Muhammad had already had many visions and revelations. His first had come ten years earlier, in 610, and it had so transformed him that, like Paul, he became the instrument for the founding of a religion. He was just an Arab merchant. He had been meditating in the hills, fasting and praying on his annual retreat, when, on the seventeenth night of Ramadan, the angel Gabriel appeared and commanded him, "Recite!"

"I am no poet," cried Muhammad, frightened at thinking of himself as an ecstatic reciter. He was afraid of possession by the demons and jinns.

But the angel embraced him, he says, until it knocked the breath out of him. "Recite!" Again Muhammad refused, and again Gabriel, the spirit of Revelation, embraced him until he thought he would die. The third time, he began to speak the famous lines from sura 96:

Recite in the name of thy Lord who created!
He createth man from a clot of blood.
Recite: and thy Lord is the Most Bountiful
He who hath taught by the pen,
taught man what he knew not.[7]

After his vision, Muhammad threw himself weeping in the lap of his wife, Khadija, undone by what he had seen. But over the next twenty-three years Muhammad wrote under Divine dictation a book so beautiful that people wept on hearing it.[8] "Never once did I receive a revelation," he said, "without feeling that my soul was being torn away from me."[9] The Qur'an, the "recitation," affected the lives of all the Arab tribes in his region and spread in only a few generations across all of North Africa and as far east as India. Paul founded a religion that counts 1.9 billion people today. Muhammad created one that now numbers more than a billion—the second largest religion. Who could do that without holy inspiration?

Here is another vision, this time from the *Shuir Qomah*, a Jewish mystical text from the fifth century. It describes Yotzrenu, the figure that Ezekiel saw on God's throne: it is a force, like Brahman, a nonfact, ineffable, illimitable, without a face or form:

> A quality of holiness, a quality of power, a fearful
>   quality, a dreaded quality, a quality of awe, a
>   quality of dismay, a quality of terror—
> Such is the quality of the garment of the Creator,
>   Adonai, God of Israel, who, crowned, comes to
>   the throne of his glory;
> His garment is engraved inside and outside and
>   entirely covered with YHWH, YHWH.
> No eyes are able to behold it, neither the eyes of
>   flesh and blood, nor the eyes of his servants.[10]

I was not thinking of such exalted imagery when I prayed in the bathtub to see God. I wanted only to fill the hollow at my heart, to satisfy an unnameable longing, the sense that there was something more than I could see, and that once upon a time I'd known it.

So who was doing the rowing, you ask, the "rowing toward God"?

Three more years passed. I forgot that moment in the bathtub. I saw no God but only my two adorable daughters growing strong, my good husband, my sister, brother, nieces, aunts, my Corgi dog. I saw only the daily struggles of our lives: my mother fighting breast cancer and lung cancer, my father felled by one stroke and then stricken by numerous tiny ones, the byways of his brain flickering out, one by one, until he could hardly move or speak. He spent his days sitting on a sofa. When we children came to visit, his face would light up. He would lean forward, his whole soul in his eyes. "Hel-lo," he would croak. I would take his hand and sit by him, and chatter brightly, while inside I felt I'd burst from pain. I loved passionately. I wrote plays, children's novels, articles, books.

But I did not see God.

Actually I didn't have any idea how God would look. What is God? I didn't even *like* the word, freighted as it was with associations of a white-bearded white male Pancreator, the Judge more than the Merciful. I preferred to call it the Universe, the Source.

It is difficult to tell my story, first because every time I begin I hesitate, thinking, No, it doesn't begin there; it all started earlier; and then, No, not there, but earlier still—until I am back to babyhood.

The second reason lies with the first person singular, this smallest and most exaggerated word in the English language, this "I." In other languages—French, Italian, German—the pronoun is never capitalized: *je, io, ich.* But in English the word puffs up and struts across the page, the pigeon-breasted Big Shot I, an intruder to this discussion of the Divine. If I say there is no "I" but only a merging into the compassionate God-ness that was shown to me; if I say there is no person separate from you and he and from the dog in the street, or the meadow where the horses graze, which are all also manifestations of the Divine; if I say I am not writing this but emptying myself in order to be written through, it sounds pretentious. As years have passed, however, this sense of communing with the Divine has deepened into gratitude, knowing all credit goes to Him, my Source, the Beloved, the Universe, the Atman, Para-atman, to the Mother; to Spirit—Yahweh, Allah, Buddha, Christ—to whatever name by which we call this God, and to the angels that sing praises to the glory of this earth and who guide and lead us where we need to go; to the masters who teach us, and to the friends and enemies, who are also our teachers accompanying us on our way.

Yet still I hesitate, aware of how little I know. I want to write of everyone else, for their stories seem stronger than mine—I'm that insecure. But there are other reasons.

The stories of others always cast light on our own. We have so many questions to cover. What is a mystical experience, to whom does it come, and at what age? What forms does it take, and especially how does it affect you afterward? In addition, I love the stories—simple as that. It's in the story that we make sense of things, and usually we don't have a full accounting until the protagonist has died. Only then can we see the completed landscape of a life. So let me turn aside for a moment and tell a little about what's happened to other people too.

CHAPTER 3

DRUNKS AND BUMS AND SAINTS

There are a thousand and one gates leading into the orchard of mystical truth. Every human being has his own gate. We must never make the mistake of wanting to enter the orchard by any gate but our own. To do this is dangerous for the one who enters and also for those who are already there.

—ELIE WIESEL, *NIGHT*

Whoever enters the Way without a guide will take a hundred years to travel a two-day journey.

—RUMI, *MATHNAVI*

I have discovered—and exaggeration is not in my nature—that He who is my sustenance will come to me. I run to Him, and my quest for Him is agony for me. Were I to sit still, He would come to me without distress.

—URWA IBN ADHINA

In 1936, Bill Wilson, a bingeing, falling-down, deadbeat, hopeless drunk, was in the hospital with delirium tremens. For years he had guzzled two and three bottles of gin a day; he had fallen so low that, for the first time, he surrendered utterly, praying on his knees to some Power greater than himself. He told the story later how "I found myself crying out, 'If there is a God, let Him show Himself.' " Suddenly the room lit up with a great white light. "It seemed to me, in the mind's eye, that I was on a mountain and that a wind not of the air but of the spirit was blowing. And then it burst upon me that I was a free man. Slowly the ecstasy subsided. . . . A great peace stole over me and I thought, 'No matter how wrong things seem to be, they are still all right.' "[1]

He wrote of it again and again. "There was a sense of victory, followed by such peace and serenity as I had never known . . . utter confidence. I felt lifted up, as though the great clean wind of a mountain top blew through and through."[2] Sometimes he wrote, as do almost all mystics, in the third person, as if the blessing had come to someone else. "In a few seconds he was overwhelmed by a conviction of the Presence of God. It poured over and through him with the certainty and majesty of a great tide at flood. The barriers he had built through the years were swept away. He stood in the Presence of Infinite Power and Love."[3]

From that day on he never took another drink. In a single moment his urge had been removed, and he experienced a profound alteration in his reaction to life. Together with his friend, Dr. Bob, he went on to found Alcoholics Anonymous, the extraordinary spiritual twelve-step program that has saved countless millions around the world. The program has been copied for all kinds of addictions: drug abuse, compulsive gambling, compulsive spending, compulsive sex, eating disorders. Bill Wilson was an outcast, and in one extravagant mystical moment he was freed.

Are there such watershed moments in every person's life?

In 1348 Richard Rolle, an English monk, was praying in chapel when Knowledge came to him, he says, "suddenly and unknown." It constituted a complete break in his life. There was no continuity, he says, between his previous spiritual life and what came after.

We tend to glamorize mysticism in our society, at the same time that we denigrate it as superstition. Perhaps it is not glamorous, but ordinary.

I know a man who years ago was sent to a treatment center for his alcoholism. At a certain moment, he walked off in disgust to find a drink. It was night. He marched across a frozen cornfield, toward a bar out by the road. As he reached the far side of the field, he looked up at the stars, and suddenly he was swept by a wave of serenity, and by the thought, unbidden, that he did not need alcohol ever again in his life. The need was wiped away. It occurred from one footfall to the next, in the time it took to lift his right heel off the ground, swing it forward, and set it down again. No angels. No glory.

He proceeded to the bar, entered, ordered a mineral water, laughed with the other patrons, and walked back across the winter stubble to his treatment center.

Thirty years later he had another spiritual experience when he awoke at four-thirty one morning and found himself engulfed in light. For a few brilliant moments he understood that everything in his past—every person, every moment—fit together perfectly, bringing him to his present place. But humility, anonymity, is the foundation of a spiritual life. He does not speak of what he saw.

Moreover, it is difficult to talk of the ineffable. How do you approach a topic so fragile that it sifts like sand through your fingers? Indeed, it's hard even to remember what you've been shown, unless you happen once again to reach that altered, heightened state. And as for those who have not seen that Light, can you say anything that they might understand? Most people stay quiet about these sacred moments in their lives.

Some years ago a reporter was interviewing recovered alcoholics about their spiritual lives. Bill Wilson said, "Oh, I don't know anything about it, but ask John over there: he's spiritual." And John answered, "No, I'm not the right person; ask Joan. She's *very* spiritual." And so it continued, each person deferring to the next, until the journalist realized that these men and women—all attempting to live devoutly quiet, reverent lives, to help others and live from the center of their highest aspirations—each believed that she or he knew nothing about what it meant to be "spiritual." No one would talk about his or her path.

I have noticed this. The most highly evolved spiritual masters deny their knowledge. Tenzin Gyatso, His Holiness the fourteenth Dalai Lama of Tibet, is considered by some a living buddha, the incarnation of wisdom and compassion. Nonetheless he thinks of himself as an ordinary monk, quite unenlightened.

"Are you enlightened?" I asked him.

"Me? No, no, no." He broke out laughing with open delight. The thing you notice about the Dalai Lama, as with all spiritual masters, is his happiness. He is very jolly, open, warm.

He took my hand in both of his, sharing his ecstatic energy. "I personally have no experience of the Awakening Mind," he confided happily.

When he was in his thirties, said His Holiness, he thought it possible to become an *arhat*, attaining the state of nirvana or personal enlightenment for himself alone. But now, nearing sixty, he says he has still not developed the Awakening Mind. The Tibetans mark twenty-two distinct categories of awakening, moving from "earthlike" to "goldlike." These may also be classified as ten buddha levels. But an *arhat* has reached only the midway point. To achieve full enlightenment one must move beyond the desire for personal liberation to that of the bodhisattva or living buddha, who brings others to enlightenment. (*Bodhisattva* means "enlightenment-being," one who agrees out of overweening compassion to be reborn in order to help all sentient beings to attain enlightenment. Like the word *buddha*, it derives from the Sanskrit root *buddh*, "to wake up." The Buddha, once asked who he was, responded, "I am awake.")

At the same time, the Dalai Lama, this extraordinary being, admits that he has "some confidence" that if he could meditate and devote himself to his studies fulltime, if he had no other work, he might reach buddhahood in this lifetime. For this is his passion: he is serious about his spiritual path.

"In my dreams," he told me, "I never dream I am the Dalai Lama. I dream of fighting or sexual things, but then immediately I remember I am a monk, because monkhood is dearest to my heart."[4]

Nonetheless, the mystical is intriguing to him. In one recent book he writes, "I wish that I had such mystical experiences myself, but—no luck! There are quite a few questions that I would like to ask! If I were to have such mystical visionary experiences, there is much that I would do . . . take the side of a scientist, be the devil's advocate and ask a lot of questions!"[5]

He notes, for example, that psychic visions require a degree of receptivity and openness, that because one person sees a manifested form or vision, it does not mean that another person in the same room would see it too. "Frankly speaking these are very mysterious phenomena, and . . . I feel these are areas that require a great deal of study and research, as well as experimentation."[6]

We have little scientific understanding of these magical experiences, and virtually no experimentation. What captures our fancy are the stories.

I think more stories are told in India than anywhere I've ever visited. People are thrilled by their guru's miracles and they talk about psychic matters constantly. How the guru walked through doors, or healed a dying man, or was seen in his hometown at the same time that he was visiting a friend three hundred miles away; how your illness lifted just on seeing him, or how he brought you money or a bride. Buddhists and Hindus both believe in reincarnation, and the more powers your guru displays, the more miracles he can produce, the more incarnations he is said to have lived. But this is deceptive proof. Having *siddhis*, or powers, does not necessarily relate to mystical experience and can easily lead to egoism and magic, as we shall see later on.

Then, too, we should take note: A spiritual awakening does not always come with a clap of thunder. It may seep into the pores of your body with so imperceptible a motion that only your friends may mark a difference; this is what William James calls the "educational variety." One day you look back and see you are different than you were five years ago. Yet you cannot remember a single mystical ecstasy that created that slow change.

After my collapse in the bathtub (was it even a mystical experience?), I returned to my ordinary life. I can't remember if I engaged in psychic exploration. I had never done the tarot cards or gone to an astrologer, or attempted to control the future with any psychic oracles.

And neither did I read about the saints of the Middle Ages, who reported such profound experiences. In fact a good deal has changed in the last twenty years, including the availability of publications for a general audience about these medieval mystics and their lives. Theirs is not the stuff of ordinary lives. Yet they are worth reading about, for they provide a point of reference, these extraordinary people who recorded their own visions and ecstatic experiences and who not only were not insane but indeed greater than the rest of us. Consider four magnificent women now long dead.

Hildegard of Bingen was a twelfth-century German nun. She was three years old when she saw "so great a brightness that [her] soul trembled." In 1106, at the age of eight, she was offered by her parents as a tithe to the nearby Benedictine monastery of Disibodenberg, she being the tenth child and tithing being a custom in those days. She entered the monastery under the care of an enclosed anchoress, Jutta, who lived walled into a tiny cell at the predominately male monastery. At the age of fifteen Hildegard took vows as a Benedictine nun, and for forty-four years she remained at Disibodenberg, eventually being elected leader of her community, before leaving at the age of fifty-nine to found the famous Rupertsberg convent for her nuns. For the last twelve years of her life, she traveled up and down the River Main, speaking both to clergy and to laypeople—and this was a courageous act, you must understand, at a time when the scriptural injunction (1 Timothy 2:12) that precluded a woman from preaching was taken seriously.

Ever since childhood, Hildegard had been clairvoyant and clairaudient. She experienced "secret and marvelous visions" of non-spatial light, sometimes accompanied by a voice addressing her in Latin.

> The visions which I saw I did not perceive in dreams nor when asleep nor in a delirium nor with the eyes or ears of the body. I received them when I was awake and looking around with a clear mind, with the inner eyes and ears, in open places according to the will of God. But how this could be, it is difficult for us mortals to seek to know.[7]

At first she "suppressed [her visions] beneath strict silence." Only a few people knew of her gifts. She herself regarded them as disabilities that threw her into illness. (In fact every major decision of her life was preceded by prolonged and debilitating illness.) Then, when she was forty-two, she received the divine command to disclose her visions (and later we shall see that the forties seems to be a watershed time in many people's lives). The command came dramatically.

> In the year 1141 of the incarnation of Jesus Christ the son of God . . . a fiery light, flashing intensely, came from the open vault of heaven and poured through my whole brain. Like a

flame that is hot without burning it kindled all my heart and all my breast, just as the sun warms anything on which its rays fall. And suddenly I could understand what such books as the Psalter, the Gospel and the other Catholic volumes both of the Old and New Testament actually set forth; but I could not interpret the words of the text; nor could I divide up the syllables; nor did I have any notion of the cases or tenses.[8]

From her knowledge thus acquired, she composed music, painted beautifully, wrote books not only about the spiritual worlds but also about the natural sciences, the human body, plants, and medicine. She corresponded with abbots, popes, and kings—and scolded them, too, when she felt them in the wrong. Her first visionary book, *Scivias,* or "Know the Ways [of the Lord]," took ten years to write; her second, *The Book of Life's Merits,* took five years; and her third and most accomplished visionary record, *The Book of Divine Works,* another ten.

Hildegard of Bingen was a powerful force in her age, traveling, teaching, writing, excoriating those whom she felt abused their power, and guiding those who wanted to deepen their spiritual path. She called herself God's mouthpiece, a "small trumpet," a "feather on the breath of God." She died in 1179 at the age of eighty-one.

But these facts reveal nothing of the raptures she must have enjoyed or the knowings and showings that made the English anchoress Julian of Norwich write, after one vision on May 13, 1373, the lines that all mystics sing after an encounter with God:

All will be well
And all will be well
And all manner of thing will be well.

Catherine of Siena was another youthful visionary. Born Catherine Benincasa in 1347, the youngest of twenty-four or twenty-five children, she had a vision of Christ at the age of six; at seven she took a vow of perpetual virginity. Later she passionately fought her family's wish for her to marry—and won only when her father saw the image of a dove hovering over her head as she prayed. At sixteen she joined the Dominicans, wore the white veil as a member of the Third Order of Saint Dominic. Thereafter she went into three years of silence, solitude, prayer, fasting, contemplation, and spiritual battles with the demons she saw around her, until she was so bonded and wedded to her Bridegroom, Christ, that in 1367, on Shrove Tuesday, the last day before Lent, she saw him place on her finger his ring—invisible to everyone but her. Later, praying for a "clean heart," she saw that he removed her heart and a few days later returned to set his very own heart in her breast.

At twenty-five she stopped eating—so filled was she by spiritual food—and this *inedia* continued until her death some eight years later. She slept one half hour out of twenty-four hours. She healed lepers, cast out demons, and nursed the sick, and so holy was her presence that in 1376 the Pope assigned three priests to accompany her when she went out in public, in order to tend the crowds who would cry out for the sacraments when they laid eyes on her. She fell into trance states so deep that she appeared dead for days on end—states comparable to the Hindu *samadhi*.

"I saw the hidden things of God," Catherine said of the experience, "and now I am thrust back again into the prison of the body."[9] She died in 1380.

We read also of Catherine Fieschi of Genoa, born in 1447, a hundred years after the earlier Catherine's birth. Another child prodigy, she had her first spiritual experience at the age of twelve and began her life of prayer. Remarkably beautiful, she was married off at fifteen to a drinking, gambling libertine, the very opposite of herself. She fell into a depression that lasted five years, then tried to console herself with five years of whirlwind social gaiety. At the age of twenty-five she grew so soul-sick that she was confined (in answer to her prayers) for three months to her room.

Finally her sister Limbania dragged her to a confessor, for apathy or despair—*accidie*—was one of the deadly sins. There, kneeling before the priest, Catherine suddenly—to her astonishment—received "a wound to the heart" from God's immense love. Knowledge of God always comes "in a rush," she explained.

"No more world! No more sins!" she cried, but nevertheless she spent the next four years practicing austerities. She wore a hair shirt, walked with her eyes downcast, slept little, abstained from meat and fruit, and enjoyed the exquisite pain of mystical ecstasies.

"My knee is God!" she cried, caught up in union with the Beloved.

Later she became director of a hospital, the Pammetone. She wrote of the fire of the love of God that draws and binds the soul to Himself "with a love that by itself could annihilate the immortal soul."[10] Then,

> The soul becomes like gold
> that becomes purer as it is fired,
> all dross being cast out.

> Having come to the point of twenty-four carats,
> gold cannot be purified any further;
> and this is what happens to the soul
> in the fire of God's love.[11]

The imagery of fire is common to mystics. Her predecessor and namesake, Saint Catherine of Siena, had also equated God's love with fire. "But as a flame burns higher the more fuel is fed it," she wrote of herself in the *Dialogue*, "the fire in this soul grew so great that her body could not have contained it. She could not, in fact, have survived had she not been encircled by the strength of him who is strength itself."[12]

But with Catherine of Genoa this fire was actual. In

1510, as she lay dying, surrounded by a circle of friends and spiritual seekers, she experienced terrible, internal burning. Her skin scalded anyone who touched her (more on this phenomenon later). Yet whenever she regained consciousness, she was found laughing—playing, she said, with angels.

Who can relate to such spiritual giants? We read of them with wonder. They seem like curiosities, queer, wondrous, historical beings, mutants almost, far removed from our everyday experience. They are interesting because they flew so far above the norm that they stand as beacons before us, calling to possibilities that we can hardly imagine.

It's easier perhaps, to consider the more accessible Saint Teresa of Avila, born in 1515, who entered a convent at the age of eighteen and despite her piety found it hard.

"All of my bones were pulled asunder," she wrote about leaving her happy home. Convent life was difficult for Teresa. She was beautiful, fun-loving, intelligent. She had to fight her liking for luxury, for brilliant company, for men, for gay, witty conversation, for the pleasures and frivolities of ordinary life. All of which seemed sins to her. In her *Life*, written many years later, she judges these normal earthly desires so harshly that we distrust, even dislike her, wondering what grandiosity might provoke such egotistical self-judgments, deciding that somehow "the lady doth protest too much." We must remember, however, that the Inquisition was peering over her shoulder as she wrote, ready to cast her into the torture chamber if she did not condemn herself first. This makes her self-incrimination more understandable, in fact quite clever. The Inquisition bore down on any heresy, including the suspect practice of interior prayer and the ways of the *alumbrados*, the "illuminists" who searched for the direct ecstatic contact with God. The Inquisition was especially attentive to the deviance of the *Judaeo-conversos*. These were the Jews who had converted to Christianity in the great sweep of 1492 and who were suspected of practicing their ancient faith; and Teresa's grandfather, a *converso*, had been stoned and spat upon.

For twenty years, in the convent Teresa found prayer difficult. Then one day, when she was around the age of thirty-eight, she walked past a statue of Christ on the cross—and found herself on her knees, in tears. After that she began to receive "delights and favors" from His Majesty, raptures and ecstasies. Sometimes when she went into trance, worshiping Christ, her body would rise from the floor and float in midair in the church. She hated levitation. She asked her sisters to hold her down forcibly, so embarrassed was she by this display, which she felt had nothing to do with spirituality.

By the time of her death in 1582, against great odds and under constant scrutiny by the Inquisition, she had founded seventeen reform convents throughout

Spain. Her Discalced Carmelites practiced strict poverty (*discalced* literally meaning barefoot, but taken to mean wearing no leather shoes: the nuns wore sandals and coarse robes).

In her forties (again in the forties!), reluctantly, and only at the direction of her spiritual adviser, Teresa began to write down what she had been graced to see, and with her sharp, disciplined mind she laid out in her books and in hundreds of letters the sacred entry to the kingdom within.

"Let us imagine that within us is an extremely rich palace, built entirely of gold and precious stones. . . ."[13]

I didn't spend much time reading about the saints. Their lives seemed far removed from mine. If I read anything it was—with fascination—about seemingly ordinary people who performed impossible deeds in the name of God. It all seemed inexplicable. Pizarro, for example, walking in full armor across the Peruvian desert, with a few horses and a tiny band of men at arms. He conquered an entire nation (bloodthirsty! horrible!) simply in the confidence that he was moved by God. Like Cortés in Mexico, he succeeded in part because of ancient Indian prophecies that a strange people would arrive like birds from across the sea and destroy their kingdoms.

What mysterious stories.

Yet it is comforting to find that even the saints quite humanly messed up. Even the disciples of Christ. If we think we have to be saints to do the will of God, we need only remember how Mary Magdalene, weeping at the tomb, met her beloved Master and thought he was a gardener. Imagine! She didn't even recognize him. Christ then appeared to two more disciples on the road to Emmaus; they didn't recognize him until he'd gone away. On the third occasion, he appeared to the eleven disciples gathered sadly in an upper room for dinner. He just walked through the wall. "Why did you doubt?" he asked, and I like to think he was laughing, enjoying the joke.

Christ told them to go out and spread the Good News. And then he disappeared and never returned in body again, but only as spiritual ectoplasm, which is how he has been appearing ever since to people around the globe.

To whom did he give this charge? To the broken ones, to women, to a former prostitute who had had seven devils cast out of her, to men who had abandoned him, run away, fallen asleep when he asked them to stay awake, cravenly denied even knowing him when their own lives might be at stake. He gave the charge to failed fishermen, to the jealous, the angry, the mentally ill. But he also added that they would not be alone. There would always be spiritual help at hand.

In the early days of Christianity, the word *saint* meant any Christian, and All Saints' Day was named in memory of any Christian who had ever died. As the centuries passed the word took on exalted shadings, so that by the tenth century, a thousand years after the death of Christ, the Church had to add the second celebration of

All Souls' Day right after All Saints' Day, to honor the ordinary ones, like us, the ones who struggle every day to subdue our defects of character and increase our goodness of heart. The good news is that saintliness is not a requirement for God's love, or for starting on the spiritual journey, or for the ecstasies that are so generously poured over us to encourage us on the path; for surely otherwise what happened next to me could never have occurred.

CHAPTER 4

THE REVELATION ON MACHU PICCHU

Who can describe a fervor that is ineffable? Who can lay bare such infinite sweetness? I know that if I wanted to speak of this inexpressible joy, I would seem as though I were trying to empty the sea, drop by drop, bit by bit, and push it down a tiny hole in the ground! It is no wonder that I, who have scarcely tasted a drop of this towering experience, cannot disclose the immensity of this eternal sweetness.

—RICHARD ROLLE

There was silence;
there was chaos,
there was a voice.
A mind went forth to form worlds:
now order reigns where chaos once held sway.

—THE TALMUD

Of all that God has shown me
I can speak just the smallest word,
Not more than a honey bee
Takes on her foot
From an overspilling jar.

—MECHTILD OF MAGDEBURG

As a child, and later as a grown woman, I knew none of what I've just described about the mystics—not even the word. Of course, I had heard the names of Saint Augustine, Saint Teresa, Saint John of the Cross, Julian of Norwich, but I had no interest in reading their work or lives, so what happened to me next came out of the blue, as it were, without warning or training, and without the discipline of a spiritual guide. I didn't know about raptures and ecstasies. I didn't know that the Way can be traced by footfalls trodden in regular exercise and following the prints of masters who have gone before.

I meditated because I could not help myself. I prayed because I loved to pray. By then, five or six years after my family had moved to Washington, after I had started meditating, I had developed some kind of faith. I attributed it in part to my beloved teacher, the Hindu sage who had first set a spark of understanding and fire into my heart.

But who was I? An ordinary woman, a wife, the mother of two beautiful daughters. I wrote books and articles, cooked meals, laughed with my husband, played with my friends, gave parties and went to them, struggled to pay the bills. I worried about my parents and read to my kids. I laughed a lot. Only, sometimes, a desperate longing filled my heart, so that the emptiness of the physical world felt heavy to me. One day I stared at my face in the mirror. "Is this all?" I asked myself.

I passed my fortieth birthday, then forty-first. I was a few months short of forty-two.

From about the age of eighteen or twenty I had known that my forty-second year would be a special one. Something special was going to happen. Even the numbers seemed magical: 3 + 3 × 7. All prime numbers, indivisible. So clear was this that on my twenty-first birthday, nearing midnight at my desk in college, I had written a letter to myself, to be opened twenty-one years later, when I reached forty-two. Myself, calling to myself across the void of future time. On that birthday, before opening the letter, I wrote another and put it in a drawer to be opened when I reach sixty-three—or perhaps, doubling forty-two, to be opened when I am eighty-four.

Forty-two. I knew it would be an exciting year.

In the course of my life I have had three prayers. When I was five I prayed to be beautiful, because I could already see that pretty girls had an advantage, had power, came out victorious in life. Later, in my teens, I prayed to *understand*, which was a Big prayer. To understand what? *Everything*. To be able to *see*, and if I could see, then, too, that I be given the talent to communicate it, to permit others to understand as well.

Later still, and with increasing longing, I had formed a third prayer: simply to serve the will of God. Because I had on a couple of occasions had glimpses—like flashes of lightning that illuminate the heavens before the black night settles in again—glimpses of the Divine, of the shining light that pervades everything; glimpses of immortality.

Now at forty-two, I prayed with an increased urgency. I wanted some indication of God's grace. I wanted to understand. I wanted to "serve"—whether as a writer

or otherwise. It sounds sentimental perhaps, overly romantic, but I meant it desperately. You see how sensitive
and open and perhaps a little loony I'd become.

A few months earlier my mother had died, and I was
experiencing all the grief that that entails. After her
death, I used to get up at four-thirty in the morning, put
on my sneakers, and run and run in the black night, the
shadow of death at my shoulder, running from my death.

With my mother gone, things changed. I decided to
give up freelancing and write the novel that I had waited
all my life to begin. Time became unutterably precious to
me: I had so little.

But I had accepted one last magazine assignment. I
didn't want to do it. I talked to my husband about returning it to the editors, moving straight into fiction. He
persuaded me to keep my commitment. Oddly, the assignment took me abroad, to Costa Rica and Peru.

It was unusual for a magazine to send me anywhere—I felt lucky to have even modest expenses paid
and enough left over to cover a baby-sitter. It did not
take long before I felt, marveling, that this trip to South
America would constitute a spiritual journey for me.
Without knowing where it would lead or why, I began
to feel the adventure was . . . "planned" is the wrong
word . . . *guided*—by the hand of God. And somehow I
knew that whatever awaited me in Peru would occur at
Machu Picchu. It was uncanny the way people kept coming up to me and telling me urgently: "Here is how you
get to Machu Picchu" or "This is the name of the person
who will get you to Machu Picchu." I felt I was "being

moved," things were falling into place, as if all destiny were determined in advance.

It was Lent. I had given up meat and was fasting, praying, and meditating for long periods.

In Costa Rica, I met three men—one Peruvian, one Scot, one Englishman—each associated with animal welfare and environmental issues. We spent three days talking about God and nature, ethics, the relationship of mankind to this little Earth. In all my life I had never heard a man—women, yes, but not a man—discuss questions of God. I drank it in.

They say that to talk of God is to talk of love, and that when you talk of love you are making love. I loved all three men, but with one, the Englishman, a veterinarian, I fell in love. It hit like a clap of thunder: Eros. One morning I was phoning home, missing my husband of nineteen years, and that same Friday in the afternoon a stranger walked into the room where I was talking to his friends. I looked at him . . . and loved. These three friends all worked in the field of animal protection. They opened my heart—quite literally, as later I would discover: the heart center opened, the chakra by which we see.

On the Monday following, when I left Costa Rica for Peru, I was drunk with love, overwhelmed by the goodness of these three extraordinary men, and in particular by that of the Englishman, whom I saw surrounded by an aura of light. I will speak more about this light in later chapters, but at the time I was confused, swept off my feet. I flicked the light off his skin and watched it scatter in the air. I was undone as well by the thought that for me he somehow stood as representative of the Divine, so that in loving him I was somehow loving God, or in loving God I was loving him. It was all confusing.

We said goodbye. I expected to see none of the three again.

I was waiting for my plane in the San José airport, which was all plastic and cheap construction. I sat down, and suddenly I saw ordinary people flaring with light: tourists, children, soldiers with their guns, Indian women carrying their babies in slings, students, and businessmen—all were shining with light. I began to shake. Light poured off their faces, hands, shoulders, wherever they showed bare skin. I sat in that grungy Central American airport, and tears of humility and gratitude coursed down my cheeks. I put on my sunglasses to hide my tears. I was trembling at the *goodness* of people, at the beauty of these luminous beings. Later I went to a restaurant (the plane was several hours late in taking off) and ordered an avocado and tomato salad, but the food was so exquisite I could not eat; it lay shining on the plate before me, light shining from the living fruit.

Since then, I have seen this phenomenon on other occasions. I have glimpsed it in a veiled or shadowed way, a quickening of light that flares up in another person and dies down again. I think it is the light of love.

In Peru I moved in a state of transport, as if carried by some mysterious force. All things seemed to work toward the perfect execution of my side trip to Machu Picchu: instant tickets, the best hotel. I was floating in some state of grace. At one point I saw two lovers kiss on the street, and my heart tilted with the sure knowledge that God loves all lovers and all who love, as I myself was flaring with love.

From Lima you fly over the Andes to Cuzco and from Cuzco you take a train down along the Urubamba River to Machu Picchu.

Cuzco lies at 11,000 feet, and the sudden change in altitude from sea-level Lima may help create the beauty of the architecture, the landscape, the people's faces. Fresh flowers and a bowl of fruit stood on tables in my hotel room, with its carved four-poster bed and lovely whitewashed walls. I accepted them as further gifts from God, as I took everything on this incredible trip—all of it from God. Yet I felt all this was only preparation, though I didn't know for what.

The first day, I went on a sight-seeing tour of the surrounding areas, and again the beauty ravished me: the hills covered with their yellow-flowering broom and blue lupin gleaming against green grass. The colors are more brilliant than the eyes can absorb, the sky as blue and hard as rock. The scenery is so magnificent that you know God took a special joy in carving those hills with His own hands, molding them to the shape of His palm, then creating flowing water, streams like silver threads, and flowers and shrubs.

The bus tour stopped at a holy spring, sacred to the Incas, where the purest water erupts from the earth, here on top of the world. The source is unknown. The water runs in a steady flow, never varying either in the dry or the rainy season. The Incas worshiped it as the most precious of waters and there, closest to God, I drank three times, and made another prayer, and left three coins in a chink as an offering. We went on to the monumental ruins of the ancient city of Sacsahuaman, and suddenly in the bus I was overcome by another fit of beauty—tears pouring down my cheeks at the ravishment of my heart. A woman behind me said, "Oh, it's raining in on you," thinking it was the open window. But instead it was the open window of my heart. The tour guide gave me sprigs of mint to inhale, in case I was suffering from the high altitude. I breathed in the fragrance of the herb.

The carved stones of the ruined fortress of Sacsahuaman stand fourteen feet high or more, great boulders that had been transported somehow from miles away over steep mountains and across gorges and chasms that are bridged only by flimsy ropes. The Incas had no writing, no wheel. How had they quarried and moved these giant blocks of stone? The stones fit without mortar one on top of another so closely that to this day a knife blade cannot slip between them.

Was it the altitude that so affected me? I stared out the bus window at this glorious landscape and marveled at the meadows with their brilliantly colored wildflowers fashioned by the most loving hand of a most loving God. I was struck by blessings I had always taken for granted: the silver ribbon of water—itself a miracle—to quench our thirst and soak the earth and grass; the generous animals given to carry our burdens, work for us, and love us, and also to provide our food; and air to breathe, and herbs for food and medicine.

Today, the memories come as a jumble, and yet each fragment is so clear that I feel my body shiver again, except now I know it was the Holy Spirit infecting me. I felt embarrassed by the depth of my emotion and grateful that the other tourists thought me so proud that they ignored me, laughing and joking with one another. I feel embarrassed now, writing all this down.

Children saw it.

At one point the bus stopped at a lookout, where everyone descended to take pictures of an Indian family and their herd of alpacas. Vibrating in my inner silence, unable to speak or indeed do more than nod and blindly follow the guide's directions to move into or out of the bus, I left the group and walked across the meadow, straight through a herd of alpacas. The animals never shifted as I passed, but continued their grazing or cud-chewing quietly. I stood at the edge of the cliff, quivering at the sight of the landscape.

A little Indian child, perhaps four or five years old, crept up to me. She had beautiful dark skin and shoe-button black eyes. I smiled. She smiled and then threw herself with all her tiny weight against me, burying her face in my skirt, while I held her head and neck. In a moment she ran off on her stubby legs, back to her family.

In my imagination, I blessed her, blessed God, blessed the landscape, blessed the alpacas as I paced slowly back through the herd. In a strange way I knew that I did not exist at all.

Back in the town I walked to my hotel, and another child of maybe nine trotted after me, caught up, and put her hand trustingly into mine, walking up the hill.

The next day our group took the switchback train to Machu Picchu.

Machu Picchu lies at 9,000 feet, much lower than Cuzco, and what happened to me there had nothing to do with altitude. From the train we transferred to a bus, and I remember thinking I was sorry not to have a chance to walk up the mountain. But halfway up we found that not fifteen minutes earlier a landslide had blocked the road; we had to climb the rest of the way. A girl nearby remarked, "Nothing is valuable without working for it." I took her words as another sign, for by then I was seeing as a schizophrenic sees: with layers of meaning, signs.

I sat on a rock waiting for the others, the elderly, of my tour group. Below me the mountain spilled straight down to the creamy Urubamba River, rushing noisily through the gorge, and high around me soared the three triangular green peaks, the Picchu, all dark greens and majestic jungle sweeps. On the train I had read a little pamphlet that said Machu Picchu had been a military stronghold. I tried to imagine myself an Incan sentry on this outpost. I was impressed at the strength of any soldier who could maintain his belligerence on this site, for I felt no military vibrations, but only waves of holiness, peace, and serenity. The air was very still and fine. Not a breath of wind.

Suddenly I felt a sound of silence hard to describe, a kind of pressing silence, a hollow roaring in both ears, like the sound inside a seashell. Frightened by it—or at least made uneasy by this dark sound—I quickly rose and went to find my group. We learned that far from being a military installation, the magnificent engineering of the lost city marked a sacred site, dedicated to fire (my sign), the sun, and served by a thousand maidens or priestesses. It was the holiest of holies, so sacred that the invading Spaniards never learned of its existence. When the last priestesses died, the jungle reclaimed the site. It was only rediscovered in the 1920s, when the first mail planes flew over it.

We saw the altar of the Sun God, the ruins of the stairwells and buildings, the astrological slit that marks the solstices. But all the while I was filled with anxiety, an increasing urgency, a sense that I had been brought here for a particular reason and I must allow time—a half hour, an hour—to find out why.

Finally I could bear it no longer. "I have to be alone," I said to our guide, Julian, himself a university-trained professor. "Where shall I go, and what time must I be back for the bus?"

He pointed to the terraced fields above us, and told me to be down at the hotel parking lot in an hour. Frantically I scrambled up the hillside, running, slipping, knowing that I had no time, though I did not know why I was hurrying or to what. The more I hurried, the more

I could feel the pressing need. I keep using this word, *knowing,* for that is what it was—a certainty, as if an external force were directing me.

I reached the right spot—Here! again "knowing" the place—threw myself down, closed my eyes to meditate, thinking I would be shown, perhaps, a special peace, and instantly was assailed by the hollow darkness of that silent roar, this time louder, overpowering.

I felt a pressure on my neck, as if a dark hand were pressing me down. Terrible and majestic it was. Nothing sweet and pretty in it, but frightening, full of force. From the midst of black roaring, came a voice: *You belong to me* or *You are mine.* Not in words, but rather as a form of knowledge, resounding in blackness. I was filled with its intent, which I understood in two ways: first that work would be required, and second that it would be hard.

For a moment I fought it, terrified. Then: "If you are God, yes," I surrendered with my last coherent thoughts. "I belong only to God." As for the work: "With your help. I am not big enough. Help me!"

With that I was immersed in a sweetness words cannot express. I could hear the singing of the planets, and wave after wave of light washed over me. But this is wrong, because I *was* the light as well, without distinction of self or of being washed. It is hard to speak of what happened at this stage. At one level I ceased to exist, was swallowed into light. How long that lasted I do not know. At another level, although I no longer existed as a separate "I," nonetheless I saw things, thus indicating the duality of "I" and "other." In that state I knew things that today I haven't even the wit to ask questions about. Some I do not remember, but I know that I saw into the structure of the universe. I had the impression of knowing beyond knowledge and being given glimpses into ALL. I capitalize because of the feebleness of words. It was knowledge untranslatable, and it filled me with joy.

I remember the destruction of planets in an encapsulation of time, with raging fires, as if of nuclear disaster, and deserts where life had been, and time passing, millions of years perhaps, and more life growing. I saw the perfection of all things that had ever happened or ever will, and how the destruction didn't matter, for energy goes on, transmuted, so that even destruction is an expression of pure God-ness, love, and creativity.

I saw that everything was perfect, and all was composed of love. I saw there is no death.

Most of it I have forgotten now. But one image remains—of sparks of light, like angels, like atoms or electrons sweeping, dancing, pulled behind the image of the Light. They were alive with praise. As solar debris is sucked across the heavens by a passing comet and pulled along to form its tail, so these dancing sparks were swept up in the wake of the Divine. And yet they were themselves composed of the Divine, as all is divine, every atom, every particle of light, singing wildly in its joy.

I did not see God, for that would have blinded me, but I saw the bending of the grasses at the passing of the hem of His garments. Everything alive with praise!

In the midst of these visions, as I was returning to my senses, I made one spotty, human, and inconsequential prayer, a speechless quiver of heartstrings (already coming out of the unitive state, you see). And then I felt the universe tilt with such joyful delicacy, such warmth of understanding, that it felt like a mother who laughingly hugs her little boy, crying, *Yes!* with unfathomable, unconditional, and insuperable love.

Slowly, slowly I came out of it, climbing like a deep-sea turtle up toward the air. I opened my eyes—and closed them instantly! Blinded by the daylight. Gradually the sound of silence faded. The black ringing stopped. After a time I opened my eyes again, and blinked stupefied against a dull and overcast pearl sky, hardly bright at all. My senses still enraptured, I was humbled by the indulgent love of the Absolute, and by a joy beyond description.

A light rain began to fall.

I stumbled to my feet. I wore no watch, and suddenly the thought slammed into me that I must hurry or I would miss the bus. I grabbed my jacket and ran down the hillside toward the hotel, leaping over the terraces. I felt myself spring down the mountain full of power and joy, to meet my group.

But what was remarkable: When I looked down I saw light streaming off the palms of my hands. I could feel it pulsating off my palms in waves, like hot currents. I could see it flaring, flashing in everything; the fields were shining with light. And so were the people gathering at the hotel, some drinking pisco sours, talking to one another and shining with their inner light.

Later, we took the train from Machu Picchu back to Cuzco. I rode in a wild and joyous state, knowing that all creation is perfect and is most perfectly composed of love.

Knowing I knew nothing.

Knowing I would never be the same.

CHAPTER 5

LIGHT AND HEAT: BURNING WITH THE FIRE OF LOVE

O Light that none can name, for it is altogether
    nameless.
O Light with many names, for it is at work in all
    things . . .
How do you mingle yourself with grass?
How, while continuing unchanged, altogether
    inaccessible,
Do you preserve the nature of the grass
    unconsumed?

> —SYMEON, ABBOT OF ST. MACROS,
>
> *HYMNS OF DIVINE LOVE*

When I flowed out of the Creator, all creatures
stood up and shouted and said, "Behold. Here is
God!" And they were correct.

> —MEISTER ECKHART

Before every human being comes a retinue of
angels, announcing, "MAKE WAY FOR AN
IMAGE OF THE HOLY ONE. BLESSED BE
HE."

> —HASIDIC TEACHING

AA nd now I must leave my own story momentarily and provide what I didn't have myself at the time: some background for the mystical experiences. What had happened? What was the meaning of the psychic powers—telepathy, clairvoyance, healing properties, auras, or energy storms—that assailed me?

In 1901 Dr. Richard Maurice Bucke, a Canadian by birth, a former railroad worker, steamboat deckhand, wagon-train driver, gold miner, and a medical doctor, brought out a small book which almost one hundred years later is still regarded as a classic of its kind. He died less than a year after publication of *Cosmic Consciousness*, but its title has gone into our general vocabulary, as another term for what is also called illumination. In Christian mysticism Illumination is considered the third stage of a mystic's progress, after Awakening and Purification, but I'm not sure the stages can be so precisely marked. They come all topsy-turvy, all the time, while the human mind, struggling to control the chaos and make God's messiness more comfortable, creates classifications. In Buddhism and Hinduism, illumination comes after long self-discipline and effort.

"Cosmic consciousness in its more striking instances," Bucke wrote, "is not simply an expansion or extension of the self-conscious mind with which we are all familiar, but the superaddition of a function as distinct from any possessed by the average man as self-consciousness is distinct from any function possessed by one of the higher animals."[1]

Bucke found fourteen cases of "full" illumination

or enlightenment in the last three thousand years of human history, including the Buddha, Christ, Saint Paul, Muhammad, Francis Bacon, William Blake, Honoré de Balzac, and Walt Whitman. Fourteen cases in three thousand years does not seem like many, but naming thirty-four more examples of incomplete or "lesser" instances of cosmic consciousness (including Moses, Pushkin, Emerson, Thoreau, Pascal, and Swedenborg), and noting the increasing frequency of these anecdotal accounts, Bucke maintained that cosmic consciousness is a natural condition into which humankind is now evolving, and that one day it will mark the majority of the human race.

Perhaps it was the culture of his times that led him to three conclusions that seem suspect to our modern eye. Still, they are worth pondering. First, noting the preponderance of men on his list,[2] he deduced that men experience illumination more often than women. Apparently it did not occur to him that men, enjoying in most cultures the advantages of literacy and power, may have recorded their ecstasies more often than women, or that women—who for centuries were burned as witches for what often earned men reverence—may have hesitated to report their experiences; or another possibility, that some women live so close to the ecstatic union much of the time that they consider it the norm. At any rate, he found the experiences reported more often by men.

Second, having confined his study principally to the Northern Hemisphere, Bucke noted that nearly all the recorded cases of cosmic consciousness occurred in early spring and late summer—one half of them in May or June.

Third, he remarked that the average age at illumination came at full maturity, which he placed at from thirty to forty, the "high water mark of efficiency," and concluded, therefore, that it was a state developing halfway through one's life. This last conclusion may have been influenced by his own experience, at the age of thirty-five, and we would have to question what happens as our life span lengthens.

Bucke received what he called a temporary illumination—the point of entry, as he termed this state of seeing. It enriched his whole life afterward. His experience occurred in 1872, some twenty-five years before he wrote his book. He was driving home in a hansom after spending an evening discussing poetry and philosophy with two friends.

I was in a state of quiet, almost passive enjoyment, not actually thinking, but letting ideas, images, and emotions flow of themselves, as it were, through my mind. All at once, without warning of any kind, I found myself wrapped in a flame-colored cloud. For an instant I thought of fire, an immense conflagration somewhere close by in that great city; the next I knew that the fire was within myself. Directly afterward there came upon me a sense of exultation, of immense joyousness accompanied or immediately followed by an intellectual illumination impossible to describe.

Among other things, I did not merely come to believe, but I saw that the universe is not composed of dead matter, but is, on the contrary, a living Presence; I became conscious in myself of eternal life. It was not a conviction that I would have eternal life, but a consciousness that I possessed eternal life then; I saw that all men are immortal; that the cosmic order is such that without any peradventure all things work together for the good of each and all; that the foundation principle of the world, of all the worlds, is what we call love, and that the happiness of each and all is in the long run absolutely certain. The vision lasted a few seconds and was gone; but the memory of it and the sense of the reality of what it taught has remained during the quarter of a century which has since elapsed. I knew that what the vision showed was true. I had attained to a point of view from which I saw that it must be true. That view, that conviction, I may say that consciousness, has never, even during periods of the deepest depression, been lost.[3]

The prime characteristic of cosmic consciousness is an awareness of the shining life and order of the universe. In addition, an intellectual enlightenment strikes "which alone," says Bucke, "would place the individual on a new plane of existence—would make him almost a member of a new species."[4] To this is added a sense of elation, an indescribable exaltation, and finally, and possibly more important, a striking new moral power combined with a sense of immortality. For Bucke, this last comes not as a conviction that he will have eternal life sometime after death, but that he has it now.

When I came down from the mountain at Machu Picchu, my heart leaping like David dancing to his tambourines, I thought, That's what happened to Moses. The leader of his people, Moses went up Mount Sinai to talk with God. He walked alone, up into volcanic smoke and fog, for the mountain was covered with a dense cloud and with smoke that rose to the sky. Thunderous growling roared about him, fire played at the summit, and the whole mountain shook, as Moses climbed alone—was he frightened?—to meet his God.

When he came back down, the light from his face shone so brightly no one could look at him. They say he had to wear a veil lest his followers be blinded by the light—though I've always thought this part was made up afterward, a tall tale spun over generations to make a point.

Well, I was no Moses, and I don't know what others saw in me that day. A friend, Sarah Michaels, tells how once in Greece she found herself in a frightening place, and how, rooted to the spot in fear, she desperately began to pray. Suddenly she felt invisible hands pick her up from behind and carry her down the road and across a footbridge. She speaks of what everyone describes on coming into contact with an angel—of feeling herself washed by light and by absolute, unconditional love, of feeling utterly safe, as if held in the embrace of Mother, or Home. All fear vanished into love.

On the far side of the bridge, the angel dropped her. Sarah skinned her knee. She scrambled to her feet and raced pell-mell up the road and into the village, up the stairs to the pension where her friends were staying. She burst into the room. Her friends looked at her. "Sarah, what's happened?"

"Oh, nothing," she said. "I just got spooked out there."

But one girl drew her aside. "No, you have to tell me. You're shining with light," she said. "You've seen God."

This light is interesting. Does it always accompany that union with the Divine which Eastern religions call enlightenment? I had thought that the term referred to an insight, an intellectual illumination, not a literal phenomenon. Yet at the hotel, and all the way back to Cuzco riding in the train, I could see light pouring off my hands and every other living thing. My heart flew out over the jungle, ecstatic with the remembrance of my vision, of the insuperable and passionate love that pervades creation.

In biology the property of certain living organisms to emit rays of light is known as photogenesis. We think of fireflies, electric eels, the phosphorescence shining off the sea at night. Moreover, it is commonly accepted that saints and mystics emit light, and this is so well known (at least it was before the skeptical and scientific humanism of the twentieth century, which itself is founded on the rationalism of the eighteenth century, paradoxically called the Age of Enlightenment) that artists have always painted halos around the heads of saints.

It is said that Saint Francis of Assisi and Saint Clare met one night, and their joy in seeing one another was so great and their discourse on God so exalted that their souls lit up the night sky for miles around.

We know this phenomenon. It is called love. "His face lit up," we say even of the ordinary man when he sees the woman whom he loves. "She was just glowing," we say of the bride.

The light is associated with auras, for when a person is deeply moved, her energy flares out in myriad colors. Clairvoyants see this light, psychics see it, and I am told that anyone can be taught to see auras, though I have never understood the purpose, if it is treated only as a parlor game. But we are talking about the person who has had an encounter with the Divine, the Atman, the Beloved; we are talking of the person who is united even for an instant with that magnificence, and enters the pure, timeless state that Buddhists call nirvana and Christians the Kingdom of God. It is the I AM. Saint Augustine called it "That Which Is"; Plotinus, "the One" and "the Supplier of True Life"; Saint Bernard, "the Energetic Word." Dante called it "the Eternal Light"; Ruysbroeck, "the Abyss"; Saint Catherine of Siena, "Pure Love"; Saint Teresa of Avila, "His Majesty." It is Paul Tillich's "Ground of Our Being," Martin Buber's "the Eternal Thou," Hegel's "Absolute Spirit." It is the Goddess. It is Yahweh, Allah, Jehovah, Krishna, Vishnu,

Buddha, Christ, and the Holy Spirit. It is called Enlightenment. The Awakening. Dieu. Gott. God.

"The world is charged with the grandeur of God," wrote Gerard Manley Hopkins. "It will flame out like shining from shook foil. . . ."[5]

It is a true phenomenon, this luminous energy. Sometimes it is accompanied by the ability to levitate, though not all those who levitate demonstrate the phenomenon of shining. Sometimes the light expands into burning heat, with inextinguishable thirst, and sometimes it is accompanied by clairvoyance, healing touch, telepathy, or the ability to perform miracles, to bilocate (appear in two places at once), or to become invisible.

The face of Saint Teresa of Avila was said to burn with light, as was that of Saint Ignatius of Loyola, who was observed by his landlady's son, Juan Pasqual: "Many nights I looked and saw his room shining with light and he, stretched on the ground crying and sighing."[6]

The face of Benedict Labre, the French mendicant saint who died in Rome in 1783, was so resplendent with light that the rays from his cheeks and brow reflected right onto the church walls. Benedict was the eldest of fifteen children of a prosperous shopkeeper. His efforts to join a religious order were rejected, and he spent most of his brief thirty-five years of life as a wandering pilgrim, an ascetic "fool for Christ," traveling on foot, sleeping in the open, his clothing in rags, his body filthy, accepting what food was given him, talking little, praying much in all the churches of Rome.

The Russian saint Seraphim of Sarov (1759–1833)

one day asked his biographer, Nicolas Motovilov, "Why don't you look at me?" Motovilov responded, "I can't look at you, Father, because your eyes shoot out lights and your face shines more than the sun, and it hurts my eyes."[7]

But this quality of luminescence is also seen in ordinary souls who are not noted for their spirituality. In 1934 the nurses in a hospital in Pirano, Italy, reported that a patient, Anna Monaro, was emitting rays of light as she slept, and that these rays lit up her dark body, especially at the heart, flaring for several seconds at a time. In confusion they called her doctor, who could find no reason for the play of light, this aurora borealis at her breast. It caused a sensation in the papers. "The luminous woman of Pirano," she was called.

The light I saw pouring from my hands, was it like this? At the time I knew nothing of these phenomena. I marveled at this *stuff* shooting from my palms. I knew that I was shining, and likewise with my spiritual eye I could see light shimmering from all the people around me, and from all the trees and grass and clouds in the sky, all living things pouring light out into light. The world was alive and flaming like that bush which Moses saw, consumed by fire and not burning. Consumed, we could say, by spiritual flames. For me all was consumed by love, the very knowledge and wisdom I had encountered in that vision. But it was only afterward that I began to read and study and try to understand what had happened there.

"The increasing intimacy between the soul and God,"

wrote Flemish mystic Jan van Ruysbroeck (1293–1381), "translates often in terms of 'light' and 'heat.' The fully unified man is illuminated. The light and heat are so intense and inordinate that the entire spirit finds itself incapable of pursuing its normal occupations, but melts and faints in the love that it feels in this unity."[8]

When Jesus led Peter and the two brothers, James and John, up a high mountain, they saw him suddenly transfigured. His face shone like the sun. His clothes became whiter than anything white on earth, white as light. Standing beside him, the disciples saw, were the two holiest of prophets, Moses and Elijah. The men were frightened, and not knowing what to say, Peter clumsily blurted out: "Lord, how good it is we're here. If you wish, I'll make three shelters, altars, one for you, one for Moses, one for Elijah." But before he finished speaking a bright cloud cast its shadow over them and they heard a voice from the cloud: "This is my Son, my Beloved, listen to him." The disciples fell to the ground in terror.

Then Jesus came up and touched them. "Don't be afraid," he said. "Stand up."

Like Arjuna with Lord Krishna, when they looked they saw only the familiar face of Jesus, the Rabbi whom they loved, standing there as usual, alone with them.

On the way down the mountain, he enjoined them to tell no one, a request which, as we know, they blatantly ignored. Yet, strange as it is, this transfiguration, this blending into the light of utter love, has been recorded in other religions too. It is a true phenomenon.

I saw it, for example, the day I met Krishna Gopol Vyasji, Maharaj, the guru who first gave me a mantra and who later became my teacher. (The root of the word *guru* means "darkness-scatterer," the one who brings light, illumination. But *guru* basically means teacher or spiritual director.)

I met the teacher on the second of his rare visits to the United States. He was staying with a distant cousin of mine in Virginia, and she had telephoned one day to ask if I wanted to meet him.

"A guru?" I laughed. "Sure. Why not?" It's not every day you get to meet a saint. This was in the mid-1970s, when gurus were rarer in the States than they were to become ten years later.

I drove down to her house. At the time I had no idea how unusual the meeting was, or how difficult it is for people to gain a private audience. Alone, I was ushered into an upstairs room, where I saw an older man sitting cross-legged on the floor. He was simply dressed in a white cotton shirt and loose white pants, and he was shining with light. My first impulse was to throw myself to the ground and kiss his feet.

The thought shocked me. People of my background and breeding do not prostrate themselves before other human beings. Holding to my dignity, I settled on a cushion on the floor. For the next hour we talked, and all the time golden tears of joy rolled down my cheeks.

Merely looking at him filled me with joy. I felt I'd come home.

A friend reports a similar experience she had with the Tibetan lama Gwendune, whom she met in the South of France. When she came into contact with his vibrations, "unbearable with love," all she could do was cry. She thought she'd met a small piece of Jesus' unconditional love.

It took years before I accepted Maharaj as my guru, so suspicious was I of cults and of the spiritual and mental brainwashing that we had heard of in the United States. I tested him at every turn. (And this is recommended: the serious seeker must constantly challenge the teacher, ever questioning and skeptical. But once you are convinced the teacher knows more than you and displays holiness, wisdom, and love, then devotion to him or her and to the teaching is appropriate.)

"Does the enlightened person know that he is enlightened?" I once asked Maharaj.

He paused, smiling at me with sweet affection. "He knows that he is different," he answered, and I was suddenly ashamed to ask anything further, all questions seeming irrelevant.

Just this past year, almost twenty years later, I asked him the same question. "Does the enlightened person know he is enlightened?"

"Of course." He laughed.

"How?"

"He cannot tell," he answered simply. "What he knows he cannot put in words. In *samadhi* he experiences bliss, joy. This is not happiness, which is a lower state; happiness comes and goes," he explained. "Thinking can bring happiness, gladness, but not joy. The enlightened person is in a rejoicing state," he said. "He lives in God, and God gives only joy."

I asked the Dalai Lama the same question: "Does the enlightened man know he is enlightened?"

"Yes, certainly!" he answered brightly, still laughing, enjoying himself. The Dalai Lama can hardly put two sentences together without bursting into laughter.

"How?"

"He knows by what kind of thinking is in the mind, what kind of knowledge he has."[9]

In Buddhist philosophy the enlightened being is free of all the hooks and attachments of negative emotions. He or she no longer feels anger, anguish, sorrow, fear, jealousy, remorse, but lives entirely in a pure and realized state of joyous love.[10] The Buddha, asked once who he was, responded, "I am awake." And here's the good news: Anyone, says the Dalai Lama, can reach enlightenment, even a soldier in the army. "We don't know who is enlightened and who is not," said another lama, whom I interviewed in the Himalayan town of Dharamsala. "You could be a buddha. Anyone."

Once a Japanese friend told me about the death of the uncle of his boyhood friend. This man was a Buddhist priest. The family gathered at his deathbed, waiting to hear his last words. They wanted to know what he had learned in his long years as a Buddhist priest, and what important thing he had to tell them. The man looked at his loving family, sat up in bed, and suddenly broke into gales of joyous laughter.

Then he fell back dead.

Enlightenment brings joy. Anyone who has been in the presence of a highly evolved or holy person has seen this. Moreover, you pick it up from him or her, as if the vibrating particles of that person's energy field excite your own and set them dancing in conjunction with his. This is why we seek out avatars, saints, gurus, to have our vibration lifted by that holy presence, and if we are lucky, we retain a bit of it when we have left, instead of sinking back to the ground state (as they call it in nuclear physics) of a resting particle.

A French writer, Isabelle Robinet, describes how in China, the Taoists purposely bring light into their souls and bodies. This technique, she warns, must be learned only under the guidance of a master, and never attempted alone. She describes the method by which the practitioner meditates upon the sun until light begins to fill his body, gradually descending right to the feet; the Taoist practices the technique until his entire body glows and pulsates with light.

Robinet relates that in another exercise the monk brings in the light of the stars of the Big Dipper or Great Bear.

The first star descends to the heart.

The second into the lungs.

The third to the liver, until the practitioner finally reaches the seventh star that descends into the eyes.

At the end of seven years of practice, the disciple

shines "with the light of seven jewels," and from his head shoots a purple ray.[11]

The Taoist saint, like all enlightened ones, can show or hide her light at will, or even make her body disappear. But the great Taoist philosopher Lao-tzu enjoined the practitioner not to demonstrate such magic tricks but to "hide your light" from unwise eyes and those who cannot understand.

We are reminded of Christ's contrary injunction not to hide our light under a bushel—in the cellar or under a meal-tub—but to set it out on the lampstand,[12] where it may shine out to all who see it, and they shall give praise to God. The enlightened ones, those whom we call saints, cannot help but shine and laugh.

When the mystic has merged with God, in the extreme ecstasy of divine union, all physical rules give way. "What do you want me to do now?" she asks her God. "Where do I go now?" For she is burning in the fire of Love.

Sometimes this burning comes literally—as a fiery inner heat. Anyone who has encountered a healer knows about the warmth of that special touch of the laying-on of hands. It can be taught. The best-known schools are Therapeutic Touch and Reiki, but healing powers also come naturally, as a God-given gift, without any formal training at all. The healer's hands become as hot as hot-water bottles, as waffle irons. She places her hands above your body, not even touching your clothing perhaps. You feel her gather your energy in her palms, smoothing and combing your aura field with her hot hands, and at the same time pouring light into your body and your soul. Or else, deep in prayer, she places her hands on your head, flooding you with light and warmth.

Light and heat. They go together, these two qualities. Once I went to a Roman Catholic healing service. The church was packed with men and women waiting for the special touch of Friar John Lubey, an old, old man at the time, very simple, very pure. I have been prayed over in other churches. But this was different. We lined up at the altar rail. Behind us stood the waiting "catchers." The priest walked down the line, lifted one hand, and touched each congregant in the center of the forehead. He held his finger there a moment only—ten seconds probably—and "slain by the spirit," smashed by the light, men and women, myself included, keeled over backward into the waiting catcher's arms. We were laid out full-length on the floor.

The man I fell so passionately in love with that weekend in Costa Rica—he had healing hands. Animals and little children crept into his lap. Later I had many occasions to observe his astonishing abilities and feel his light and heat. Once I watched him on a dare telepathically call to his side two dogs that were a good quarter-mile away (they were not even his dogs; they belonged to a stranger walking them in the park). He sent out some kind of silent signal, and the dogs suddenly began to romp with each other, bounding in wider and wider circles, until in a matter of minutes they were at his side, jumping and greeting him, before taking off again in a straight line, dashing back to their master. He emitted so much heat that sometimes I couldn't sit beside him comfortably. Panting, I would move away. If I remained too long in his presence, a rash broke out on my arms. I spoke earlier of how he emitted light. Yet curiously he wasn't aware of either the light or heat, and he couldn't tell me exactly what he did to call animals to him or help wounds quickly heal.

On the other hand, the medieval mystic Richard Rolle described the phenomenon in detail:

> I can't tell you how astonished I was when I felt my heart grow warm for the first time. It was a real warmth, too, not an imaginary one: I seemed kindled with a fire that I could feel with my senses. I kept feeling my chest over and over again to see if this burning sensation had a physical cause. But when I realized that it came entirely from within myself and that this fire of love had no sensual or sinful origin but was a gift from my Creator, I melted with joy and wanted my love to increase still more, especially because of the pleasurable sensations of interior sweetness that poured into my soul with this spiritual flame. . . . It set my soul ablaze, as though a real fire were burning there.
>
> . . . Others have said, there are certainly people

who are afire with love for Christ . . . but I am arguing that a loving soul feels a heat that is as real as that felt by a finger that is thrust into the fire.[13]

Light and heat both come as a consequence of meditation. The Sufis, members of the mystical branch of Islam, spend their days silently absorbed in chanting the remembrance of God: *La ilaha ill-Allah*. "There is no god but God and his name is Allah; and Muhammad is His prophet." When the Sufi shaykh is meditating, his breathing slows to such a point that he is said to be able to repeat the *dhikr* twenty-one times on a single breath. The first result of these prayers is that the heart catches fire. The Sufi becomes a living flame.[14]

The holy Sufi Shaykh Sharafuddin ad-Daghestani, meditating one winter in seclusion, the ice thick on his beard, attained such a state of pure love of God that—his body on fire—he raced outside, throwing off his clothes, and dove into the ice-cold waters of a nearby river. His followers heard the sound of steam rising from the river.

High in the Himalayas, the Tibetan monks train themselves to generate heat. Here, where the mountains soar 11,000 to 18,000 feet into the sky, and the winter winds whip the snow in long white streamers around their isolated huts and hermitages, the monks practice a discipline called *tum-mo* or *g tumo* (the *g* is silent), and they can raise their body temperature so high that the snow melts around them.

Many years ago, I heard how after long practice the initiate is taken at night to the side of a river or a lake.

He is clad in only a sheet, about three feet wide and five or six feet long. His brother monks chop a hole in the ice, dip his sheet into the freezing water, and wrap him in the cold, wet material. Then the aspirant must dry the cloth with his own body heat. When the sheet is dry, it is dipped again in the water, and this practice continues all night. According to one rule, he must dry at least three sheets in one night in order to be a true *respa*, entitled to wear the insignia of proficiency.

If he succeeds, he is elevated to his new position at a great feast, with the blowing of trumpets and joyful clanging of brass. During the festivities one monk after another comes up to congratulate him on his success. If ever he agrees, "Yes, wasn't I great!" he is instantly demoted, for he forgot that all credit for his accomplishment belongs to God.[15]

The lamas whom I've met, however, insist the *g tumo* has nothing to do with spiritual development, although it comes through secret initiation and must be guided by a master. I found this interesting, for I had read that the feat is a technique acquired for spiritual liberation, and that practiced at its highest level its purpose is to enable one to reach the highest buddha-nature and become a bodhisattva, who can teach others the path to enlightenment and joy.

Apparently, then, there are two kinds of *g tumo* (or two motives for acquiring it): one which arises spontaneously in the course of ecstasies and rapture, when you find yourself burning in the love of God, and another which keeps the hermits warm on winter nights.

This latter requires discipline as well. Alexandra David-Neel, the French orientalist and explorer who spent fourteen years in Tibet in the early part of the century and claimed to speak fluently all the Tibetan dialects, wrote that once initiated into *g tumo*, the monk renounces all fur or woolen clothing and never approaches a fire to warm himself. He never practices the exercises inside a house or near inhabited places, where smoke and smells may interfere with his success, but instead he climbs to a cave or hermitage above 10,000 feet, where in silence, seeing no one, he begins his disciplines well before dawn and must finish before the sun comes up. There in solitude he maintains his ability to raise his inner heat.

I know of only two medical studies of *g tumo*, and both are inconclusive. The French author Hélène Renard in her book, *Des Prodiges et des Hommes,* writes that Dr. Raphael Bastiani obtained permission from the Dalai Lama to study a monk in the Himalayas who practiced *g tumo*. This lama, then about fifty years old, lived as a hermit in total isolation in a sort of stone hut inside a grotto at about 3,000 meters (approximately 10,000 feet) altitude. He passed his days in almost constant meditation. Two young monks accompanied Dr. Bastiani to serve as translators. Together they watched the lama dry a handkerchief in about fifteen minutes.

The doctor expected that he would find the lama's body transformed into a kind of radiator, with temperatures higher than normal. To his surprise, the man's temperature remained at 37° C (98.6° F). Yet the hand-kerchief dried.

Asked how he did it, the lama answered that he did not know exactly. He said that he enters into meditation and concentrates all his energy on a point around the navel. There he starts to light a fire that becomes always more intense and that grows according to the measure of his concentration, kindling a spiritual ecstasy so rich that he experiences a kind of spiritual orgasm. The fire, the flames are not only an image, a psychological or symbolic construct, but create a physiological change as well: of purification, heat, exaltation, illumination, transfiguration. These become reality, drawn from the fire of love; and this interior light and heat constitutes the source of his ability to dry the cloth, melt snow, and survive the winter.

G *tumo* brings visions and intense sensual pleasure, said the lama, but he too warned that it is dangerous to practice without guidance. He said the practitioner must have compassion, love for others, and the desire to help all sentient beings to attain enlightenment.

The second study is the result of four expeditions, the most recent in 1988, when the Dalai Lama, who is forward-thinking and scientifically inclined, gave permission to Dr. Herbert Benson, chief of the section on behavioral medicine at Harvard Medical School and New England Deaconess Hospital (now Beth Israel Deaconess Medical Center), to study Tibetan monks in g *tumo*. Accounts of the expeditions can be found in Dr. Benson's

Beyond the Relaxation Response and also in his *Timeless Healing*, written with Marg Stark.

First he documented that, yes, the monks could indeed dry long, cold, wet sheets measuring three feet by six feet that were wrapped around their naked bodies time and again in freezing temperatures. Within three to five minutes steam rose from their sheets; within forty-five minutes the sheets were dry. He observed monks in Ladakh who wore only sandals on their feet and thin woolen robes, who lived at 19,000-foot heights in the Himalayas in sub-zero weather—and kept warm with the "fierce woman," or heat yoga of *g tumo*. As a woman protects her young, he was told, *g tumo* burns away "defilements." The monks explained that *prana*, or life force, is focused into the "central channel" inside the body, then ignited, producing incredible heat. In one study, performed in February 1981, Benson found that the monks could raise the temperature of their fingers and toes by as much as 8.3° C—roughly 16.5° F— enough to keep anyone warm.[16]

Benson and his team expected to find in *g tumo* the usual changes associated with meditation—decreased oxygen consumption and a general slowing of the nervous system. Earlier, he had measured meditative patients in Boston whose oxygen consumption dropped by 10 to 17 percent. Yet the Tibetan monks experienced so sharp a drop in metabolism that the oxygen consumption of one monk dropped 64 percent—the lowest level ever documented in a human being. This is enough to permit a yogi to survive for hours buried alive, merely breathing the oxygen in the loose soil around him. To confuse the issue, however, in another study one monk's oxygen consumption actually *increased* momentarily, leaving us to conclude with Benson how little we understand about the mechanisms involved in producing *g tumo* heat.[17] Is it a sign of spiritual development? Or is it, as the Dalai Lama and other monks assert, a natural physiological activity, unrelated to compassion or the love of God?

Nonetheless, let's not be misled: Some mystics, in their sensual union with God, do literally burn with love. In the Christian faith, it is called *incendium amoris*, the fire of love. Sometimes the burning reaches levels of intolerable pain.

The saintly monk Padre Pio lived for fifty years in a monastery in the remote village of San Giovanni Rotondo in southern Italy. Born in 1887, he was the only ordained Roman Catholic priest and one of only a few men (for usually women evidence this gift) to have received the stigmata—the bodily wounds of the crucified Christ—on his hands, feet, and side. He saw angels. He fought demons in his cell and would rise in the morning from his bed black and blue from the beatings he'd received. He lived in constant pain. Blood poured from his hands. The bandages had to be changed several times a day. In addition, his body temperature rose sometimes to unimaginable readings, and in this he differed from the Tibetan Buddhists who practice *g tumo*.

Normally the temperature of humans is 98.6° F, and it must not exceed 109.4° F. The extreme limit registered

even in the course of the death throes is 111.2° F. Padre
Pio's temperature was usually a little lower than 98.6° F.
But it could rise as high as 119° F. The standard fever
thermometer does not even reach that high; his temperature was taken with a bath thermometer. Padre Pio
died—much studied by doctors—in 1968.

I spoke earlier of Saint Catherine of Genoa, whose
skin scalded the sisters attending her at her death. Less
well known is Catherine of Geneva (d.1551?), who was
subjected in her mystical raptures to such terrible burning that she would cry aloud. Her skin was so hot that
no one could touch her, and the blood from her stigmata
heated the bowl in which it was collected. Her tongue
was a hot iron, and during her extreme fasts she drank
only a vinegary liquid that she seemed to find refreshing,
though the nuns around her could not imagine how her
stomach could support the drink. Catherine of Geneva,
however, was living in joy, for nothing inhibits the wild
God-ecstasy, the abandonment of the mystic's view. "Put
out my eyes," wrote the poet Rainer Maria Rilke in *The
Book of Hours,* "and I can see you still."

> Put out my eyes, and I can see you still;
> slam my ears to, and I can hear you yet;
> and without any feet can go to you;
> and tongueless, I can conjure you at will.
> Break off my arms, I shall take hold of you
> and grasp you with my heart as with a hand;
> arrest my heart, my brain will beat as true;

and if you set this brain of mine afire,
upon my blood I then will carry you.[18]

Light, heat, levitation, fasting (in one known case, the saint ate *nothing* for ten years),[19] bilocation, clairvoyance, clairaudience, telepathy, prophesy: These are some of the by-products of the mystical way. Others can be learned. You go into a trance and walk on fire, sleep on a bed of nails, pierce your cheeks, unharmed, with thorns, or run a sword through your belly and pull it out without a trace of blood. Or you whirl around on one foot, lost in dizzying meditation and subject to almost erotic spiritual orgasms and to wisdom that cannot even be expressed.

I'm told we use only about one-tenth of our brains. Who knows what powers might be ours if we had access to it all? And if we understood that when bonded to God, absorbed in ecstasy, we would find treasures beyond imagining, would any of us waste time on merely mortal realms?

We read of Tibetan men or women, the *lung-gom-pas*, who run faster than a horse for days and nights without stopping to eat or rest. They cover huge distances by foot, leaping in a kind of trance, almost weightless, and moving across the plains at extraordinary speeds. You must not greet or interrupt one of these individuals if you see him striding toward you, eyes fixed on the horizon, one hand moving up and down as if holding an invisible staff, for the shock to his senses can harm or even kill him. Seeing nothing, eating nothing, drinking nothing, they stride like supermen, crossing in a few days distances that ordinarily would take a month.

Or we read of Hindu yogis levitating, in the fashion of Teresa of Avila, and I imagine their weightless bodies floating like helium balloons and bouncing gently against the ceiling. I myself have never seen this. But after I returned from Peru, when I had begun the stately questioning and study of what had happened on that mountaintop, I was browsing in a bookstore one day, when a young man approached me to talk. It turned out he was a follower of the Maharishi Mahesh Yogi, the guru who developed TM, or transcendental meditation, and who had founded in Washington, D.C., the Maharishi International University (now the Maharishi University of Management). At the time the Maharishi was building a huge structure in downtown Washington, and this young man told me in all seriousness that it called for extra-heavy steel beams.

"Oh? Why?" I asked.

"Because of the falling bodies."

"What falling bodies?"

"The bodies of the people falling when they're practicing levitation."

"You're not serious!"

"I am."

"Can I see it?" I asked, choking with laughter. "Can you get me in to see them levitate?"

"Oh no," he answered seriously. "I haven't ever seen it myself, but you can hear them practicing in the room upstairs. Big thumps, when they fall."

He didn't see the humor in it.

Paramahansa Yogananda describes a similar though more serious and also more successful levitation in his beautiful *Autobiography of a Yogi*. He tells of visiting in the 1920s the wife and holy companion of the enlightened master Lahiri Mahasaya. She told Yogananda how one night she dreamed that there were angels in her room and awoke to find the room filled with a dazzling light and her husband levitating. Up in the air. Surrounding him were angels, palms folded, worshiping his worship of God.

Lahiri Mahasaya spoke to his wife, saying she was not dreaming, whereat she fell to her knees and begged her husband's forgiveness for not having recognized him for the saint that he was. He asked her to do reverence then to the angels, too, who returned her greeting with celestial songs—and disappeared. The room returned to the blackness of deep night.

She became her husband's disciple, and he never slept in her bed again.

Stories about saints circulate in India. The holy ones have power. A sweater picks itself up like a Disney cartoon and slips itself over the guru's head. *Malas* grow.[20] Photographs change. The guru passes through locked doors, heals illnesses, drives out demons, materializes objects. It is commonly accepted that a master emits waves of light or currents of energy so great that all physical barriers fall before its force. Merely by sitting in his presence you are washed clean—all sins forgiven, to use the Christian term. By the fire of his projected thought alone, he can guide, refresh, and invigorate his distant disciples or produce what we call a miracle. The same powers were attributed to certain medieval Christian saints—and to those of other religions too.

Once a passerby saw the eighth-century Sufi master Jafar as-Sadiq at prayer, invoking God repeatedly. "O God, I have such longing for grapes, O God give me some grapes. And my robe is becoming old and tattered. Please, O God, grant me a new one." He had hardly finished praying when a basket of grapes appeared, and then two cloaks more beautiful than any ever seen before. Then Jafar as-Sadiq gave the grapes to the passerby and the cloaks to the first two beggars who approached.

Questioned about these prodigious powers, one Buddhist lama grew very quiet. The powers, he said seriously, are meaningless, even dangerous, and to pay any attention to them is to lose the point. Instructive in this regard are two stories, one Christian and the other Buddhist. Both deal with the seductive powers of walking on water.

The Christian tale: Once, two learned monks sailing to the Holy Land came to an island deserted except for one old hermit, who ran down to the seashore, his rags flapping, to welcome his visitors. He took them into his hut and prepared for them his best food and gave them pure spring water to drink.

"Teach me to pray," he implored the monks. "I live here all alone. You can't imagine how lost I am, with no one to teach me what I need to know."

The monks exchanged a superior look, but they were happy to teach him the Lord's Prayer and various church chants and litanies, and so the three talked all evening about the best way to pray or invoke Christ to one's side. They told him that if he practiced faithfully, praying night and day for a long time, someday, after many years, the Lord God would favor him with preternatural powers that would indicate his spiritual state.

The next morning after breakfast the monks went on their way. As they sailed off, one of them looked back and saw the hermit. He was running after their boat across the surface of the water.

"Wait! Wait!" he called. "I've forgotten the words to the prayer."

The Buddhist story makes a different point. Once the Buddha, traveling with his disciples, met a yogi in the woods. He asked how long the man had been there alone, practicing his disciplines.

"Twenty-five years," answered the ascetic.

"And what power have you acquired by such long discipline?"

"I can cross a river," said the *sadhu*, "by walking on water."

"Ah," sighed the Buddha with compassion. "Have you really wasted so many years for such a trifling result? Why, the ferry man can take you to the opposite bank for a small coin."

Charged with performing miracles, my Hindu teacher, on the other hand, just laughed.

"How could that be?" he teased. When pushed, however, he grew serious. There are no miracles, he explained, but only natural causes which we may not yet understand, and all credit, he said, belongs to "Almighty God."

He might as well have quoted Saint Augustine, that "miracles do not happen in contradiction to nature, but only in contradiction to that which is known to us of nature."

We are reminded of Our Lord feeding the multitude with two fishes and five loaves of bread. Christ glowed with that same inner burning light. When the woman who had hemorrhaged for twelve years came up behind him in a crowd and merely touched the hem of his robe, she was healed. Such was the power of Christ. "Who touched me?" he asked. He was being jostled by a crowd of five thousand people, yet he could feel the current of his healing energy flow out into her.

It's important to understand the difference between the powers of magic and mysticism. In magic the sorcerer is interested in playing with or using the powers he has developed for his own benefit, or sometimes for the benefit of others. "My will be done," the magus says. The mystic has no interest in these lesser pleasures, for she has subsumed her self entirely into the magnificent energy of the Source, the Light, which is the One she serves: "Thy will be done," she cries in utter abandon, gratitude, and trust. She (or he) may have the powers but cares nothing about using them either to bolster her ego or to control events or other people's lives. "What do you want me to do now?" she asks her God, her Beloved. "Where do I go now?"

Meanwhile, I was not bilocating, levitating, predicting the future, or searing people with the heat of my skin. All that happened was that for a moment I had been embraced by the Divine, and I woke up a different person. In that moment my life turned upside-down. I'd already experienced Bucke's "lesser" cosmic consciousness. I wrote about it in *A Book of Angels*.[21] I had lived familiarly in that wider, unitive state, but this revelation in Peru went to something beyond, and it would take all my faculties in the next few years to stay on my feet.

For years I had prayed with all my heart and devotion to see God. Now, as with Semele, it threatened to burn me up, me and my whole family, to burn us up with fear and love and joy.

CHAPTER 6

COMING DOWN, GOING OFF

I trust all joy.

—THEODORE ROETHKE

The Prophet has poured into my heart two kinds of knowledge: one I have spread to people and the other, if I were to share it, they would cut my throat.

—SUFI ABU HURAYRA

My heart is fixed, O God, my heart is fixed: I
*   will sing and give praise.*
Awake up, my glory; awake, psaltery and harp: I
*   myself will awake early.*
I will praise thee, O Lord, among the people: I
*   will sing unto thee among the nations. . . .*

—PSALMS 57:7–11

When, as I said earlier, I came down from the mountain, our tour group was gathering at the hotel, some drinking pisco sours. It was exactly three-fifteen—the very time we'd been told to meet, and my heart laughed, *knowing* I was cared for—for had it not begun to rain (and it had already stopped), I would have missed the bus back down the mountain to the train. I was beaming, lighthearted in the pleasure of God, released from all my spiritual longings, released even from that trembling and fragile exaltation of the last few days.

No one could see that light was pouring off their hands and skin. No one knew that we were all shining like gods with this spiritual matter, with love.

On the train back to Cuzco, I saw that a blood vessel had burst on the back of my right hand. It formed a round purple bruise about the size of a quarter. It served as a memento of my experience. Looking at it, then, I knew that something real had happened on the mountain. It was not my imagination; this vision had had a physical side to it.

Already intellect was taking over. On the train I asked three others on my tour if they had heard that hollow roaring in their ears, the silent wind; no one had.

Hours later, back in the Cuzco hotel in my lovely, flower-filled room, I wrote an account of the experience on a yellow legal pad. Now I had no more roaring in my ears, no more tears or visions of light. I had returned to the higher altitude of Cuzco, breathless again from lack of oxygen. But I felt calm and uplifted, a quiet, ringing joy, serenity. I wrote objectively, not doubting, yet not daring to believe.

Saint Teresa spoke of this quality of trust. "The soul," she writes,

> neither sees, hears, nor understands anything while this state lasts; but this is usually a very short time, and seems to the soul even shorter than it really is. God visits the soul in a way that prevents it doubting when it comes to itself *that it has been in God and God in it*; and so firmly is it convinced of this truth that, though years may pass before this state recurs, the soul can never forget it nor doubt its reality.[1]

But like other mystics she is also aware of the importance of differentiating between the various types of rapture. Visions, voices, ecstasies must all be subjected to unsparing criticism before they are recognized as divine.

"The great doctors of the mystic life," says one French writer,

> teach that there are two sorts of rapture, which must be carefully distinguished. The first are produced in persons but little advanced in the Way, and still full of selfhood; either by the force of a heated imagination ... or by the artifice of the Devil. These are the raptures which St. Teresa calls ... Raptures of Feminine Weakness. The other sort of Rapture is, on the contrary, the

effect of pure intellectual vision in those who
have a great and generous love for God.[2]

Was the light inside my head or outside? Had I had a
seizure of some kind, an epileptic fit? Was it due to
nerves and over-excitement, combined with a reaction to
the altitude? I have heard that an epileptic just before a
seizure feels his mouth filled with an exquisite honey, and
he himself, or she, is caught in rapturous light. Was that
what had happened? Or did the revelation come as the
result of my months of fasting and praying, my an-
guished searching, so that I was more exhausted than I
had recognized—and stressed, too, by suddenly having
fallen in love so openly, vulnerably—so passionately—
swept off my feet by love. Was it an hallucination? I remembered only one or two images from the vision, and
these could not have lasted more than a few seconds—a
minute or two at the most. Yet the entire experience had
lasted almost an hour. Where was I the rest of the time?

I decided that if the vision were real its effects would
be evidenced in my life, and if it were not, it would pass
away or turn to ashes in my mouth. If it were an hallucination, caused by ego or some chemical eruption in the
brain, then it would not change the way I thought or
acted or viewed myself and others.

"Time will show me if it was real," I wrote. Better
tell no one, I thought, lest I be ridiculed.

Or confined as mad.

———

How can we speak of what cannot be apprehended? We see it like a shadow out of the corner of our eye, and when we turn our head to confront it—it's gone. It is approached in poetry. In music. In the eyes of a good dog. In the little hand of a trusting child.

Otherwise, in words, it just sounds mad.

In a sense, it is mad. They say that only another mystic can understand the mystic's view. Can anyone who has not had a glimmering of truth comprehend the love songs of the Indian poet Kabir (1398–1518)? Kabir was a weaver, an ecstatic, laughter rising up in him:

> Oh friend, I love you, think this over
> carefully! If you are in love,
> then why are you asleep?
> . . . .
> Kabir will tell you the truth: this is what love is like:
> Suppose you had to cut your head off
> and give it someone else,
> what difference would that make?[3]

Or this one, translated, like the above, by Robert Bly:

> I don't know what sort of a God we have been
>   talking about.
> The caller calls in a loud voice to the Holy One at
>   dusk.
> Why? Surely the Holy One is not deaf.
> He hears the delicate anklets that ring on the feet of
>   an insect as it walks.[4]

When the prophet Muhammad came down from Mount Hira and told what he had seen, only his wife; one friend, Abu Bakr; and one boy, Ali ibn Abi Talib; accepted his word. Later, enraptured by the music of the Qur'an, many listeners wept and were instantly converted to belief in one God, *the* God, which in Arabic is named Allah (a contraction of *al-ilah*, "the god"). But others were enraged, their values threatened. His converts were tortured and beaten, their children killed, their wives and daughters raped—so much did the new prophet anger people with his talk of surrender to one God. That's what the word *Islam* means—"surrender to God"; *Muslim* means "one who has surrendered."

The psychologist and philosopher William James, brother of Henry James, wrote *The Varieties of Religious Experience*, published in 1902. Unequaled for its depth, beauty, and clarity of discourse, it is a classic of mystical literature, and I will quote from it often. Writing of another religious leader, George Fox, James remarks how

A genuine first-hand experience like this is bound to be a heterodoxy to its witnesses, the prophet appearing as a mere lonely madman. If his doctrine prove contagious enough to be spread to others, it becomes a . . . labeled heresy. But if it then still prove contagious enough to triumph over persecution, it becomes itself an orthodoxy; . . . its day of inwardness is over: . . . the faithful live at second hand exclusively and stone the prophets in their turn.[5]

Thus it happened with Muhammad, as with Jesus before him, persecuted for blasphemy.

In fear of his life, Muhammad fled Mecca with Abu Bakr and was forced to hide in a cave. Then a miracle occurred—the kind we hear about when someone founds a religion.

His pursuers rode right to the lip of the cave yet saw neither the two men nor their camels. It is said that a spider had woven a huge web across the opening to the cave and a dove had built a nest at the exact spot where one's foot would fall to climb up to the cave. The vigilantes rode on past. Muhammad and Abu Bakr mounted their camels and continued their flight.

In India one doesn't hear of saints, sages, *rishis,* and gurus being tortured or martyred. They use their miraculous powers to escape, for they are One with God. They are God-ness incarnate, as it were. But Christianity (and I live in a Christian society) carries a history of persecution, the killing of brothers because they believe in the "wrong" God, or in the wrong way, or in a different path to God. The victims, true saints, leap joyously into martyrdom, the moth to the candle, refusing to escape.

Well, not I. I wasn't about to tell anyone about what had happened. Many visionaries are tortured and defiled, their beautiful insights despised, and some of them with cause. They set themselves up as better than others, perhaps, having been taken to the edge of the unknowable. Or they go crazy with God-knowledge, hearing voices or wandering naked in the streets.[6]

James Fletcher, one early Quaker, thought he was Jesus Christ and entered the city of Bristol riding on a donkey while his followers sang, "Holy, holy, holy." The authorities took care of the problem with their usual dispatch and Christian humility: they cut off his ears, bored his tongue with a hot iron, and branded his forehead with the letter *B*, for *Blasphemer*.

George Fox (1624–1691), founder of the Quakers, the Society of Friends, seemed not much saner, refusing after his mystical revelations to bow to superiors or doff his hat to any man. He addressed everyone, whether rich or poor, inferior in station or of a higher rank, with the intimate and familiar "thee" and "thou" instead of the formal "you."

"Oh! the scorn, heat, and fury that arose!" he wrote.

Oh! the blows, punchings, beatings, and imprisonments that we underwent for not putting off our hats to men! Some had their hats violently plucked off and thrown away, so that they quite lost them. The bad language and evil usage we received on this account is hard to be expressed . . . and that by the great professors of Christianity, who thereby discovered they were not true believers.

It came out all right in the end, however, when many, Fox said, "came to see the vanity of that custom of putting off hats to men, and felt the weight of Truth's testimony against it."[7]

Fox put his English compatriots to the test. In the early days of his searching for God, he fasted and walked about in solitude with his Bible, sat in hollow trees until night came, and wandered mournfully about in those owl-hours. "For I was a man of sorrows in the time of the first workings of the Lord in me." He refused to profess any religion, but gave himself only to Christ. He was afraid of all talk and conversation, for he saw only corruption around him, from layman and preacher alike. From today's psychological view, Fox would be called "disturbed" or "depressed," or perhaps he would be said to be "having a psychotic episode."

Mental illness is often accompanied by increased religiosity. Therapists say that they can tell when things are getting worse for a schizophrenic or manic-depressive: the person suddenly becomes especially religious. I heard of one woman who in the midst of a manic episode decided that she was having a spiritual experience, as she wandered homeless through the streets, subject to energy waves. In these distorted states, the spiritual imagery may include satanic encounters, strange dreams, or the idea that everything is fraught with meaning. The shoes lying on the floor or the magazine opened to a certain page are speaking to you. Everything becomes a message from God. One friend of mine who suffers from bipolar disorder was hospitalized years ago for a manic episode. He didn't think he had *merged* with God. He thought he *was* God. Given Thorazine, he dropped into a depression so severe that it lasted for a year, which he called "the worst time of my life." The manic episode so frightened him that he "got into Christ." As he told me later, "I needed to get out of the driver's seat. I needed a Savior in place of Me. I need to be under a Higher Power, because the bad thing about a manic episode is that I lose the Higher Power. I eclipse it with my own I AM. It's enjoyable, but underneath the No-Fear lies the fear."[8]

There is nothing this deeply spiritual man wants less than another full-blown manic attack like that. The line between manic and religious is sometimes thin, for in the midst of a spiritual experience the recipient may become intensely sensitive.

George Fox is an example. One day, caught in a trance, he took off his shoes, left them with some shepherds in a field, and walked barefoot into the town of Litchfield, crying, "Woe, to the bloody city of Litchfield," for he saw a "channel of blood running down the streets," and the marketplace was running with blood. "Woe to the bloody city," he shouted; and in this instance no one accosted him or threw him in prison. The vision passed. He walked back into the pasture where he had left his shoes, put them on, and continued on his way, baffled by his own behavior. Was he abashed? I don't know. Later he discovered that Litchfield had been the site of a massacre hundreds of years before, and he felt comforted that he had perhaps plugged into that ancient memory.

Well, George Fox founded the Quaker religion. I, on the other hand, had no such distinction. I decided to hold my experience to myself, and like Mary to ponder it in my heart. I didn't trust how others would respond.

They say that when the ascetic prince Siddhartha Gautama sat down under the Bodhi tree in northern India, he was only a seeker on the path to awakening. When he stood up he was the Buddha, fully enlightened. He had been transformed in one long session.

"At that sacred moment [of his enlightenment]," writes Sogyal Rinpoche in *The Tibetan Book of Living and Dying,* "the earth itself shuddered, as if drunk with bliss."[9] At that moment no one was angry, ill, sad, or proud, or performed any malicious act. Everything stopped, resting in utter quiet. In the mind of the Buddha.

In Christianity we have no equivalent for the Buddhist concept of enlightenment. But we speak of grace, of being inspired by the Holy Spirit, or of the gifts of the Holy Spirit. We speak of the Kingdom of God. I think the meaning is much the same.

For most people, even the highest souls, there are many awakenings, and no ending to the journey to God. The awakening comes gradually. The teachings pass directly from master to student, but they seep in slowly, drop by drop; each one must be tested by the passage of time, until one day you look back five years and notice that you have changed. You are able even in times of difficulty to hold the teaching. Nonetheless, you still continue, "practicing the presence of God," as Brother Lawrence, a seventeenth-century Carmelite, called it. Brother Lawrence was assigned to kitchen work. He hated it. Humbly, he practiced the presence of God while slicing, chopping, praying, talking with friends. Practicing the presence is no different from loving. When eating you notice the sacredness of your food, when sleeping you remain in prayer, unshakable.

When I was growing up, we hadn't heard about the "crack in the cosmic egg," through which the Divine is revealed. In the 1960s and later in the '70s and '80s, many people experimented with the spiritual journey, with Eastern or Native American religions, with peyote or pot, with gurus and hippie communes. Often "mysticism" became negatively associated with charlatans and cheats, with magic and sometimes with the more disreputable fringe of charismatics, astrologers, tarot card readers, psychics, palmists, and mediums who dabble in the occult. But I define mysticism as the unmediated experience of God, however that word is defined; of spiritual encounters transcending human comprehension. It hardly matters how the experience comes—but always it leads to joy and heightened or expanded energy, to increased compassion for others and deepening capacity to love.

According to the Oxford Universal Dictionary, a "mystic" is one who "seeks by contemplation and self-surrender to obtain union with or absorption into the Deity, or who believes in the spiritual apprehension of truths inaccessible to the understanding." Twenty years ago, the practical and Protestant society I moved in did not easily recognize these spiritual states. If anything, they were reserved for saints, poets, and failures, not for the better lot, people with responsibilities, children, and a stake in a community.

So I was almost as confused by what had happened in Peru as elated. I had no idea mine was just a common, everyday, garden-variety mystical experience. As ordinary as a weed. Like weeds, such experiences crop up helter-skelter in a variety of forms.

Some are conversion experiences, like Saint Augustine's—made unusual only by his later acts. Augustine was born in A.D. 354 in what is now Algeria. He studied at Carthage, moved to Rome to teach rhetoric, and then to Milan, leading a dissolute, degenerate life. His mother, Monica, a devout Christian, prayed continually for his conversion and followed him to Milan. There Augustine came under the influence of the saintly Bishop Ambrose, struggled with the question of the Incarnation of Christ, which he found intellectually offensive, and fought against the horrible pull of chastity—a state which he felt was required of the Christian life.

"Give me chastity and continence, but not yet," he prayed throughout his twenties. Then at the age of thirty-two he had his conversion experience.

It was a hot August day. He was in the garden of the house he shared with his friend Alypius. Filled with self-loathing, Augustine was trying to force his mind to serve the Lord God as he would have liked.

"My inner self was a house divided against itself," he later wrote in his *Confessions*. He "twisted and turned" in his chains. He tore his hair and hammered his forehead with his fists. He locked his fingers and hugged his knees, struggling to dedicate himself to a lifetime of chastity, but shrinking back. "Somehow I flung myself down beneath a fig tree and gave way to the tears which now streamed from my eyes. . . . In my misery I kept crying, 'How long shall I go on saying tomorrow, tomorrow?' "

At that moment he heard a child's voice in a nearby house: *Sume, lege*. "Take it, read; take it, read." He looked up, opened a book containing Paul's Epistles, and read the first words his eyes fell on: "Not in revelling and drunkenness, not in lust and wantonness, not in quarrels and rivalries. Rather, arm yourselves with the Lord Jesus Christ, spend no more thought on nature and nature's appetites."[10]

Instantly he crossed the line. Converted. He rose to his feet to tell his friend Alypius, who, deeply moved, likewise took up the book, opened it to read his own sentence, and was immediately converted as well.

Was this a mystical ecstasy? I think not. Certainly it came as a directive from the Divine, full of magic and mystery, but Augustine's true mystical union with the Divine did not take place for several more months.

He was in the port of Ostia, talking about God with his mother, when simultaneously they both experienced a transport of rapture, climbing higher and higher, he writes, "as the flame of love burned stronger in us," until at length, "we came to our own souls and passed beyond them." For a moment he reached out and touched the seat of silence, wisdom.

Suppose . . . that the tumult of a man's flesh were
to cease, and all that his thoughts can conceive,
of earth, of water, and of air, should no longer
speak to him; suppose that the heavens and even
his own soul were silent . . . ; suppose that his
dreams and the visions of his imagination spoke
no more . . .[11]

In that silence he and his mother stood entranced.

I have a friend who was converted just as fast. In a
flash. She did not believe in God or Christ, but had
agreed to join three women friends as they prayed for
her. She says that she was standing in the circle, when
suddenly she felt a warmth fall on her shoulders. Tears
sprang to her eyes. She knew Christ. Simple as that.

These "touches" of the soul by God "enrich it mar-
velously," wrote Saint John of the Cross, adding that a
single one of them may abolish imperfections at a stroke.

Often these experiences, conversions or otherwise,
are preceded by a sense of failure, hopelessness, despair.
The heavyweight boxing champion George Foreman told
about his conversion on *60 Minutes*. As a prizefighter
he lived in hunger, anger, and fear. His fists were
weapons. He fought everything that moved. He wanted
to kill everything, he said, including women. In 1974 he
arranged a match—the "Rumble in the Jungle"—with
Muhammad Ali in Zaire. Ali demolished him.

"It drove me nuts. I almost lost my mind," Foreman
said. Losing threatened his identity, his very survival.

For the next three years he tried to regain his title. In

1977 he lost again, this time to Jimmy Young in Puerto Rico. Afterward in his dressing room, at his lowest moment, when he felt he could not take another step, he was swept by a mysterious force.

"Jesus Christ is coming alive in me!" he cried. "Hallelujah, I'm clean. I've been born again. I'm dying for God." He told his doctor, "Move your hands. The thorns on his head are making him bleed."[12]

From that time on, the killer Foreman no longer existed. He gave up boxing, gave up watching TV. He began to preach on street corners, wherever he could draw a crowd, then at his own church in Houston. Later he opened the George Foreman Youth and Community Center to keep kids out of trouble. What had happened? He'd had a vision of God, that's all. He'd become a different person.

Jakob Böhme (1575–1624), the "inspired shoemaker" and one of the giants of mysticism, had such a vision at the age of twenty-five, in which he was

> surrounded by the divine light, and replenished with the heavenly knowledge; insomuch as going abroad into the fields to a green . . . he there sat down, and viewing the herbs and grass of the field, in his inward light he saw into their essences, use, and properties, which was discovered to him by their lineaments, figures, and signatures.[13]

"In one quarter of an hour," the German mystic later wrote, "I saw and knew more than if I had been many years together at a university. For I saw and knew the being of all things." He understood that there were three worlds, an external physical world, a spiritual world, and a third that existed inside himself. He saw how the physical world and all things in it were the creation of the other two, and he understood how the whole worked together, both "in the evil and in the good."

"But it was impossible for me," he wrote, "to explicate the same."[14]

Such moments come to both ordinary and extraordinary people, to the famous and the unknown, to rich and poor. They come at any age. But it often takes years before the person dares to set it down in writing—and even then he or she often writes in awe, sometimes using the third person, as if writing of another.

I mentioned Jean Houston earlier. In her book *A Mythic Life*, she describes a mystical encounter she had as a child. She had heard that if she prayed, the Virgin Mary would come to her. She prayed to exhaustion, and then, discouraged, wandered to the bay window of the family's Brooklyn house and sat there.

> I must in my innocence have unwittingly tapped into the appropriate spiritual doorway, for suddenly the key turned, and the door to the universe opened. Nothing changed in my outward perception. There were no visions, no sprays of golden light, certainly no appearances by the Virgin Mary. . . . Yet everything became part of a single Unity, a glorious symphonic resonance in

which every part of the universe was a part of and illuminated every other part, and I knew that in some way it all worked together and was very good. . . . I had awakened to a consciousness that spanned centuries and was on intimate terms with the universe. Everything mattered. Nothing was alien or irrelevant or distant. The farthest star was right next door, and the deepest mystery was mystically seen . . . as if I knew everything, as if I was everything.[15]

A door slammed and her father entered the house laughing. Everything exploded into laughter. "Great roars of hilarity . . . Laughter leavened every atom and every star until I saw the universe inspirited and spiraled by joy." Later she learned that the mystical experience "is not something to be kept sacrosanct in esoteric cupboards. It is coded into our bodies, brimming in our minds, and knocking on the doors of our souls. It is our natural birthright."[16]

My friend Gabrielle Hill tells how she too had an overwhelming experience as a child. She was eleven years old, a student at the Sacred Heart school in Honolulu. Gabrielle had an unhappy childhood, tainted by her father's sexual abuse and, at that time, by the cruelty of two or three girls at school. One day, kneeling in morning chapel, she was gazing at the baroque interior of the dark chapel, the gilt flooded with candlelight, when suddenly she experienced a moment that "lasted an eternity." She felt part of everything: the candles, the wood, all were dancing, moving. Time stopped. "I could have stayed on my knees forever," she says, and today the tears pour down her face as she remembers this moment from forty years before, a union that she often reexperiences now in meditation or as a spiritual healer but that never loses its power over her.

The day after my rapture I left Cuzco for the hot desert along the Pacific coast. The beauty of the landscape no longer reduced me to tears. Nonetheless, I felt different— alive and calm and filled with ringing joy.

One event happened on the return journey so unusual that it merits mentioning, though I have often wondered whether it had any meaning at all or whether its significance was created afterward by my fevered imagination. Simply, I lost my ring. The circumstances surrounding its loss were strange.

The ring was a sapphire flanked by two pearls. It had belonged to my mother. I always wore the ring on the little finger of my left hand and I treasured it for its sentimental more than its monetary value. I'd already lost the ring once before, several years earlier, on a trip. I had searched for it frantically, telephoned my hosts, asking them to check their guest room. I opened my suitcase again and again for weeks, compulsively unzipping the bag, to look inside. The suitcase had no hidden pockets. Finally I had accepted the fact that the ring was gone. But I'd also prayed for its return.

Months later, I opened the suitcase—and there lay my ring in plain view. Impossible!

I had taken its return as a special gift and guarded it thereafter with particular care.

Now I was in the desert of Peru. On my last morning there I awoke with a clear knowledge: *Today you will lose your ring.*

It was not a voice in my head, but simply a "knowing."

I slipped on the ring as I dressed, thinking, I have to be careful; I must not take it off today.

A driver drove me five hours through the red sands of a desert drier than the Sahara, up toward Lima. We took only one rest stop, and I remember reminding myself as I washed my hands at the primitive and none-too-clean porcelain sink, Don't take off your ring. Don't risk losing it.

An hour later, back in the car, I looked down at my hand. The ring was gone.

Many times I have wondered about its loss. Was I really so thoughtless as to have removed it from my finger at that dirty rest stop? I hope the ring was found by someone who needed it more than I. But then, I wonder whether the ring was removed to symbolize the completion of one phase of my life, the beginning of a new one.

Whatever the reason, I returned to Washington a different woman from the one who had left it two weeks earlier.

CHAPTER 7

THE SWEETNESS OF THE PAIN OF LOVE

In Thy wind—in Thy light—
  How insignificant is everything else,
how small are we—and how happy in that
  which alone is great.
                    —DAG HAMMERSKJÖLD, *MARKINGS*

There is no need for temples; no need for compli-
cated philosophy. Our own brain, our own heart
is our temple; my philosophy is kindness.
                              —DALAI LAMA XIV

After my return to Washington, I could not read a newspaper or look at the TV news without bursting into tears. It was as if a layer of skin had been removed, I was so open. I could not read novels anymore, not even great literature. My husband was confused.

"What's wrong?" he asked.

I shrugged. "Nothing. I don't know."

I sighed a lot. I strained for silence, longed to be alone. The company of others worked on me as a kind of torture, and a social occasion, a dinner party with all the gay, intoxicating chatter, seemed intolerable. Yet we had always entertained: we loved people!

Now I wanted only to be alone.

I wanted to withdraw into the golden light, or walk in silence, communing with this interior silence, this radiant calm bliss that I remembered, thirsted for, thought that I could touch at any time, if only people would leave me to myself.

The slightest movement brought me to tears: a blue jay in the garden—the intense blue feathers against the green of grass. The leaves of trees quivering in the springtime wind, waving their fragile new green fingers in psalmodies of praise. Or the scent of the apple blossoms. Or music. I was hearing as if sounds had architecture and emanated from inside my head, the notes like falling stars. I was seeing as if the view penetrated me or arose as the creation of my mind. From earliest childhood I had envisioned numerals as colors (making math next to impossible). Now musical notes sometimes took on tints as well. One Sunday morning, I lay in the hammock on our back porch listening to Beethoven's Fifth Symphony, and as the last note faded, a church bell rang out down the street. I burst into tears, it was so beautiful.

I cried a lot. Is this too part of this ecstatic journey? Only recently have I heard the story of the soldier—later saint—Ignatius of Loyola. In 1521, as a young man, he was wounded in battle, and while recovering he had a mystical experience that left him shaken, disoriented. Afterward he could not stop crying. His tears fell so hard and for so many days that his friends were afraid he would go blind.

"My soul is the silence of a bell ringing," I wrote in my journal, and when I wrote it the words made sense.

"Joy! Joy! Joy! Joy!"

There is a story of a Hindu saint who wrote constantly in his notebook. He never allowed anyone to read the book that he carried with him wherever he went. The others in the community whispered among themselves, wondering what he was writing—about them perhaps! On his death they grabbed the book. Every page was filled, top to bottom, with one of the thousand names of God: Ram Ram Ram Ram Ram Ram Ram Ram Ram Ram Ram Ram Ram Ram Ram Ram Ram Ram Ram Ram Ram Ram Ram Ram Ram Ram Ram Ram Ram Ram Ram Ram Ram Ram Ram Ram Ram Ram Ram Ram Ram Ram Ram Ram Ram Ram Ram Ram Ram Ram Ram Ram Ram . . .

Ram, the name of God.

"God God God God God," I wrote, seeing only bliss.

Surely I went mad. Nothing of the physical world attracted me, not clothes or *things*, not food or the company of my friends. I had no interest in sports or games or parties or movies or any of the pursuits that keep normal people involved in life. To go to the market or into a store to shop felt like torture.

Then, too, the tears. I was so sensitive, so emotionally raw that if someone angry walked into the room, even holding his temper, curbing his rage, I felt as if I were being whipped with barbed wire.

There is a book, *Pilgrims of the Stars: Autobiography of Two Yogis,* by Dilip Kumar Roy and his disciple the guru Indira Devi, in which Devi describes how one day she saw a man beating a bullock in a field, and how she felt each blow of the whip fall on her own skin. When she got back to her house and removed her clothes, she found her back covered with bleeding welts. I was not so sensitive as that, but I could not tolerate the commonplace abuses of ordinary life.

And yet, I had never felt more alive.

The Buddhists say that the Awakening provides the confidence needed at the beginning of the journey, and the visions provide encouragement to make us pursue the teaching. But the moments themselves are impermanent. Even the great wild insights, eternal truths that we think are so important—all shift and transform into other states. We cannot hold on. Instead we follow the counsel of William Blake, that

He who binds to himself a joy
Does the winged life destroy.
But he who kisses the joy as it flies
Lives in eternity's sunrise.[1]

Father Thomas Keating, an author, teacher, and monk, has worked for many years to foster understanding among the world's religions. A member of the Cistercian order, founded by Saint Bernard in 1098, he directs retreats in the practice of "centering prayer," and he too explains that the vision is an invitation only, after which the true journey begins. The journey may be hard and long, wearing through your iron sandals and your iron staves. It takes time to integrate a massive mystical encounter. Still, it's hard to ignore what Saint Teresa calls the "favors of His Majesty."

At night, going to sleep, and sometimes also early in the morning just on awakening, I would feel wave after wave of light pour through me, pulsating, as if I were being washed inside and out by light. I felt I was being made love to by God, and with an intensity and radiance so sweet that my body could hardly bear it. I thought my bones might break with the sweetness of the pain. My mouth was filled with a taste more exquisite than honey—the kisses of God.

"I'm jealous," said my husband, the companion of my life. "How can I compete?"

Truly, he could not, and this upset me as much as it did him. Neither of us understood what was happening. We had never heard of it before.

I had the impression of understanding Gospel passages at deep, deep levels—wisdom hitherto hidden from my sight. Whether the impression was founded in reality I cannot tell you, but the words, striking my heart like golden arrows, reduced me often to tears of humility and brave gratitude. (Always tears.)

And all the while these mystical ecstasies were confused by my having fallen in love with a married man who lived on another continent. It was in this period I learned to discount the folk wisdom that claims you can only love one man at a time. It's simply wrong. You love because love is pouring out of you. You cannot help but love. And anything in sight is covered by your love.

One day I telephoned my friend Elinor in New York and told her about the man I'd met in Costa Rica, and some of what had happened to me. I burst into tears. "I didn't know how lonely I have been."

But whether it was for a man or whether it was loneliness for God I could not say. Everything was mixed up, the spiritual and physical, erotic and immaterial, love spilling out of me.

Today, I have had a little more experience. I know some of the landmarks on this path, this razor's edge, and I know that these ecstasies have come to many people and in such wide range and diversity of form that we can hardly count the ways. Some experiences are sweet, some frightening, and some just surprising. Not all become life-transforming watersheds.

I have a friend, Constance, an Episcopalian, who on a visit to India saw the Hindu god Ganesh in her bedroom. Ganesh, the son of Shiva, is beloved by everyone. He is the plump, happy, elephant-headed boy who brings creativity, wisdom, and good luck. My friend saw him with her eyes open. He hovered at the ceiling then slowly disappeared. She felt surprised, of course, and then awestruck, enchanted, and humbled. She told me about it later, with a shy laugh, but she never doubted for a moment that she'd actually seen the god.

I know another woman to whom Christ appeared one Easter Monday morning, walking across her lawn. She, too, saw him with her eyes open. Like Ganesh, the Christ did nothing in particular. He walked toward her, bathed in radiant light. A few steps later, he vanished in the air, leaving her filled with sweet tranquility. Afterward she tried to reconstruct his face, wondering how she knew it was Christ, rather than an angel or any other spiritual being. She remembered only the long, white, unbleached robe, the sandals, the featureless, shining face. Mostly she remembered light. And that she just "knew."

Neither of these visions changed the person to whom it came, perhaps because each woman already had deep faith. The vision of Christ did not send my friend into paroxysms of joy. She saw, remarked, acknowledged him in her heart, and when he vanished, she returned—with a little smile—to washing the dishes.

A Jewish friend, on the other hand, once saw Christ while taking marijuana—the face of Christ seen through a windowpane. It shook her to the core. But she did not become a Christian because of it, just as my friend who saw Ganesh did not convert to Hinduism.

Some mystical encounters build on prior imagery, such as this one described by a former divinity student in Berkeley, California, a woman now living "in religious monastic vows, alone." She prefaces her account with the observation that her visions come to her during periods of deep silence and prayer. She must remain very deep for them to come, and often they give a warning signal or aura beforehand—and then they arrive. This one, however, left her shaken.

> As usual I was in silent prayer. All of a sudden I saw pink all around me where before it had been solid black. It was a wonderful shade of pink. I sensed moisture as well and a kind of translucent quality to the color. Christ was very near. As quickly as I was placed in the pink, I was taken out of it to be shown just where I was: I was in the wound. The pink was his blood and the moisture sensation was his flesh. With my exit came the words, "Learn from this." How long all this took, I don't know: one second, ten, a minute; it is hard to say. Time stopped for me. The vision left me visibly shaken and in tears. It has been a year now and I have hesitated to go too deeply into prayer, although I believe it is God who decides who is to receive a vision.[2]

Some ecstasies bring simply peace. The brilliant writer Arthur Koestler, in his book *The Invisible Writing*, recounts a series of mystical experiences that came on him when he was captured by Fascists, imprisoned, and sentenced to death as a spy during the Spanish Civil War. In one, he writes:

> I was floating on my back in a river of peace under bridges of silence. It came from nowhere and flowed nowhere. Then there was no river and no I. The I had ceased to exist. . . . When I say "the I had ceased to exist" I refer to a concrete experience . . . because it has, by a kind of mental osmosis, established communication with, and been dissolved in, the universal pool. It is this process of dissolution and limitless expansion which is sensed as the "oceanic" feeling, as the draining of all tension, the absolute catharsis, the peace that passeth all understanding.[3]

And some ecstasies rock the recipient, bathing him in light, as I was for weeks after my return from Peru. William James records such an experience by Mrs. Jonathan Edwards.

> Last night was the sweetest night I ever had in my life. I never before, for so long a time together, enjoyed so much of the light and rest and sweetness of heaven in my soul, but without the least agitation of body during the whole time. Part of the night I lay awake. . . . But all night I continued in a constant, clear, and lively sense of the heavenly sweetness of Christ's excellent love, of

his nearness to me, and of my dearness to him; with an inexpressibly sweet calmness of soul in an entire rest in him. I seemed . . . to perceive a glow of divine love come down from the heart of Christ in heaven into my heart in a constant stream. . . . At the same time my heart and soul all flowed out in love to Christ, so that there seemed to be a constant flowing and reflowing of heavenly love, and I appeared to myself to float or swim, in these bright, sweet beams, like the motes swimming in the beams of the sun. . . . It was pleasure, without the least sting, or any interruption. . . . The sweetness was greatest while I was asleep.

Mrs. Edwards goes on to describe her feelings of humility, awe, and gratitude upon awakening, and the realization that the glory of God had swallowed up every desire of her heart. All she wanted was to do God's will.

I used to think of living no longer than to the ordinary age of man. Upon this I was led to ask myself, whether I was not willing to be kept out of heaven even longer; and my whole heart seemed immediately to reply: Yes, a thousand years . . . in horror, if it be most for the honor of God. . . . The glory of God seemed to overcome me and swallow me up, and every conceivable suffering, and everything that was terrible to my nature, seemed to shrink to nothing before it.[4]

Sometimes such ecstasy shifts all perception and atti-
tudes, as with one Jewish correspondent, Aryeh Faltz,
who after a mystical rapture turned from atheism to
prayer and who eventually converted to Christianity.

It happened in the evening, while my first wife
and I were visiting a friend in Cambridge, Massachusetts. I was lying, eyes closed, on my back on
a couch in the living room, listening to J. S.
Bach's Prelude and Fugue in D Major. Suddenly I
felt as though a wave of cosmic or holy force
went through me. I did not actually hear a voice,
but I understood that God was calling me to love
and worship Him. This confused me greatly:
what I was experiencing contradicted the scientific, university-educated circles I moved in. Did I
even believe in God?

Yet God's goodness was so palpable that I was
filled with tremendous joy. My heart melted. I
knew that Heaven was real. I felt my body lifted
up. I was surrounded by light. Some of this light
was inside me, so that I became not only lighter
in weight but also filled with light. But, along
with this, I became aware of a hard, rocklike
lump inside of me that held me down. It was the
sin and evil in me.

I distinctly heard the words "Flesh and blood
cannot inherit the Kingdom of God," but I was
also told that this heaviness could be removed to

allow me to enter a tiny bit of Heaven. I would have to allow God to transform me, so that I would be fit for the experience. Even so, I would not be able to endure more than a glimpse.

I agreed, and immediately I felt the lump of sin dissolving inside of me. I was changed into an angel.

It is not possible to describe the actual experience. I was filled with the worship of God—I *was* worship, adoration, praise, love. I was astounded that it was possible to be alive without any evil inside me, to desire exactly what God desires and nothing more, to live and still be perfect, holy, eternal.

As the light of the sun is felt as heat by our physical bodies, so the light of God is felt as love by our heavenly bodies. As an angel, I felt that God, the source of light, was inside me as well as outside; I was God's love itself.

This ecstasy lasted only a brief time, but before I returned to my usual earthly state God drew my attention to certain signs of the angelic transformation. Each of these signs had special meanings which I understood mystically but cannot explain. My earthly "self" was embarrassed at the literalness of this imagery, but I also understood that it was real.

At this point I was brought back to my normal state just as the D major Prelude and Fugue was ending. There remained a tremendous feeling of joy and liberation.[5]

Faltz's experience took place in March 1967. Afterward he decided he had to nourish his spiritual life. It was not an easy road. He had to fight his own cultural prejudices against anything religious, as well as those of his immediate circle. But seven years later he converted to the Roman Catholic faith.

Today he says he worships at the Episcopal church more often than at his more rigid Catholic parish church, but he maintains his prayer life as the path of faith. "In all of this, my 1967 vision remains an ever-present source of joy," he writes, "and surprisingly it helps me see the things of Earth with greater clarity and certainly with greater love."[6]

After my return from Peru, I felt disoriented. I didn't doubt what I had seen, I only wondered what to do with the new information, how to live. I felt that everything I had previously understood had been swept away and I had no foundation on which to stand. At the same time, I saw that everything was good, indeed was perfect, even wars and conflict, loss, destruction, death. I understood the sweetness behind the concept of Lord Shiva, the destroyer. Or the Hindu image of God as a little boy building castles in the sand when his mother calls. He turns and runs to her, kicking over his sand castle in his heedless rush . . . and it is perfect.

Or Christ dying on the cross. Perfect, and no sacrifice. Perfect. All of it.

The only problem is that you can't live easily in this world thinking in this way, thinking with the heart, I mean. At first you can't live comfortably.

CHAPTER 8

HOLY CRAZINESS, CRAZY HOLINESS

Saints have no moderation,
nor do poets,
just exuberance.

—ANNE SEXTON,
"THE SAINTS COME MARCHING IN"

Much silence makes a mighty noise.

—AFRICAN PROVERB

I felt alone. I had no formal guide. In part this was my own fault, because I didn't want to tell anyone what I had seen. Why not? First, out of fear and shyness, a cringing from criticism. I couldn't have stood anyone diminishing or ridiculing what I'd seen, or worse, perhaps, actually taking it seriously and *talking* about the vision, which would somehow diminish it even while giving it too much weight. Or even worse, blabbing my secret to some third party. I held it to my heart.

The second and contradictory reason for keeping it secret was an instinctive recognition that the vision itself was not significant. The experience picked me up, shook me until my teeth rattled, set me down disoriented. But at some deep level I understood the danger of becoming attached to the revelation itself, or the images that followed. I distrusted them.

The third reason for secrecy was the fear of becoming spiritually proud, as if the hallucination imparted a special merit or conferred some privilege.

Whatever I wanted, it was not to be "special."

Add, too, the fear of ostracism, of being cast out of the human race: my great fear—separation. Who would not be afraid of rushing out to proclaim what she had seen?

Look at John the Baptist, thrown in prison, head sliced off; or the two saints, Peter and Paul, both killed in Rome; or martyrs burned, maimed, beheaded, shot with arrows, fed to lions for their faith or heresy.

Not I.

Not coward I.

Keep mum, I thought.

And finally, who did I have to turn to anyway? I had wandered away from the formal worship of the Episcopal Church, and though I knew several ministers to nod to on the street, I didn't care to entrust them with my secret.

Why didn't I tell the guru back in India? Shame. Diffidence. He'd given me a personal mantra with the express promise that it would deliver the experience of God. But I'd only met him briefly twice and had no reason to presume he even remembered my name. I didn't know how to describe what I'd seen or if he'd understand my English. Moreover, I still distrusted authority then. I accepted that he was a wise teacher but not necessarily of me.

As it happened, months later I did confess a part of the vision to my cousin Gita, one of his followers. But even there I shied away from the full account; I reported hearing the hollow wind and cut out all the part about the light. She forwarded my letter to India. "A demon," came back the report.

By the time this pronouncement reached me, months later, I'd forgotten I'd only revealed the dark opening of the vision. I took offense, and knowing the glory that I'd seen, and disliking superstition (*demons?*), I righteously ignored that sensible interpretation.

I told my husband, my darling best friend, Elinor, in New York, one dear friend then in her eighties who lived next door. But we were all ignorant, all stumbling down the same dark road, and the most we could do was to call out blind encouragement to one another: "Are you here?" "I'm beside you, still." "Are you all right?"

I say I had no guide. Yet, looking back, I see that beloved teachers came as needed, one by one, edging into my life, for a few months or a few years, each one more advanced than I on the spiritual path, each leading me to the next stage of self-knowledge. I was never alone—not even counting the Presence which walked beside me all the time. There was Gina, a lover of Christ, to whom I went once a week for more than two years for spiritual direction. At a time when I could not afford therapy, surely she saved my life. There was Gita, who listened tenderly and counseled me on this strange journey, loved and cherished me. There was my husband, and then this extraordinary soul, my new friend the vet, the gentle healer and wildlife expert, who was writing me from England and whose vibrations so filled me even across the ocean that sometimes others came in on the open channel of our love, overwhelmed themselves by love. A few years later a carpenter appeared, and later still a brick mason completed the circle of those who led me along the Way. But now I'm ahead of myself, for the last two came later, after my marriage had broken up, and I had spun out into orbit, on my own.

The Reverend Dr. Tilden H. Edwards, executive director of the Shalem Institute for Spiritual Formation in Bethesda, Maryland, says there is a holy craziness. Or crazy holiness. I mentioned it in passing earlier, but it takes powerful forms.

You want crazy: Look at young Francis, long before he was named a saint, stripping off his clothes and standing naked in the cathedral in front of the archbishop and all the people of Assisi, publicly disowning his father, who wanted only that his son act like a normal businessman; Francis running away with two or three hippie friends to live in poverty. They were flower children. They rebuilt old chapels with their bare hands, went barefoot, begged for food, and talked of reforming the Catholic church (which, in fact, they did). Crazy.

Or look at the teachings of Zen. What seems crazier than that?

Stephen Mitchell tells us that when the Zen master Dok Sahn was asked a question, he answered by hitting the student.

Zen Master Ku-ji, when questioned, would silently lift one finger.

Zen Master Lin-Chi, when questioned, would shout: KATZ. Ask any question, and he shouted KATZ! What is Buddhism? And he shouted KATZ! Or, What is the enlightened mind? KATZ! Sometimes Lin-Chi would shout KATZ and the confused student would shout back KATZ![1]

Frankly, that sounds bizarre. Then you read other books and discover that in the world of Zen, the word *Katsu*, like the silent lift of one finger or the blow on the back, is equivalent to "Ho!"—the shout given by the Japanese master that throws the student into the intuitive mind. It's actually a sensible instruction, meaning, "Look deeper. Stop struggling to understand by *thinking*."

The way to God cannot be found by the cognitive or analytical mind, but comes in a sudden burst of understanding, after you let go. Katz!

Or you want crazy: From the second to the fourth century A.D. and probably for hundreds of years before, thousands of anchorites and hermits moved out into the rocky red caves and cliffs of Egypt and the Sinai desert. Some became famous as the Desert Fathers; their sayings helping to found the Christian church. Some of them lived in little communities of five to twenty brothers (or sisters: there were anchoresses, too, though we hear less about them). They lived in silence, in contemplation, in prayer, searching for the experience of God. One class of ascetics sat for years on top of pillars; of these Simeon Stylites of Antioch (d.459) is best known.

Now that's crazy. Moreover, these actions have nothing to do with enlightenment, as the Buddhists call it, or self-realization, as the Hindus name it: that state in which the person, aware of the divine aspects of his or her own nature, lives continually in the presence of the Divine.

Once when I was in India I saw a contortionist outside a temple. He balanced on his buttocks, with his legs hooked firmly behind his ears, feet crossed at the back of his neck, and a wild expression in his shifting, piercing eyes. His arms swung freely, moving in little helpless circles, like sea plants waving in the dust, or else they searched the dirt around him to lift an apple peel to eye level and examine it wonderingly. His beard was scraggly and unkempt, his loincloth gray with dirt. In front of him sat a little cup for donations. He did not seem particularly spiritual.

My guru passed him by with a scorn and contempt that seems unseemly in the light of holy compassion.

Maybe the contortionist was crazy. Or maybe he was just earning his living.

But the hermits who lived on the tops of pillars—how did they survive? Did their children or uncles have to tramp across a dry field to the foot of the pillar, and up the dunghill that must have lain around it, to bring them food? And did the hermit pull up water in a little basket on a rope? Or did he live there thirty years under the blistering sun without speaking, eating, defecating, without water, as his lips cracked and peeled and his hair grew thick and dirty and his uncut fingernails curved into spikes the length of bear claws?

Today we would send such a person to a mental institution. In those days, he was permitted his God-craziness, sitting on his pillar, waiting for enlightenment.

And what if he didn't get it? How sad. Five hundred years before Christ, some seekers pierced their tongues or lips, held stones in their mouths, beat themselves until they bled, cried out in loud voices as they wandered praying in the woods, trying to induce an altered state of mind. And we are reminded of the Christians who six hundred or a thousand years after the death of Our Lord wore hair shirts against their skin to remind themselves of the suffering of Christ. To this day there are secret societies in Mexico and the Southwest of the *flagellanti*, who beat themselves with leather whips or reenact the tortures of the Crucifixion, in order to induce a mystical trance. Other seekers engage in Native American ceremonies, hanging in the hot sun by the thorns that pierce their skin.

In the sixth century B.C., Siddhartha Gautama searched for enlightenment in similar fashion. For six years he and five companions disciplined themselves with merciless austerities. He was not yet a buddha but merely the troubled former prince who had left the luxury of his palace and abandoned his wife and child to search for peace of mind. He went out into the forests and practiced asceticism, fasting, starving, not moving, depriving himself of sleep.

One day Siddhartha saw a boatman floating down the river, playing on a stringed instrument, and suddenly the young man understood the concept of moderation. For if the sitar's string is too loose, it will not make music; too taut and it will snap. The body works the same way. He abandoned his forced disciplines of the string-too-taut, and sat down under the Bodhi tree. He vowed not to move until he reached enlightenment. You would think his sitting might be considered another stubborn expression of forced discipline, but fortunately for him (and for the rest of us), on the sixth day his eye rested on the morning star and he found that "what he had been looking for had never been lost." Thus did enlightenment come on December 8, 528 B.C., according to the Western calendar, and he became Shakyamuni, the Sage of the Shakyas, the Buddha, the Awakened One.

"Wonder of wonders," he is reported to have said, "this very enlightenment is the nature of all beings, and yet they are unhappy for lack of it."[2] He was thirty-five years old.

Another person might have stayed there thirty years, loyal to that promise, and like the poor fakir on his pillar never once achieved an ounce of joyous God-realization. Craziness becomes less crazy only with success; after his enlightenment the Buddha taught for forty-five more years to crowds that reached into the thousands.

"A journey to the depths of the mind," writes Karen Armstrong, "involves great personal risks because we may not be able to endure what we find there. That is why all religions have insisted that the mystical journey can only be undertaken under the guidance of an expert, who can . . . guide the novice past the perilous places and make sure that he is not exceeding his strength, like poor Ben Azzai, who died, and Ben Zoma, who went mad. All mystics stress the need for intelligence and mental stability."[3]

E. D. Starbuck, in *The Psychology of Religion*, describes how sanctified persons often show signs of abnormality. "They get out of tune with other people; often they have nothing to do with churches, which they regard as worldly; they become hypercritical towards others;

they grow careless of their social, political, and financial obligations."

Starbuck met a woman of sixty-eight who had once been an active member of a progressive city church, and who had grown more and more censorious, until at last she withdrew from the fellowship of other people entirely and lived alone in a little room on the top story of a cheap boardinghouse, happy in her own spiritual blessings. She spent her days contentedly writing booklets on sanctification—page after page of dreamy rhapsody. "While listening to her own story," reported Starbuck, "one was tempted to forget that it was from the life of a person who could not live by it in conjunction with her fellows."[4]

Another example was Count Leo Tolstoy, the great Russian writer, author of *War and Peace* and *Anna Karenina*, whose creative works take up forty-five volumes, his diaries and letters another forty-five. Born in 1828 to the aristocracy, he joined the army and led a debauched, wild, heedless life. Today he'd be called a sexaholic. If he were out riding on his estates and overtook one of his woman serfs, he would throw himself off his horse, take her forcibly, and ride away cursing, consumed by one of his black rages. Again and again he promised himself he wouldn't rape the women—and then he would.

In 1862 he fell in love with the lovely and innocent eighteen-year-old Sophia Andreyevna Behrs. She had led a sheltered life in Moscow and she returned the love of the dashing and romantic, famous soldier-author. On the night before their wedding Tolstoy, in a misguided fit of honesty, gave his bride his journals, and all that night the young girl read, weeping with horror, one sexual, drunken exploit after another, disclosing the character of her husband-to-be. The next morning, dressed in her heavy Russian wedding gown, she stood, near-fainting, beside him and took the all-day vows of the Russian Orthodox Church.

That night he leapt on her in bed and took her as he had the serfs.

Sophie bore him thirteen children, and in addition to running the family estate, Yasnaya Polyana, and educating her children, she copied out each night by hand the work that her husband had written by day. It took five to seven years to write each of his novels. So the first years of their marriage passed happily.

At the age of fifty, Count Tolstoy fell into a depression, marked by questioning, fear of death, of nothingness. He was rich and famous. Yet life had become meaningless. He contemplated suicide.

For two years he remained in this confusion, until he suddenly realized that his only hope lay in the irrational spiritual faith of the common people, that his despair came not from the world but from the stifling conventions of aristocratic life.

One day in early spring, walking in the woods, he had a blinding revelation.

"Everything in me awoke and received a meaning. . . . Why do I look farther? a voice within me asked. He is there: he, without whom one cannot live. . . . God is what life is." And then, "as insensibly and gradually as the force of life had been annulled within me, and I had reached my moral death-bed, just as gradually and imperceptibly did the energy of life come back."[5]

From then on he wanted only to live as an ascetic. Now he made his wife's life another kind of hell—as she made his. He wore only peasant clothing—the loose pants tucked into soft boots, the collarless shirt with its billowing sleeves. He insisted on eating with the peasants (the serfs had been emancipated in 1861), and worse, in his wife's eyes, he invited any beggars and servants to sit at the same table as his family. His fame as a holy man began to spread. He wrote tracts denouncing private property and kept trying to give away his money—an act which his more worldly wife, fighting on behalf of her children and grandchildren, constantly thwarted. Poor, gentle man, struggling to live a simple, humble, godly life! He became as passionately ascetic as before he had been passionately libertine.

Years passed. In the evening of his years, he turned against all sexuality and began to write fierce Christian essays about the necessity of chastity and celibacy, a public denunciation of marriage which so humiliated his wife, mother of thirteen, that she took up her own pen angrily to defend herself.

They fought continually. All because he had gone God-mad and wanted to live the life of Christ, the unencumbered life that his contemporary, Gandhi, was living (to the dismay of *his* wife, too, let me add). In 1901 Tolstoy was excommunicated by the Russian Orthodox Church for his rejection of both church and state.

When he was an old man, dying at the age of eighty-two, he ran away from home, fleeing his wife and the possessions and responsibilities that he felt prevented his immersion in the God-ness and goodness that he sought. His wife came after him. By now he was one of the most famous men in the world, recognized at every little train station, and the story of his flight into Egypt, pursued by the Herod of his wife, was telegraphed by the press to waiting listeners everywhere. His wife wanted him to return to Yasnaya Polyana to die properly in his own bed, on his own estate, as befitted a man of his rank. She caught up with his train, had him forcibly removed, while he struggled, poor, sick, dying man, shouting, *Kidnap!* It did no good. He died in 1910 at the little railway station of Astapovo.

Was he godly or crazy? Or was he both? Casting aside convention, repudiating the church of their times are common themes among people who are crazy for God. We find it in every culture.

The Chinese Zen master Xu-Yun (Empty Cloud), who died in 1959 at the age of one hundred twenty-two, had been a Buddhist monk for one hundred years. He reached complete enlightenment at the age of fifty-six (only midlife to him), and he describes the sensation clearly in his autobiography. But by ordinary standards he wouldn't be called completely sane. He walked across China, down into India, over to Burma, sometimes going on four-hundred-mile journeys, prostrating himself at every third step. Except for boats on which to cross rivers and seas, he used only his own two feet. Later, he got it into his head that out of the great love he felt for his mother, who had died in childbirth when he was born (so much had she loved him that she gave her life for him), he must do something to keep her from the terrible cycle of rebirths. So he cut off one of his fingers out of love for his mother, who had died for him. He laid his hand on a chopping block, cut off his own finger, cauterized the wound with a candle flame, and returned to his meditation seat.

Holy craziness. Crazy holiness.

Or consider the life of Meher Baba, who died in 1969 and is worshiped by his followers not as a man who became united with God, but as God brought down and made man. He spoke six languages. Yet, for the last forty-three years of his life, Meher Baba lived in "thunderous silence." He wrote instructions on a slate, or used a sign language interpreted by a trusted devotee.

The name Meher Baba means "compassionate father." He was born in 1894 in Poona, India, and named Merwan Sherianji Irani. Quick and intelligent, athletic and playful, he had a happy childhood.

In 1911, at the age of seventeen, he started college. Biking back and forth to school each day, he passed an aged woman, Babajan, who lived in a lime tree. "An emperor," he called her, "incomparable" and "matchless." It was known that Hazrat Babajan had been born one hundred twenty-two years earlier, in 1790. She had run away from home at the age of fifteen, to escape an arranged marriage, and she had wandered for fifty years before she found a master to guide and teach her. At the age of sixty-five she had achieved spiritual enlightenment. She was Muslim, and the young Hindu boy, Merwan, loved her with all his heart. One day, while he was biking past, Babajan called the boy to her and kissed him on the forehead.

Instantly he went God-mad. He bicycled home and lapsed into a coma that lasted four days. Then he roamed the house in a trance, unable to eat or drink anything more than a little tea, "lost in that state to which very, very few go." If food were put before him, he gave it away to beggars or dogs, or else he put it in a bureau drawer, where it rotted and stank. He seemed never to sleep. His parents didn't know what to do. After a time, instead of living in Divine Bliss, he began to suffer extreme anguish. He banged his head on the floor or on the window glass. He broke windows with his forehead. "It was as if the whole universe was on my head," he wrote later, and "my sleepless, staring, vacant eyes worried my mother." His mother went to Babajan and demanded to know what the woman had done.

"This child of mine," the old woman is reported to have said, "will after some years create a great sensation in the world and do immense good to humanity."[6]

His madness continued nine more months, until November 1914. Merwan was then twenty years old. Gradually he began to return to normal consciousness. In later years Meher Baba would explain that the kiss had carried him into the bliss of the Divine, and the intensity of his sufferings came from his struggle to come back down to normal life for the work he had chosen to do.

He left college, though, and for several years more he wandered, searching. He met another renowned saint and master, this time a Hindu named Upasni Maharaj, who had been living for three years on water alone. Upasni Maharaj was just as queer as the incomparable and aged, beautiful Babajan. At one time he had lived for fourteen months in a cage 3 feet × 3 $\frac{1}{2}$ feet. When he saw Merwan, Upasni Maharaj picked up a stone and threw it at the young man with all his force, hitting him in the middle of the brow, exactly where Babajan had kissed him.

Holy craziness.

It drew blood. It also brought the boy sharply back into the physical world.

A few years later, Merwan went to live with the Hindu master. At the end of a year Upasni Maharaj handed authority over to him, saying, "This boy will move the world." He referred to Merwan as a *sadguru*, meaning one who has become one with God but remains on earth to guide others. (In Buddhism, such a person is called a bodhisattva.) Later still the master termed him an avatar—not man become God, but God himself incarnated into man. The best known and most accepted avatars or manifestations of God have been Zoroaster, Krishna, Buddha, Jesus. Today the devotees of Mother Meera in Germany claim she is an avatar (though others charge she is a fake). The Hindu guru Sai Baba is called an avatar. The Dalai Lama is revered as the incarnation of Avalokiteshvara, the Buddha of infinite compassion. But he would be the first to tell you he is only a simple monk.

Whatever happened to me was nothing compared to these—was the smallest drop in the ocean of God-knowledge; was perhaps my imagination, nothing more. But I was crazy nonetheless, crazy in seeing the world as perfect—not only as Voltaire's "best of all possible worlds," but as Whitman's shining miracle. One day, cutting an eggplant for dinner, I suddenly became my hand, the knife, the purple vegetable, the movement of the knife. No separation. From a conventional point of view, the world was divided into dualities: I/you, me/it, right/wrong, good/bad, either/or, black/white. From the spiritual view everything had become a single unity and whole. The Buddhists speak of the "emptiness" of all phenomenal existence, wiping out the illusion of space— a spiritual insight.

Likewise I saw that of course we must struggle for justice, social change. Yet I could hardly take care of myself. How could I do anything to change the world?

I think what hurt me most at this period of intense, raw, thin-skinned sensitivity was the lack of communication between people, the gross misunderstandings, the grasping, frightened, greedy, deluded clutching that informs our human touch. And then my own moral failings, all the petty, selfish, ignorant, well-meaning yet misguided things I did that caused another person's heart to hurt.

I felt crazy, finally, from the paradox of time. I had seen into eternity. Yet suddenly I was aware of how short life was. I could not expect to live more than forty or fifty more years. I was torn between my responsibilities toward my family and my need for other things. I had no *time*!

CHAPTER 9

CHAOS AND DISINTEGRATION

Before anything is brought back into order, it is quite normal for it to be brought first into a kind of confusion, a virtual chaos. In this way, things that fit together badly are severed from each other; and when they have been severed, then the Lord arranges them in order.
—EMANUEL SWEDENBORG, *ARCANA COELESTIA*

We awaken in Christ's body
As Christ awakens our bodies,
And my poor hand is Christ, He enters
My foot, and is infinitely me.
I move my hand, and wonderfully
My hand becomes Christ, becomes all of Him.
—SYMEON, ABBOT OF ST. MACROS

If you love a being for his beauty you love none other than God, for he is the Beautiful Being.
—IBN AL-ARABI

Now my marriage was breaking up, and this was another cause of suffering. You'd think the mystical vision would bond two loving people, not wrench them apart. A few weeks before leaving for Peru I had asked my husband to marry me again, to renew our wedding vows for our twentieth anniversary coming up. He was lying on our bed at the time, reading. I sat on the bed beside him, hugging my knees to my chest. He looked up from his book with that quizzical expression a man gets when his woman has just said something that makes no sense to him and he is struggling for the right response. "If you want," he said, amused.

Now I looked at my husband and knew our relationship was in jeopardy.

Three things had happened to me within a six-month period. I think our marriage could have withstood any two of them, but not all three descending on us at once.

The first was the death of my mother. It had hit me harder than I recognized at first. Yet the death of one's mother is commonplace. It happens to everyone. It's not a cause for divorce.

The second was that I had fallen in love—violently, passionately. But falling in love is no reason to break apart a good marriage either, not by my canon, and anyway the man was married and lived on another continent. Still, it confused the issues, loving two men at the same time.

The third and most powerful event was the spiritual revelation on Machu Picchu.

Twice during that early after-period, I was awakened by a voice, and this was not a simple urge, that gentle tap of intuition on your shoulder, or an angel's whisper in your inner ear. This was an external voice, awakening me out of sleep. The first time:

"You must leave," it said, and then it repeated the command in case I hadn't heard. "You must leave."

By then I was fully awake and shaken. Leave what? My marriage? (I had a horrible idea that that was what it meant.) I decided it was a dream, a fantasy to be ignored. I had no intention of leaving my marriage. I said my prayers, committed myself to God, and returned to sleep.

A few nights later—a few weeks?—it happened again. This time I was just falling into sleep, rocking in that hypnogogic half-awake, half-sleeping state. The voice spoke only once, insistently.

"You must leave."

My husband lay asleep in bed beside me. I was appalled. I spoke back silently: *Leave, why? Where would I go?*

It did not respond.

I sat on the edge of the bed in the dark. It is important to add that this voice did not come with any sense of joy, warmth, light, or angelic radiance. Just a direction in the night. But it came with an authority that could not be set aside. I remembered how in the Bible the young boy Samuel is awakened by a voice calling his name, "Samuel, Samuel." It happens twice. Each time he thinks it's his foster-father calling and goes to his guardian's room.

"Did you call?" he asks the old priest Eli. The third time Eli tells him that it's God, and that he must ask the voice to tell him what it wants. Well, I didn't believe in those things, actually. I did the sensible thing.

I went to a therapist.

I had never tried therapy before, had always believed that asking for such help was for weak or even "sick" people, and that the simple act of going to a therapist might be construed not as a sign of health but as proof of its lack.

I interviewed several therapists before selecting one, and that was an interesting experience in itself. One woman listened with attention to the entire story, and told me that she didn't think she could work with me, because she, too, had once been smitten by Eros—seen horns of fire flaring in the hair of a man she loved. Eros is the Greek god of love. He is armed with a bow and arrow, and they say you can fight against Eros, but he always wins. Love always wins. I didn't know what to make of her rejection, but moved on in my search.

The therapist selected was a Jungian, a lucky accident (if there are accidents), for the followers of Carl Jung are steeped in the spiritual and mystical side of human nature and in the importance of dreams.

To my surprise he took the voice seriously. I expected him to tell me to set my steps firmly on the path of Duty and repress this sick meandering of the mind. I knew Duty. At school, hadn't we memorized the "Ode to Duty" by Wordsworth?

Stern Daughter of the Voice of God!
O Duty! if that name thou love
Who art a light to guide, a rod
To check the erring, and reprove.[1]

My therapist settled down to a long year of intense probing, guiding me to new levels of introspection. Everything was confused in those days, as if the mystical vision had sent up volcanic lava and debris, and I was walking through the burning ash, trying to keep my footing on the shifting soil.

The disintegration of our marriage hurt: my husband and I had taken vows. "For better or for worse . . . in sickness and in health . . . Those whom God has joined together, let no one put asunder." Neither of us took these promises lightly—nor the effects that separation would have on our children.

To me, this dismantling felt inexorable, as if we were being physically picked up, my husband and I, and against our wishes thrown down two divergent paths, and we were each of us looking over our shoulders, reaching back toward the other as we were swept apart.

Today, years later, I justify myself, make excuses, take comfort in his happy remarriage to a beautiful and warm-hearted woman, or in the fact that none of my subsequent work and probably none of his could have been done while we remained together. But at the time it was all confusion, guilt, anger, fear, wrenching pain, and tears—exactly as it is for everyone whose marriage

breaks apart. It is a common story, filled with recrimina-
tion and remorse, with what-if's and if-only's. For six
years I played and replayed the tapes of our separation
and divorce, trying out different scenarios: Was this the
truth? Was that what really happened?

If I was thrown into confusion, so too were our two
beautiful girls. They are grown now. I purposely avoid their
story in this account, not out of disregard for how they
were hurt, but out of respect for them and for their privacy.

"I feel I must destroy all preconceptions," I wrote in
the journal that I started at the time and that I have kept
for most of the past seventeen years. "Tear down the
memories and façades, and only then will we be able to
see each other clearly, as new souls, rebuild a relationship on new love. D. sees only the destruction in that,
selfish, ruthless cruelty, and no creation. Is he right? Am I
simply looking for punishment?"

For the first time in fifteen years, I could not work.
Poetry came pouring out instead, a flood of words that
ended a year later as suddenly as it began. I went mad.
Or perhaps I went sane; who knows? Intoxicated with
the beauty of being alive.

"I am a river flowing to the sea," I wrote,

I am the sky tossed over fields
the very canopy of sky
that trees—who are also I—
hold up with dazzled fingers, frayed and tassled
    shields. . . .

My marriage was not the only thing destroyed. As if intent on breaking apart every relationship in my life now that my mother had died, I found myself unraveling the knitted strands of my life. I resigned from community boards, fired my literary agent, withdrew from friends, turned away from the magazine editors who had provided my livelihood, deliberately wiped out working relationships built up painstakingly over more than ten or fifteen years. Agent, marriage, community boards, friends: everything tossed overboard. Was I just burned out?

I longed to go *sunnyasi*, have no possessions, no responsibilities. I wanted to be free from the fatigue of discriminatory thought, the strain of constantly having to use the logical, analytical, critical faculties that I have spoken of earlier, the *thinking* mind, by which we see the world and all actions as divided into judgments: I/you, me/it, either/or, good/bad, right/wrong. Yet didn't the longing for that simplicity represent merely another form of judging and discrimination? I wanted to be free to move intuitively, "in the flow," to act without acting, to know without knowing, merging with the physical world as easily as I merged sometimes into the meditation of artistic creation. I wanted to ring all the time with this newfound, fearless joy. I was aware these moments came as gifts and not by will.

One day, for example, I stepped out of doors and my heart lifted as I felt myself become the wind, the space between the branches of the trees, the crows flapping through the space to land upon the branch. Yet curiously, all of these images were taking place, it seemed, inside my head and had no other solidity: the dreams of the gods; as I, too, held no existence separate from my mind.

Such an instant might last one second or less, but it felt like an eternity, timeless, rich, and pure. No words, no cognitive thought accompanied this perfect state. Returned to my body afterward, I felt invigorated, awake in ways that made me think I'd walked half-dead through half my life. It was *That* which I wanted all the time and wanted to pursue. And every other pursuit seemed an irritant, a distraction to the goal.

Mother Teresa says that "the more we have, the less we can give," that poverty provides freedom, for when all that's left is to be yourself, you can only receive. I think that's what we all want: we are hungry for spiritual sustenance, for the Word of God. We are thirsty for serenity, peace, knowledge, truth, compassion, confidence; for unconditional love.

I didn't know where I was going. I watched myself destroying my past, helpless to do otherwise. And was I all alone? Did no one share these experiences? Who could I talk to about what was going on?

In 1973, Father Andrew M. Greeley and William C. McCready, both social scientists at the University of Chicago, carried out a survey of mystical experiences of Americans. They asked only one initial question, deriving the wording from classic Christian descriptions of mystical experiences.

"Have you ever felt as though you were very close to

a powerful spiritual force that seemed to lift you out of yourself?" They asked 1,460 people, chosen in a National Opinion Research Center poll. The survey covered all age groups from teenagers to octogenarians, and the results, published first in a long sociology paper, were also reported in *The New York Times Magazine*.[2]

Six hundred of the respondents—about 40 percent—admitted such an experience, and they were then asked many further questions about their spiritual lives. Three hundred had had mystical interludes several times, and seventy-five people, or .5 percent of the almost 1,500 total, said they had them "often." Two-thirds placed the experience at the top of a seven-point index of intensity. But most of the mystics had never revealed their ecstasies, not even to their closest confidants, and none had discussed them with their clergy.

Greeley now says that reports of ecstatic experiences have increased today, perhaps because people feel freer to talk about the mystical than they did twenty-five years ago, when he undertook his questionnaire. But one recent TV survey reported the numbers of those having a mystical experience in the United States as 40 percent—no change from the earlier study. In England one half the population say they have experienced the mystical.[3] These percentages are probably very rough at best: So much depends on how the questions are phrased, and Greeley and McCready are the first to admit their survey may have been inadequate; it represented one of the first attempts at classifying the ineffable.

What had the respondents experienced? "A feeling I couldn't describe," or "the sensation that my personality had been taken over by something much more powerful," or "a sense of being bathed in light." Greeley and McCready found, as others had before them, that in general these intensely emotional experiences involved *knowing* something, and also that the true mystical encounter is marked by changes of personality, either subtle or striking. Nonetheless, sometimes these flashes of grace effect no change, and sometimes the changes are not permanent.

"I know people," said Greeley, "with authentic mystical experiences who have still messed up their lives."

As for who has such experiences, Greeley found, as had Dr. Bucke seventy-five years earlier, that the mystics were predominately male. They tended to be "disproportionately male, disproportionately black, disproportionately college educated." Disproportionate, that is, to the general population. They were likely to be in their forties or fifties (43 percent), although the differences are not great, and such experiences happen to those in their seventies as well as to those in their teens. Protestants seem more likely to have mystical experiences than Jews, Jews more than Roman Catholics—which is strange indeed, given the rich mystical heritage of this original Christian church. Of the Protestants, curiously, it is not the Baptists and fundamentalists who most frequently report ecstatic experiences but the Episcopalians, Presbyterians, and other mid-road groups. One half of those queried in these denominations had had ecstatic interludes. "The notion of mysticism as a fundamentalist experience," say Greeley and McCready, "is badly shaken in this table."

What are we to make of that? Is the mystical encounter thwarted by authority—a priest or minister, or church law, standing between the recipient and his God?

And were the respondents crazy or unbalanced? No. The survey found those confessing to mystical encounters were psychologically strong, confident, and optimistic. Nothing indicated that they were either socially deprived or psychologically disturbed. They were creative, dynamic, happy, balanced individuals. Indeed, Greeley administered one brief test of psychological well-being, developed by Professor Norman Bradburn, and found the highest possible correlation between spiritual ecstasies and psychological well-being.

Some seventy years earlier William James had reported a similar finding. The more authentic the experience in classic mystical terms, the more likely the person is, said James, to show a "positive affect balance."

Greeley and McCready's survey found that the responding mystics tended to have had warm and happy childhoods in "a supportive and religiously joyous family atmosphere."[4] But who could say if it was the mystical experience that induced life satisfaction or whether greater pleasure in life created a personality open to mystical experience?

We know so little about these ecstasies that almost all we do know is the need for more research. How do we even phrase the questions properly? In the pre-test phase,

Greeley and McCready first asked, "Have you ever had a religio-mystical experience?" Fifty percent of the respondents answered yes. On a hunch that the figure was too high, they reformulated their query: "Have you ever felt as though you had become completely one with God or the universe?" This time 45 percent insisted that they had; and again the surveyers threw out the results. Eventually they developed the classic question used: "Have you ever felt yourself very close to a spiritual force that seemed to lift you out of yourself?" This time they were relieved that only 35 to 40 percent of the respondents could answer in the affirmative, and judged the response correct. But was it?

If you asked a more open-ended question, or if you asked a series of questions, would you find that more people would admit to experiencing these moments of deep, ringing peace or of exalted rapture? I can think of phrasings one might try: Have you ever felt the presence of an invisible loving Force or companion beside you? Have you ever seen or felt an angel? Had a vision of religious significance? Been embraced by a sense of divine light that comes combined with unconditional love and a feeling of safety and of peace? Have you ever felt that something intervened in your life to produce a "miracle"?

I find it fascinating that Greeley's mystics, unlike psychics and other sensitives, were predominately male. What does that mean? Do women have different raptures than men? Would woman respond to questions differently phrased? Greeley and McCready asked if the respondents had been "lifted out of" themselves. What

of powerful spiritual forces that descend into you, bringing "showings and knowings" that benefit your life?
What of dreams or other visions? These, too, make striking changes in one's life.

The following almost classic mystical encounter
comes from a woman, Debbie Matthews, sent hand-
cuffed and shackled to a county jail in 1992.

After being taken through two large, time-locked,
steel doors, I took in the dingy sour-smelling sur-
roundings that would be my new home for the
next eight months. . . . At that particular time, I
really never gave much thought to God or angels,
but my belief stood solid for both. I began to sink
into a deep depression, including thoughts of suicide. I cried for two days, unable to eat, my head
pounding from lack of sleep. I had given up hope,
when the thought to pray occurred to me.

I prayed briefly for God to remove my pain
and misery, and it seemed instantly that I experienced the most wonderful sensation. I could not
"see" anything, but I could feel a presence in that
cell. It is difficult to describe this feeling that began at the very top of my head and slowly descended down my body and finally to the tips of
my toes. With this sensation, I felt an utter calm
come over me, together with the thought that
everything would be all right. I bowed my head
again, thanking God for sending one of His angels to me.

Afterwards Debbie Matthews began to read as much as possible on supernatural events. "I've come to realize that many things happen to us for a reason, and that we are supposed to 'learn' from them. I now don't take life so seriously and enjoy myself more," she wrote. "My faith holds strong that God and the angels keep a silent vigil over all of us, and things will really be all right."[5]

My revelation in Peru represented only a moment of my life. Many other experiences still lay ahead. I had had a certain type of vision, been absorbed for an hour into the light. But I was not "enlightened," make no mistake, and certainly I knew it.

Today, years later, I have had time to learn a little more about these ecstasies and what they mean. Many religions describe two, three, ten separate levels of illumination. In the first a person becomes conscious of his relationship to the universe, living in Bucke's cosmic consciousness. In this state he is simultaneously aware both of himself, the doer, and of the deed—two separated things. At later stages he lives on the level of angels, always observing and worshiping the Divine. I forget which Christian mystic would only pray: "O thou my Joy! O thou my All!" Caught up in mystical rapture, he still sees himself as separate from God, for his soul is playing with God. Or is the bride of God. But there is an even higher stage, in which the mystic merges utterly with the Divine. No longer a separate ego, the soul becomes subsumed in both the All and Nothingness. In classic mystical terms his soul *is* God. "My *me* is God," cried Saint Catherine of Genoa, "nor do I know my self-hood except in God." Is it these last two states to which Christ refers in the *Apocryphal Gospel of Saint Thomas*?

A lamp am I to those who see me,
A mirror am I to those who know me.

Hindu philosophy describes two stages of absorption into the Divine. The one is a kind of waking state, in which knowledge enters by intuition. "All ideas are gradually generalized into one, which [appears] as a stationary spectacle before the spectator."[6] In the second state even this view of something disappears, and the yogi is so absorbed into the Divine that to the outward eye she appears unconscious and inwardly she has merged with the Divine. This is "*samadhi* without seed."

The Sufi Muslims also define two stages of illumination. The first begins with revelations and visions, in which the mystic in a waking state beholds angels and prophets and hears them speak. A higher stage cannot be expressed, except to say that some nearness to God occurred, and it brought knowledge untold.

"Of the things I do not remember," wrote the renowned Sufi al-Ghazali in his *Confessions*, "what was, was; think it good; do not ask for an account of it."[7]

Always you fall back again into the normal world. In *The Common Experience,* J. M. Cohen and J. F. Phipps tell the story of a lonely, bored young mother pushing her baby carriage during a bleak moment in the first World War. "For a split second, there upon the shores of the Firth, I *understood*. What I understood I don't know. I don't know now. I *know* I understood then and I have remained firm and calm and unshaken upon that rock— i.e., that once I understood—ever since."[8]

Buddhists, as I've said, mark many levels on the Way to full enlightenment, but the important thing for the Buddhist is not which level you are on, anyway; for once having realized that all phenomena are creations of the mind and have no separate existence, the practitioner simply continues to practice deepening her compassion, devoting every thought and action to the benefit of all beings—since the process is the goal.

Finally, the Christians, too, name various stages of mystical ecstasy. The unitive state is highest. The German mystic Sister Katrei, a disciple of Meister Eckhart (1260–1327), went into such depths of divine union that once she had to be carried from the church. She lay three days inert. The nuns thought she had died. Without her confessor, Meister Eckhart, himself a mystic, they would have buried her. On the third day she came back to her senses. "Alas, miserable me," she cried. "I am back!"

"Permit me to taste divine truth in the revelation of thy experience," said Eckhart.

"God knows," she said, "I cannot. My experience is ineffable."

"Did you receive all that you want?" he asked.

"Yes," she answered. "I am confirmed."

Another time Sister Katrei went into the solitude of her meditation, only to reappear:

"Sir, rejoice with me, I am God."

"Glory to God," cried Eckhart, justifying the charges of heresy later leveled against him. "All joy be yours, and may you remain God."[9]

Saint Teresa, in her autobiography, compared the successive degrees of orison, or the prayer of quiet, to four ways of watering the garden of the soul. The first, she said, is contemplation of a religious object, in which you are still thinking; this is the slowest and most laborious of the four. The second is the orison of quiet, in which the soul receives some help; the well has been fitted with a windlass, and more water comes with less labor, "for grace now reveals itself more distinctly to the soul." In the third stage the gardener no longer depends on her own exertions, but makes contact with the Divine without strain, and now the irrigation of the garden is easy. In the fourth and highest stage, she says, God Himself waters our garden with rain "drop by drop." Then individual activity sinks into the "great life of the All." *Samadhi*, as with Sister Katrei.

When I came down from Machu Picchu, wondering if the experience was real or evidence of some malfunction of my brain, I understood instinctively that only time would tell. If what I had seen were true, the effects would be demonstrated in my life. Indeed all authorities agree. "By their fruits shall ye know them." William

James speaks of a new ardor, a love of living that overcomes the mystic, and of magnanimous actions once impossible to contemplate that "with this shifting of the emotional center" are now made easy. He speaks also of "a melting mood" that overtakes one, and the special grace that is traditionally revered by the Church, the gift of tears. The person having a "real" spiritual encounter undergoes

- A feeling of being in a wider life than the world's selfish interests,
- A sense of the goodness and friendliness of the universe, and a surrender to that will,
- An immense elation and fearlessness in acting; a shedding of all vain, selfish, or egotistical goals,
- A tenderness toward all things; a shifting of the center toward loving and harmonious relationships, toward (in James's words) "yes, yes," and away from anxious, prideful "no."

Certainly I found it so. I sprang out of bed so happily each morning that my husband commented on it. "No one gets out of bed like that," he said, bemused. One day I saw an eighty-five-year-old neighbor sweeping her front steps. I'd always laughed at her a little snidely, but this day I bounded up to greet her, overjoyed. "You acted as if you really *wanted* to see her," said my husband in surprise. And then it was my turn to look at him in surprise, for yes, I had been glad. I hadn't realized how much I liked her. I decided to take the old lady under my wing, as a special volunteer project, since she lived alone. There was still a certain smugness in the decision, or sense of superiority. Little did I know she would become my close, dear friend who, before she died twelve years later at the age of ninety-seven, gave back to me a thousand times more than I could offer her.

Carl Jung says that if you think you've had a spiritual experience, then you have. But James, the intellectual, offers three criteria by which afterward to judge one's ecstasy. First is *immediate luminousness*. Was the experience accompanied by a wider vision, wisdom, and, at the physical level, by love and light? Second is *philosophical reasonableness*. Does its insight conform to what is considered morally and philosophically "good"? Does it set the mystic's foot on the path toward becoming a better person, more generous, tolerant, self-effacing? Third is *moral helpfulness*. Do the effects represent the highest social virtues, the desire to help others even at personal cost? In the end, even James reverts to examining the effect of the mystical consciousness on the individual herself.

If the experience was real, says James, the person now "reborn" demonstrates five qualities:

- Strength of spirit
- Equanimity
- Tolerance
- Purity
- Charity

And also happiness, for the person having such an encounter is often of a sunny, happy disposition. James makes the point that *sanity*, coming from the Latin *sanus*, means "healthy," and that health can be defined as happiness. The sane person is happy.[10]

I think that after a violent mystical encounter, however, there also comes the kind of scathing self-doubt and introspection that hit me, a remorseless moral inventory. So much is happening.

One night I lay weeping in bed beside my husband, and he, dear man, put his arms around me and held me while I cried. He knew the cause: that our marriage was finished, that I was scared and felt only failure and loss. Who was the more "spiritual" in that little scene?

I must have been intolerable to live with. I consumed spiritual books. William James, Krishnamurti, Evelyn Underhill, Yogananda, Reshad Feild, Muktananda, Richard Bucke, C. S. Lewis, Martin Buber, Simone Weil, Teilhard de Chardin . . . I marked up the margins of my books. I could not get enough of the ecstatic passages.

"I am God," says Love, "for Love is God, and God is Love. And this soul is God by condition of love: but I am God by Nature Divine. And this [state] is hers by righteousness of love. . . . This [soul] is the eagle that flies high, so right high and yet more high than doth any other bird; for she is feathered with fine love."[11]

"Yes!" I wrote in the margins. Ram Ram Ram Ram Ram, wrote the Hindu saint, and my soul wrote on the prayer wheel of the turning sky Love Love Love Love and God God God. I felt as if I could taste the color red, I could hear the apple blossoms opening in the warm spring sun. All senses were quickened in the love of God.

Perhaps I was thrust too quickly into waters that threatened to drown me. Nothing was clear. Moreover, I was getting sick. More and more frequently I felt physically ill. I thought if I continued my life as I was leading it—a life of Washington politics and investigative journalism, of chic dinner parties and intelligent, well-meaning friends talking intently at superficial levels about politics or money, carping and criticizing instead of appreciating—I thought if I continued, then literally I might die. But how could I leave my husband, my children, my friends? And for what? God may have revealed something, but He didn't tell what lay ahead.

The stress erupted as pure physical pain. I lost ten pounds. One day I was walking up the hill to the park that spread above my house. I hurt so badly I could not stand up straight, but moved bent over by my stomach cramps. My shoulders ached with tension, as if I were heaving a yoke up that hill. Suddenly the thought occurred to me: This is what Christ must have felt like, carrying his cross to Calvary.

Instantly, another thought rose up: that I am always willing to accept my joys and happiness as coming from the gifts of God, but never the fire of His love. Ridiculous!

If this pain is an expression of Your love, I said

inwardly, then I can take *much* more. Give me more! Give me a thousand times more!

Instantly the pain was gone. My shoulders eased. I could straighten my back, hold up my head again. The burning in my stomach left, never to return.

That day I learned about the fire of God's love, although the lesson has had to be repeated over and over, for I forget, every time, that just as ancient swordsmiths used to make the finest Damascus blade by heating a lump of iron to intolerable temperatures and thrusting it into ice-cold water, so are we tempered in the forge of God's love to produce a weapon both whiplash flexible and strong. In the same way, pain is given to us, sometimes as a signal that something needs to be addressed, sometimes in order to teach us how to love.

One day, standing in the kitchen, thinking of this man in England, I felt my love for him streaming out of my heart in a tangible fierce current. It was so palpable that I thought he must be able to feel the energy three thousand miles away, and then in curiosity I wondered what it would be like to feel it myself. I stood there a moment allowing the outpouring of love to gather force, streaming out to him . . . then switched it around onto myself.

A blast furnace! I was hit by a wall of heat! It so surprised me that I stopped.

So that's what love is like, I thought.

Yet all this time, even while confused, struggling to keep my head above water, to keep my feet steady on the shifting sand, even while weeping in my husband's arms,

I knew a curious core of happiness, like an iron rod running down the center of my body, and radiating . . . joy!

I meditated now for long periods, with deeper and more concentrated attention, for in these moments the taste of God prevailed. As the months passed I found I did not want to eat meat anymore, or drink wine or other alcoholic beverages. It was not that I renounced them for religious principles, but simply that *they* gave *me* up: my body revolted. Gradually I shifted to a mostly vegetarian diet, modified by fish. But this change took time, came over me imperceptibly. Other things occurred with dramatic force.

I could not tell a lie anymore. I could not kill an ant on the kitchen counter. If a spider came in the house, I would capture it on a paper towel (to my family's amusement) and carry it out of doors. (And still do.) I spent time catching flies on the windowpanes with a water glass and a piece of paper. It was not that I necessarily believed in reincarnation or that this fly or ant was my reborn grandmother, simply that I didn't want to kill. I was not afraid of dying, but life had become inconceivably precious; in fact the very words *life*, *kill*, *squash*, had taken on new meaning, for it seemed that to kill an enthusiasm or a dream with a negative word or a flashy remark was almost as cruel as to take a physical life. I hadn't noticed before how often, thoughtlessly, we crush the human spirit, put people down. I started listening to how I spoke. In my family we generally blurted out the first thing that came to the tongue, especially a quick retort. It was considered witty. I determined to learn to speak in such a way that the person I was addressing could actually hear what I wanted to express. This meant framing my thoughts according to the nature of the listener. (It's been a lifetime job: I still don't do it well.) Likewise I began to watch my own unspoken thoughts: Were they negative, directed against myself, lowering my self-esteem? When were they supportive? When scolding, judging, "killing"? And concerning other people, when were my thoughts or words just gossip, or motivated by my need to feel superior?

And so I lived for the next months in this new mystical awareness, loving so deeply you'd think I had shed my skin, and quivering with newly discovered psychic abilities—telepathy, clairvoyance, prescience, healing properties—sometimes seeing my future path clearly, sometimes walking in the dark. Confused. Elated. Tender. Sad. Full. Empty. Erotic. Chaste. And wishing I knew others on the path.

CHAPTER 10

THE HIDDEN MYSTICS

There are only two ways to live your life. One is as though nothing is a miracle. The other is as though everything is.

—ALBERT EINSTEIN

There are hundreds of mute and unnamed mystics for every one who writes a book. In fact, the most important interpreters of mysticism in all periods are those persons who quietly practice the presence of God . . . without even being conscious that they are rare and unusual persons and often without knowing the meaning of the word 'mystic.'

—RUFUS JONES

Though a man be soiled
With the sins of a lifetime,
Let him but love me,

. . . .

In utter devotion:

. . . .

That man is holy.

. . . .

The man that loves me,
He shall not perish.

—BHAGAVAD GITA

All around us live the hidden mystics. They walk down the streets of New York in shoes with worn-down heels. They beg on street corners. They drive fast cars through Chicago or L.A. They run multimillion-dollar businesses, and when they go home, their heads whirling with figures and finances, they catch their breath at something so simple—the ringing of a bell, the light-struck pigeons flying upward in a flurry of wings, a fragment of music—and in that moment they remember . . . what? They cannot say. Some sign, some glimmering that points beyond themselves to things not of this world.

Some of their mystical experiences are dramatic, passionate events that wash away all prior conceptions, firm ground. Others come as softly as the whisper of silk, a moment of mere harmony. . . . You aren't even certain anything happened there in that time-suspended second, but your spirits lift as you proceed. Sometimes it is so casual, you step out of your house one morning, and out of the blue, for no reason, you are washed by joy, brushed by an angel's wing. A spiritual event.

Seeing deities, hearing voices, having ecstatic experiences does not make you spiritual. I know brilliant people who have never had a vision, who practice no religion, but are more spiritual than many religious practitioners. They work in the world, saving children, forging social change, or simply raising their own or foster children—most lovingly. No big deal. Just drawing water at the well.

"When God wants an important thing done in this

world," wrote Edmond McDonald in *Presbyterian Outlook*,

> or a wrong righted, He goes about it in a very sin-
> gular way. God simply has a tiny baby born, per-
> haps of a very humble home. . . . And God puts
> the idea or purpose into the mother's heart. And
> she puts it in the baby's mind, and then—God
> waits. . . . For each child comes with the message
> that God is not yet discouraged with humanity.

Some people never even think about God. They take
a walk, or work on carpentry, or they weave, garden, or
cook. Some meditate just by waiting in silence for a few
minutes, and some, like Brother Lawrence, simply "practice the presence of God." No big deal. Are they the truer
mystics, these humble, silent ones? Others throw themselves into all the healing arts, intent on becoming better
than they are, on transforming the very cells of their bodies into light.

We know certain things of the ecstatic journey. Yet
the more we know the more questions arise. For example,
as noted earlier, the sociologists Andrew Greeley and
William McCready discovered in their survey that those
admitting to mystical encounters tended to have had
happy childhoods, loving parents, and especially a father
who expressed religious joyousness. But does that signify?
Since those responding affirmatively were predominately
male, the fact of a religiously joyous father might also be

interpreted as meaning no more than that the son had received parental permission to testify openly and without embarrassment to his own spiritual life. I have only anecdotal evidence to draw upon, but I submit that a happy and a spiritually rich childhood are not prerequisites. Many of the letters I receive are from women who were neglected or abused in childhood, or reared in an atheist or nonbelieving environment, and who nonetheless relate their sweet experiences.

Catherine Brown, for example, wrote from North Carolina, and despite her spiritually barren childhood she is one of the 5 percent (according to Greeley and McCready) who have been blessed with many ecstasies. "Mystical experiences," she says, "have punctuated my life for over ten years." They began with a request—a prayer made directly to God, and "have continued through meditation and many conscious efforts to remain open to the miraculous in daily affairs." The prayer—that longing of the heart—is important, for God is usually too courteous to barge in uninvited.

Having been raised by parents and grandparents who were atheistic secular humanists, I entered adulthood a skeptic who became an increasingly angry cynic. My awakening came about one night as a result of a chilling fight with my husband. After I had made one too many scoffing remarks about his faith in the Divine, he let me know he was closing off that side of himself to me. A deep shiver of fear ran through me and caused me to do a strange thing: I prayed. I asked simply, "God, if you're there, please let me know!" The extraordinary answer I received came immediately.

My reclining body felt as if each and every cell was being filled with helium. The lightness and expandedness was so real I thought I'd float up to the ceiling. A powerful stillness covered me, combined with a tingling sensation (as if my blood had been replaced with champagne). I don't know how long I remained in that heavenly embrace, but I remember not being able to speak or move or to tell my husband that I finally understood and was sorry I had hurt him.

Afterward, her brushes with the Divine took other forms, including seeing the beings of immeasurable love.

In deep states of meditation my soul or spiritual essence takes me to what I know are sacred spaces. Although my soul does not leave my body (as in astral travel), it moves into a position as my lens. From this point of view, I often experience spaces best described as angel-flanked altars, refulgent with light, colors, and a rarified air (which I can only explain as an atmosphere with infinitely refined but intense energy vibrations). The angels do not speak. They emanate awe and unconditional love.

She ends her letter with the ineffable: "The magnitude of this love and energy is not comparable to any ordinary waking consciousness and is not effectively translated into words."[1]

My friend Elinor likewise forms an exception to the Greeley-McCready rule, having had a difficult childhood. Her independent mother was distant and busy, her famous father absent, and neither parent indicated any interest in a spiritual dimension. As a grown woman, at the time when we were writing long letters to each other in an effort to understand how the spiritual journey tangled with our marriages, children, and work, she had left her Jewish roots to explore Buddhist and Hindu teachings. At a weeklong meditation retreat, as she writes in an as-yet unpublished memoir, she experienced what Hindus call the rising of Kundalini.

On the fifth day of the retreat, her teacher laid both hands on the crown of her head. Elinor turned around, took a few steps through the lawn of meditation cushions, and then:

> A surge of energy was pouring through me. It pounded against my head and forehead, gushed from the center of my heart, sluiced down my arms, and ran out of prickly electric sockets that appeared to have opened in the palms of my hands. My God, I was running and running with the stuff. I was pouring. I was throbbing with it. . . . I was lined up like rifle sights with the universe and open to it. There was no spiritual

realm, no earthly realm, it was all here, and in me. I was a walking transformer, running with what felt like love, in elemental, particulate form. . . .

That evening I sit at my teacher's question-and-answer period, taking notes in my 5 × 8 spiral notebook, the dutiful scholar, and those same hands taking notes are on fire with a high voltage current passing steadily through them. When I close my eyes, the energy purrs up to the top of my head and pushes to get out, like a child at birth, and when I open them it runs down my arms and out my tingling palms. That morning my first impulse had been to hang on to this stuff. . . . But I saw beyond any prior clarity I had had about "being here now," that all this energy was only coursing by a moment at a time. I couldn't catch it, it wasn't mine in any sense; it was just passing through.

She understood at a deep cellular level the Buddhist teaching about attachment and suffering, and how not clinging—letting go—leads to emotional freedom and happiness. As the retreat continued she sensed the hidden energy in her fellow meditators.

Passing by Eugene, a New York lawyer, I placed my buzzing hand lightly on his bald head. I felt a virtual conflagration under my hand. Where had this energy been hiding in us? Were we all walking electrical fields, but living too coarsely to know it? Myself, I felt like a great milk-cow seeking relief: I wished someone would draw off a little of this invisible swollen stream, this energy that longed for milking. Hadn't I seen it years ago the night of my vision of the Mother? Then I *saw* it, now I *was* it. The whole astral spin-out, even Christ, came down to such a simple thing. Merely our own nature, correctly perceived.

For days the energy flow didn't seem to end. For weeks that included a trip to Los Angeles and back, she felt as if her being was all but dissolved into the great river of existence. Slowly she returned to "normalcy," until she could write of the separation. "Every street is no longer a river at every step. I live in a body, in a family, and a society. And pavement is real."[2]

Howard Thurman was an African American, born in 1900 and deeply influenced by an eminent Quaker mystic, Rufus Jones. Author of fifteen books, he describes a quieter experience than Elinor's. "As a child," he wrote,

I was accustomed to spending many hours alone in my rowboat, fishing along the river, when there was no sound save the lapping of the waves against the boat. There were times when it seemed as if the earth and the river and the sky and I were one beat of the same pulse. It was a time of watching and waiting for what I did not know—yet I always knew. There would come a moment when beyond the single pulse beat there was a sense of Presence which seemed always to speak to me. My response to the sense of Presence always had the quality of personal communion. There was no voice. There was no image. There was no vision. There was God.[3]

Sometimes God comes as fire—beyond all philosophy. Until his death, Blaise Pascal carried sewn in the pocket of his clothing a description of the two-hour period he could not forget:

Fire. God of Abraham, God of Isaac, God of Jacob, not the God of philosophers and scholars. Absolute Certainty: Beyond reason. Joy. Peace. Forgetfulness of the world and everything but God. The world has not known thee, but I have known thee. Joy! joy! joy! tears of joy![4]

What brings on a mystical encounter? Why does it come at one time and not another, to some people and not to others? Why must it be invited in, first by the loneliness that aches to be filled, then by surrender, a crying out for help? And why do the mysteries present themselves in such vast and varying forms? Wind, light, fire, peace, love, Christ, angels, guides, knowings, or dark nothingness.

It comes like a blow in the night, the mugger sneaking up behind you, and suddenly you are flooded with delights. The writer Joan Borysenko remembers that between the ages of forty-two and forty-six, during a particularly difficult period of her life, she had three and four dreams a night—all of them experiences with the light. "I was rewarded by four years of grace. For a time, as the Buddhist saying goes, mountains and rivers were not just mountains and rivers but something spectacular; until slowly the mystical and magical withdrew, and mountains and rivers went back to being mountains and rivers again."[5] There is a Zen saying to the same effect: Before enlightenment, chop wood, draw water; after enlightenment, chop wood, draw water.

By no means do mystical experiences arrive only in middle age.

In 1940, when Thomas Merton was twenty-five years old, he went to Cuba to recuperate from an appendectomy. Two years earlier he had been baptized a Catholic. He was in a church in Havana when he felt as if he were "suddenly illuminated by being blinded by the manifestation of God's presence."

> But what a thing it was, this awareness: it was so intangible, and yet it struck me like a thunderclap. It was a light that was so bright that it had no relation to any visible light and so profound and so intimate that it seemed like a neutralization of every lesser experience.
>
> And yet the thing that struck me most of all was that this light was in a certain sense "ordinary"— it was a light (and this most of all was what took my breath away)—that was offered to all, to

everybody, and there was nothing fancy or strange about it. It was the light of faith deepened and reduced to an extreme and sudden obviousness.

He continues, describing how

> A door opens in the center of our being, and we seem to fall through it into immense depths which, although they are infinite, are all accessible to us; all eternity seems to have become ours in this one placid and breathless contact. . . . It is useless to think of fathoming the depths of wide-open darkness that have yawned inside you. . . . These depths, they are Love, and in the midst of you they form a wide, impregnable country.

Writing afterward, he decided the light was a metaphor. "It was knowledge and Love—especially Love . . . and it was something I have never forgotten."[6]

Sometime later Merton joined the silent Cistercian (Trappist) order of monks. He wrote copiously. He corresponded with presidents and popes, and studied the interwoven threads of Christianity, Buddhism, Hinduism, and other religions. Then in his forties he fell in love with a young nurse—the flare of erotic love in the midst of the spiritual. He took a sabbatical to travel in Asia. He had been questioning his calling and monastic life. In 1968 in Ceylon (now Sri Lanka), he went to visit the gargantuan carved statues at Polonnaruwa, the ones of standing and reclining buddhas. There he had another epiphany, sweet and clear as glass.

> Looking at these figures I was suddenly, almost forcibly, jerked clean out of the habitual, half-tied vision of things, and an inner clearness, clarity, as if exploding from the rocks themselves, became evident and obvious. . . . The thing about all this is that there is no puzzle, no problem, and really no "mystery." All problems are resolved and everything is clear, simply because what matters is clear. The rock, all matter, all life, is charged with dharmakaya . . . everything is emptiness and everything is compassion. I don't know when in my life I have ever had such a sense of beauty and spiritual validity running together in one aesthetic illumination. Surely, with Mahabalipuram and Polonnaruwa my Asian pilgrimage has come clear and purified itself. I mean, I know and have seen what I was obscurely looking for. I . . . have seen and have pierced through the surface and have got beyond the shadow and the disguise.[7]

"Why does God come in different forms?" I asked my guru. "It is like your clothing," he said. "When you get up in the morning, you put on a bathrobe to wash, to eat breakfast, and then you get dressed suitably for work. In the evening after work you change to play tennis, and perhaps you change again to go out to dinner.

Each dress is suitable to its own occasion. You don't go to the theater in tennis whites.

"Think of it like your hand or leg," he continued. "You are not your hand, but your hand picks up a scrap of paper on the floor. You are not your legs, but your two legs carry you to pick up the paper. So it is with God. Many hands. Many eyes. Many legs."

Mirabei, the Hindu saint, worshiped Krishna in his form as an infant and fell into such ecstasies, mad with love just thinking of the babe, that she left her husband (who adored her) and the intolerable comfort of her family to wander India as a *sadhu*, a holy one.

Sometimes the visions come in the form of angels and sometimes as imageless ecstasies—David dancing to the cymbals before the altar of God, as the whirling dervishes still do today. Sometimes they come as simple knowledge. I spoke earlier of George Foreman the boxer, to whom the vision came as Christ; and I will tell more stories later of the appearances of Christ, and his Mother, Mary.

Here is one such story, modern and classically correct. Nellie Lauth was living in Gainsville, Florida, attending an Episcopal church. As the congregation stood up to approach the altar for communion, she no longer saw human beings, but row after row of great beings of sacred light. They stood twelve feet tall, approaching for the Eucharist.

I myself was a bride in a white bridal gown, waiting to commit myself to Christ as the Eucharist.

By the time it was the turn of my row, I didn't know if I could walk up the aisle. But I did, and Christ awaited me in the minister's hands. I do not know to this day how I negotiated that walk to and from the altar. The choir and congregation sang 'Holy God We Praise Thy Name.' Then all became quiet again and I returned to myself. Everyone returned to their form. I was trembling like jelly.

She stayed after the service. She felt the need to speak to the minister, but she did not describe her vision.

"Father, today I realize the greatness of my soul," Nellie said.

He responded with a truth she says it took years to understand. "Be patient with your experience," he said.[8]

Many mystics are simply ordinary people, churched or unchurched, born to enjoy these gentle and intuitive altered states of consciousness. They make no dramatic mark in the world. One such woman is my friend Naomi. To talk with her you'd think that nothing displeased her, that she was satisfied by everything she saw or had.

As a young girl she lived with her family out in the country. One day when she was thirteen she went to the well to get butter, because the family had no refrigerator and kept the bacon and milk and butter in the well-bucket, down in the cold. Her married sister lived over the hill and shared the well with them. On this particular day this child, age thirteen, was pulling up the bucket at the well, when over the hill came the handsomest boy she'd ever seen. He was the brother of a neighbor, much older, eighteen or twenty.

It's like a Bible story.

They talked at the well.

The next day he moved to a dairy farm far away. She thought she'd never see him again.

Then one day when she was sixteen, she went again to the well, and over the hill walked this young man, "Tater" (which was his nickname), coming to meet her, and her heart leapt up. A few years later they were engaged, and then married. They were lucky all their lives, she says, eyes glowing as she tells her story. Her husband worked as a tenant farmer.

The first house they lived in had kerosene lamps for light, and it was pretty as could be, with the soft light shining on the walls. They moved to another farm and this one had gas.

Now we are talking about the 1940s and '50s, not the nineteenth century, but this woman is so good-hearted and so unassuming that she views everything as a gift, including her husband, "the sweetest man ever born."

They moved up, job by job, into houses with electricity and running water and flush toilets, and each one came as a blessing, because to her the entire world is shining with divinity and nothing exists that is not good. They had children. Their children grew and went to school. They in turn married and had children; there were deaths—one son and her husband—while throughout she maintained a trust as wondrous as a child's.

You could listen to her for hours, and you'd come away feeling you'd been touched by something precious. I think that every moment of her life was spiritual; I know she had deep trust in God. Whether it came in moments of ecstasy and rapture I never asked. And I doubt she'd call herself a mystic or a saint.

I know another hidden mystic, Bessie, an African-American woman, pretty as a flower, and so filled with the Lord that hardly a phrase can fall from her lips that does not begin or end with "Bless the Lord. Praise God!" So high is her faith and love of God, so vivid are her experiences, that for years she went to night school after work to qualify as a clergywoman of her church.

One day I telephoned her, discouraged. "Rejoice!" she told me, and "Give thanks!" Every morning she wakes up, she says, and her first thought is of her Lord, "because I don't own me anymore," she said, and I could hear the lilt in her voice. "I am living for the Lord, going where he wants me to go, needs for me to go." Her relationship is strictly personal, one of intimate simplicity.

She laughed. " 'Husband,' I say, 'are we going out tonight?' Sometimes I get angry and tell him what to do: 'Husband, you better pay attention now!' God loves it when I tell him what to do." We laughed into the phone. "God is working things out," she continued. "Don't worry. I can't do nothing, He does everything. 'Show it to me in a dream,' I say, and, 'Thank you, Lord!' Letting go and trusting him. If I lose this body today, I wouldn't mind, because I'd be with God." Everything is preordained, she said; her task is only to step out each day in faith.

I put down the phone that morning, laughing, my despondency forgotten in her simple trust and gratitude. All through our conversation my pen had been scribbling down her words in the automatic writer's activity, the journalist's reflex. I slipped the paper underneath my desk blotter, and it still sits there to this day. Over the years I have referred to it every now and again, reread her faith and always found my heart uplifted, and as the years have passed I've noticed that sometimes now I talk like this myself to my Beloved, who is husband, mother, sister, brother, father, lover, friend, my very self, it seems.

I have an image: that we spend our lives climbing the winding staircase of a high, glass tower. Sometimes we stand on one step, sometimes on another, and outside the windows, the land spreads gloriously before us, different vistas opening, according to the height of the step we stand on and the direction of the view. We see pine-covered mountains or tropical vegetation, deserts or snow, rivers or seas, flat plains or rolling hills, each step presenting a different sight-line as we circle the tower, sometimes climbing high, sometimes dropping down ten steps on the journey of our lives. With each stair-step the landscape appears mysterious and new, although only the viewing point has changed.

Or perhaps this magical stairway forms a double

helix, like two strands of DNA, winding and intertwining, or like a deceptive Möbius strip, so that on our journey we not only move up and down the stairwell but step forward onto the other ribbon as well, twisting in constantly changing circles. We think we've never seen this vista before, while in fact only our position on the stairwell lends the countryside its awe.

I have spoken so far about inviting in transcendent grace by silence, solitude, and prayer. But there are other ways, known for centuries to travelers on this road, to induce ecstatic states. Some we have already mentioned—such as the austerities of the ancient Hindu ascetics, who pierced their tongues or beat themselves, or of medieval Christians who wore hair shirts against their skin and fasted to the point of starvation. Native Americans attempt the same transcendence with sundance rituals, or shamanistic rituals, for I think the urge to transcend self-consciousness is a universal longing of the soul.

The fact is that if the discipline is approached as a holy endeavor, a sacred undertaking, such torture can produce a heightened, exalted—could we say, endorphinated?—transport of the soul, and this is far beyond the mere happiness of the runner's high. Blanche Gamond, "a humble sufferer," was persecuted as a Huguenot under Louis XIV. She wrote later of how

They shut all the doors, and I saw six women, each with a bunch of willow rods as thick as the hand could hold, and a yard long. He gave me the order, "Undress yourself," which I did. He said, "You are leaving on your shift, you must take it off." They had so little patience that they took it off themselves, and I was naked from the waist up. They brought a cord with which they tied me to a beam in the kitchen. They drew the cord tight with all their strength and asked me, "Does it hurt you?" and then they discharged their fury upon me, exclaiming as they struck me, "Pray now to your God." It was the Roulette woman who held this language. But at this moment I received the greatest consolation that I can ever receive in my life, since I had the honor of being whipped for the name of Christ, and in addition of being crowned with his mercy and his consolations. Why can I not write down the inconceivable influences, consolations, and peace which I felt interiorly? To understand them one must have passed by the same trial; they were so great that I was ravished, for there where afflictions abound grace is given superabundantly. In vain the women cried, "We must double our blows; she does not feel them, for she neither speaks nor cries." And how should I have cried, since I was swooning with happiness within?[9]

There are three ways of courting holy ecstasies: through the age-old religious disciplines of prayer and fasting, the expression of the longing heart; through sacred dance and ritual; and last by ingesting intoxicants or hallucinogenic substances. For centuries people have entered the sacred mysteries by taking sacred herbs or experimenting with chemicals and drugs: ether, opium, chloroform, belladonna, morphine, heroin, cocaine, LSD, ecstasy, marijuana, peyote, alcohol, glue; there are an infinite number of substances. Alcoholic beverages provide a high, as, more mildly, do nicotine and caffeine. William James was experimenting with nitrous oxide when he wrote *The Varieties of Religious Experience*. He confesses that he never had a mystical experience. His experiences on nitrous oxide, like those of others taking drugs, converged toward a kind of metaphysical insight, the keynote of which was *reconciliation*, whereby the opposites of the world were all "melted into unity." Nothing persuaded him to count it "spiritual." Still, he writes,

one conclusion was forced upon my mind at that time . . . that our normal waking consciousness, rational consciousness as we call it, is but one special type of consciousness, whilst all about it, parted from it by the filmiest of screens, there lie potential forms . . . entirely different. . . . No account of the universe in its totality can be final which leaves these other forms of consciousness quite disregarded.[10]

The wisdom-bearers, the shamans and priests, magi and spiritual diviners would agree. They never used drugs recreationally. The Aztecs called cocaine the "divine leaf of immortality," and psychedelic mushrooms were known as "flesh of the gods" and "vine of the serpent."

In the 1960s Richard Alpert, a psychologist on the faculty at Harvard University, took LSD with Timothy Leary. He used to laugh that the tiny white pill was the Second Coming of Christ. Certainly it changed his life. He left his teaching position at Harvard, changed his name to Ram Dass, and set off on a rollicking spiritual journey, through Buddhism, Hinduism, and back to his Jewish roots, always pulling others in his charismatic wake.[11] I have friends who speak longingly of the spiritual highs and insights found with pot, LSD, cocaine, and heroin. "The only thing is," said one, still struggling hopelessly to escape her addiction, "they don't last."

Here is the story of the ecstasy experienced by J. A. Symonds while anaesthetized with chloroform, and his subsequent horror and dismay.

"After the choking and stifling had passed away," he wrote,

> I seemed at first in a state of utter blankness; then came flashes of intense light, alternating with blackness, and with a keen vision of what was going on in the room around me. . . . I thought that I was near death; when, suddenly, my soul became aware of God. . . . I felt him streaming in like light upon me. . . . I cannot describe the ecstasy I felt. Then, as I gradually awoke from the influence of the anaesthetics, the old sense of

my relation to the world began to return, the new sense of my relation to God began to fade. I suddenly leapt to my feet on the chair where I was sitting, and shrieked out, "It is too horrible, it is too horrible, it is too horrible," meaning that I could not bear this disillusionment. Then I flung myself on the ground, and at last awoke covered with blood, calling to the two surgeons (who were frightened), "Why did you not kill me? Why would you not let me die?" Only think of it. To have felt for that long dateless ecstasy of vision the very God, in all purity and tenderness and truth and absolute love, and then to find that I had after all had no revelation, but that I had been tricked by the abnormal excitement of my brain.[12]

At least in the beginning, before reducing the individual to a jelly of addiction, inefficiency, and paranoia, hallucinogens produce brilliant, short-term ecstasies. The problem is that the experience can't be replicated except by taking more, and then later, not even the drugs that induced the highs seem to work anymore.

Nonetheless, sometimes they change the person taking them. A botanist I know (who does not take recreational drugs) believes that 30 million Americans took drugs between the 1960s and the 1990s, and that the visions the drug users had while in that altered state account for the utterly new sea-change of attitude that we find today at the end of the century: a deep and reverent regard for our planet and for those others out in space, for our environment, for the rain forests and both wild and domestic animals, for the idea that the Earth itself— Gaia—is breathing, has consciousness, and that all living beings, all rocks and plants and sentient beings are inextricably entangled; that we humans are now evolving to a higher plane of divine consciousness.

In some cases the visions seen on drugs have had profound effects. Here is the revelation of another friend of mine, seen while "tripping" on LSD. Lily was twenty-two when she came from England to San Francisco, attracted to the hippie life. It was March 1970, and at a Grateful Dead concert she was given three "orange barrels," a very pure form of LSD.

A week later she decided to "drop one barrel." She had the impression it was a holy act, a sacrament that she was undertaking. She fasted beforehand—no breakfast— she wanted to be pure. She took one pill and telephoned a young friend of hers, Bill, and asked if she could come to his house. She wanted someone with her as she "tripped." She hitchhiked over. She hitchhiked everywhere in those days. By the time she arrived she was already "coming on." There was a taste in the back of her throat, and on her empty stomach it made her feel fuzzy. She recalls: "I have no idea how I found his place; I'd never been there before. I told Bill I'd already started. He was shocked I'd already taken it."

The drug came on so fast that she got scared. She tried to throw up. She sat on the floor by the toilet and put her finger down her throat, but she couldn't vomit.

She thought she would die, then thought, "This has to be okay. It was my choice. What will be will be."

It was early spring and the trees were just blooming. The next thing she knew she was sitting on the lawn looking up at a flowering tree, and it was glorious. She remembers it still as gorgeous, psychedelic explosions of pink light.

A moment later: "I was in heaven. I was on a cloud, certainly no longer on Earth.

"I remember saying, 'I want to see God,' There was a Voice or Knowledge over to my left. It said, *I am God.*

"I turned and saw a bright, BRIGHT Light! I was quite matter-of-fact. 'Why am I alive?' I asked. 'What is the point of my life?'

"Then I was taken to the edge of the cloud and shown a Vision. I saw a long rope, and Jesus at the front of it had the rope over his shoulder, and he was pulling humanity by the rope. Humanity in the form of thousands of people stretched out in a long V, like a cone or the point of a pencil if Jesus were the lead at the tip. I couldn't see the end of this huge mass of people. I was up toward the point, and all of us were pulling humanity toward this . . . toward God! Toward the Light! But the Light was on the cloud with me. There were other Beings up on the cloud, full of light. I don't remember features. They were separate from the Light Source. They moved around. I felt that one of them looked over the edge of the cloud with me.

"This cone, this mass of humanity, was coming through a narrow cleft or gorge carved between high cliffs. I was also down there, fairly near the front of the cone, helping to pull it to a lighter, happier place.

"I had no more questions to ask God. God was in the Light where there is no Time. Then I had to come back into my body, which had now moved to a chair in the kitchen. I kept repeating, 'I don't want to go back.' But I was given the information that without a body you can't take action on the earth. Therefore I had to return. It was emotionally painful, sad. I felt constricted in my body. I didn't like it. I loved the spacious, open feeling of heaven."

Later Lily remembers being on BART, the Bay Area Rapid Transit, and looking at her body. She would move her hand, watching it touch her skin. "All I wanted to do was move my hand over my skin."

The experience changed her attitude, she said, and affected her deeply. Immediately afterward, still blissed out, she tried to tell a few people she'd met God. They laughed. She was shocked and hurt. She thought this was a religious experience that anyone could have and she wanted to spread the news. She was dissuaded from telephoning her parents in England to tell them to take acid. The next day caution reappeared. She remembered how in the Bible "Mary pondered these things and held them to her heart." She also felt that despite her own conviction of what she'd seen, because her experience had been prompted by a drug, others might invalidate it, diminish it as a mere hallucination.

She had two "barrels" left. She thought when she took them she would meet God again. It didn't happen a second time. Eventually she heard that you can find God through meditation, and retain more permanent results. She studied with Swami Satchitananda in Los Angeles, who taught her breath meditation, mantra meditation, hatha yoga, blending-with-the-guru meditation, and more. She did not stay with the guru. One day she had the experience of falling into his eyes as if into a vast space, somersaulting in his eyes. It felt intrusive, and she left.

Now she practices the Buddhist *vipassana* meditation described in chapter 1. She feels safer on her own, she says, not tied too closely to one teacher or one path.

"Years later, though," she says, "when my father was dying in a nursing home, I found I could speak to him, out of the experience of my vision, about this passage out of his physical body. And by the time I left, he was reconciled to leaving: he had seen in a dream how to die."

Today she says she has a deep faith in the fundamental goodness of the world, of people, of the universe, all nurtured by her experience. She has a deeper concern to do something for the planet, and feels that she'd better, as her mother would say, "buck up and DO it."

"Sometimes when I'm confused about whether I'm doing it, I ask for guidance, and then I get another piece of the puzzle—what comes next. But it's so vague, helping pull humanity to God . . . and so *huge*."

Lily is a vision therapist, helping people see better. One woman came to her concerned that she was seeing spirits, ghosts. Because of her own experience, Lily could comfort her: it was okay. "And psychotic episodes, I'm not afraid of them. I see that nothing is weird unless it's warped. Out-of-body experiences, miracles, mind-expanding experiences all seem normal to me now. I feel a calmness. Death in and of itself is not frightening."[13]

Aldous Huxley writes in *The Doors of Perception* of his experience with mescalin, which covered a period as long as eight to ten hours and which Huxley felt was safe since mescalin creates no craving for repetition. He felt that the visions were caused by cerebral sugar shortage created by the mescalin. Looking at a chair during his experience, he found himself on the brink of panic, the same as that found in religious literature when one approaches the *mysterium tremendum*. "In theological language this fear is due to the incompatibility between man's egotism and the divine purity," he wrote.[14] But Huxley, like William James, gave it no such significance.

Here is one last story about the altered vision induced by drugs. It is told by W. T. Stace in a book published in 1960, *Mysticism and Philosophy*. His story concerns "N.M.," who insists the mescalin did not produce the vision but rather "inhibited the inhibitions" which had previously veiled his eyes.

The room in which I was standing looked out onto the back yards of a Negro tenement. The buildings were decrepit and ugly, the ground covered with boards, rags, and debris. Suddenly every object in my field of vision took on a curious and intense kind of existence of its own; that is, everything appeared to have . . . a kind of individual life, and every object, seen under this aspect, appeared exceedingly beautiful. There was a cat out there, with its head lifted, effortlessly watching a wasp that moved without moving just above his head. Everything was *urgent* with life. . . . All things seemed to glow with a light that came from within . . . and I was filled with grief at the realization of the real situation of human beings living continuously in the midst of all this without being aware of it. This thought filled my mind and I wept. But I also wept over the things themselves which we never saw and which we made ugly in our ignorance, and I saw that all ugliness was a wounding of life. . . .

Afterward he began to reflect on the experience: "I had no doubt that I had seen God, that is, had seen all there is to see; yet it turned out to be the world that I looked at every day."[15]

CHAPTER 11

ANGELS AND
VISITATIONS

Beauty is reality seen with the eyes of love.

—EVELYN UNDERHILL

*So many gods, so many creeds, so many paths . . .
while just the act of being kind is all the world
needs.*

—ELLA WHEELER WILCOX

*Do not attach yourself to any particular creed ex-
clusively, so that you may disbelieve all the rest;
otherwise you will lose much good, nay, you will
fail to recognize the real truth of the matter. God,
the omnipresent and omnipotent, is not limited
by any one creed.*

—IBN AL-ARABI

I wrote earlier about how much I needed solitude during those early months. I wanted only to be alone. I began to see the subtle energy that envelops and pulses in all living forms, and later, after my marriage had broken up, when I was on my own, I began to study in order to intensify these perceptions and increase the power of the healing touch.

But for a couple of years after that ecstatic revelation in Peru, my marriage occupied my thoughts. We understood, my husband and I, that there is a healing way to separate, just as there is a nurturing way to come together. We had been married for twenty years: you don't just walk away from that. For two years we talked and talked.

Somehow we both understood that if we did not do this painful, frightening "work" while we were still together, then it would come whipping back like a scorpion's tail to poison our future lives. We'd just have to repeat ourselves in other relationships, until we learned the lessons, worked out karma. We didn't necessarily believe in karma, but we did believe that what goes around comes around.

Parts of the story were poignant, parts sad, parts just funny.

Other times we were ready to kill.

We saw the world entirely differently—he as a normal man, walking on a physical world, and I with a double vision of our physical existence, which seemed to me now half-dead and shadowy in comparison to the gleaming and miraculous inner spiritual world that had lit my eyes and heart.

Two years later, in the fall of 1980, my husband and I went away for a weekend. We borrowed the pretty country house of some friends and spent the weekend walking hand in hand down the pastoral lanes, or reading in the little clapboard house with its gingham curtains. We agreed we would stay together through Christmas, a family time, and afterward we would have a trial separation for a year.

Surely the Universe (God—Providence—luck—the Creator—the Source) was moving us like chess pieces on a board. No sooner had our decision been made than everything combined to execute the separation gracefully. A few days after we returned from the country my husband received an invitation to teach for a semester at Stanford University, beginning right after Christmas. Then the very day that he returned I moved to Baltimore for rehearsals of a play I'd written, and no sooner had that ended than a friend loaned me his apartment a few blocks from our house to use on weekends and at night. He was an artist. By day he painted in his little studio, but the rest of the time he stayed with his spouse in her house. My office was still in our house. I slept, therefore, in his studio, and every morning we nodded to each other as our paths crossed, walking to our respective work. The arrangement allowed me to be home when the children returned from school. At six P.M., just before my husband arrived, I would leave for the artist's studio, my temporary house.

I spent the summer in England to be with the man with whom I'd fallen so passionately in love, telepathically, magnetically; in the autumn I went to a writers' colony in New Mexico. At no time was our trial separation forced.

At the end of the year we decided to separate for good.

Twenty years have passed since the revelation on Machu Picchu, and many other favors have since been shown to me: dreams, visions, voices, insights and coincidences, raptures and revelations. God's marks lie everywhere, like paw prints in the snow—evidence that something passed that way . . . if we could only read the signs.

But first came the Fall. First, I found myself stripped of everything by which I identified myself: as writer, mother, wife, daughter, businesswoman, as struggling artist, as sexy or attractive—anything in which I took pride was removed. If I were to put it in a spiritual context I would say that so good was my Lord God, so loving, that He took from me everything by which I kept myself separate from Her, any false sense I held of self. I've already said, I wanted to go *sunnyasi*. I lost my marriage, my place in the world, my friends (the friends of our marriage largely chose my husband), my house, even my children for a time. I lost my comfort and security, except in God. I lost my confidence. Sometimes I had the image of myself as a lonely child, swinging naked in a lunar landscape alone against the black infinity of the pinprick stars. "Enlightenment includes an insight into the nature of self," wrote Carl Jung. "It is a liberation of the mind from deception regarding self." I learned over the next few years all that I was not. Today I can give thanks for that period, the crisis of confidence, but at the time I was thrown even further into confusion, struggling to keep my footing. My one hold with steadiness lay in the strength of my belief in what I'd seen, in faith.

In the midst of this turmoil, I wrote as if possessed. I wrote seven books in eight years—novels, essays, non-fiction works.[1] No sooner was one finished than I began another, heedless of success. Most concerned the spiritual path.

For eight years I worked without lifting my eyes. One day I woke up to find the obsession lifted. The drive was gone. I looked around me, startled, and realized that it had been ten years since I'd published a book, that I had worked eight years—and no one wanted what I wrote. But that is another story: how the books were published later, in good time.

I did not marry my English friend. After my divorce, after the longing for stillness had been satisfied, new doors opened and I moved (sometimes forcibly dragged forward while I clung to the door frame by my nails) into further avenues of investigation and integration, worlds of magic and mystery. Some involve the healing arts—acupuncture and Chinese medicine, polarity, Cranio-Sacral work, Reiki, Sukyo Mahikari, Therapeutic Touch; others, physical movement—the Alexander Technique, tai chi, qigong, Synergy Dance. And then there are all kinds of practices designed to reveal the present or unveil the future—by astrology, psychic readings or mediumistic channeling, through the I Ching, runes, tarot. I have walked barefoot on coals of fire, participated in Native American ceremonies, traveled in India, and altogether lived in charmed and fascinating times. Yet keep in mind none of these substituted for the Light. I wanted *That*! I prayed for that, and having seen into the Divine even for that moment, I now had different prayers. I said earlier that I used to pray to *understand*. Now, that goal seemed too exalted for my poor mind. Now I prayed to be *awake*! I prayed that every moment I might see as if with the eyes of God, hear with the ears of God, that I might be open to the miracle of living in this world. For our senses are given to us in order to feel and praise God's world, and most of the time I walked about numb to what was going on. In addition, I prayed to serve, whatever that might mean. I thought that such service might be to write, for I wanted to write with an intensity I had not ever felt before, a longing to touch the minds and hearts of people everywhere, to tell what I'd been shown. Mostly I wanted to see as a child again. I wanted the gift of being loved, and especially the gift of loving utterly, in wonder and innocence.

You can see that having embarked on the ecstatic journey did not wipe out desire.

Years earlier, when my mother died, I had woken up at four or four-thirty every morning to run through the black night, running from my fear. Now when I woke up at four-thirty, immediately alert, it was sweetly, as if shaken by an invisible hand, to meditate. At this pre-dawn hour, when all is black and still, concentration goes very deep. You can hear the silence of the swinging stars, the low rumble of the very rocks and stones, and sometimes it seems the music of the spheres will fill your soul. At five-thirty A.M. would come the familiar far-off roar of the first public bus passing several blocks away. The sound only pushed me deeper into that dark, exquisite place where all things ignited in white light, and I was lost in love.

The question remained: Had I gone mad?

William James devoted an entire chapter in *The Varieties of Religious Experience* to the question of religion and neurology: What happens physically? James found the question simplistic: "Medical materialism seems indeed a good appellation for the too simple-minded system of thought which we are considering," he wrote.

Medical materialism finishes up Saint Paul by calling his vision on the road to Damascus a discharging lesion of the occipital cortex, he being an epileptic. It snuffs out Saint Teresa as an hysteric, Saint Francis of Assisi as an hereditary degenerate. . . .

And medical materialism then thinks that the spiritual authority of all such personages is successfully undermined.[2]

Every single one of our states of mind, high or low, healthy or morbid, has some organic process at its root. Therefore, to suggest the organic cause of a spiritual state, he found illogical and arbitrary.

> Otherwise none of our thoughts and feelings, not even our scientific doctrines, not even our *dis*-beliefs, could retain any value as revelations of the truth, for every one of them without exception flows from the state of their possessor's body at the time.[3]

In the end, says James, we pass judgment on all spiritual experiences, as on all others, circuitously, based first on our own immediate feelings and then on our own moral code and what we hold to be true.

Nonetheless, my bulldog intellect shook the rat of materialism in its jaws. My soul knew what it had seen, and it was singing with its joy. My mind worried. What happens to the brain during a mystical experience? Do all the fuses blow? Why is it flooded with light? And why had a blood vessel burst in my hand?

Only in the past two years have I found any information, and that is disarmingly scant.

Not far from Charlottesville, in the Blue Ridge Mountains of Virginia, the Monroe Institute has been studying shifting states of consciousness for more than thirty years. Anyone can take a program there. You lie down in a soft-lit cell equipped with headphones and there you listen for predetermined periods of time to carefully selected blends of sound patterns—a different frequency and volume in each ear. The process is trademarked Hemi-Sync, meaning hemispheric synchronization, since what the Institute claims to have discovered is that the brain, accommodating to the two different sounds, moves to a balanced state in which the two hemispheres operate in equilibrium. This is the state of the artist; this is the unitive, timeless state in which tasks are accomplished easily. Gradually the participant learns without the assistance of the headphones to dive or climb (how hard to find the verb) into altered states of consciousness. There is nothing spiritual or religious about it. The Institute claims that with practice anyone can gain access to the full range of our brain waves, always remaining in equilibrium.

Normally we operate in the beta or stressful waking state, with brain wave frequencies in the range of 12 to 30 hertz (cycles per second). This operates in the front of the brain. Eight to 12 hertz marks the deeper alpha state of REM (rapid eye movement) or dream sleep, with the most activity occurring in the occipital lobe, or back of the brain; this is also, I am told, the state used in various mind-control programs. In the theta state, at the frequencies of 4 to 8 hertz, you have visions, hear voices, have out-of-body experiences; little children spend lots of time in theta. And beneath that, at 2 to 4 hertz, in delta, we enter deep restorative sleep and unconscious thought.

The Monroe Institute claims that by introducing sound waves at the theta frequencies of 4 to 8 hertz in a binaural beat (it doesn't work with just any music), the brain will accommodate itself, pick up the frequency, and move into what researchers call dissociative states. Carried further the participants slip into "transcendent" states as well. The Institute has studied healers and found they display bursts of gamma waves, higher than 30 hertz, while, curiously, those engaged in psychic activity or remote viewing show no deviance from ordinary brain wave activity. But the Institute has not mapped the brains of meditating gurus in *samadhi* or people in states of rapture.

Can a spiritual experience be induced? Yes, sometimes. But every artificial way of producing an altered state of consciousness, whether by drugs or sensory disciplines, differs from spontaneous transport in one simple way: it did not strike spontaneously. Does it produce the same conviction of having the soul lifted up in rapturous ecstasy and delivered back into your hands, refreshed, reborn, washed permanently clean? And are you forever and instantly transformed? We don't know. When I took the course of treatment, I had visions, it is true, but none burst over me with the power of the hand of God, though who could say what mystical rapture might occur to someone else? I would speculate that such visions are more like listening to a dream. Dreams themselves are very powerful, fragile as they appear, but not all dreams have a permanent effect.

I know a woman who had a dream about her

estranged ex-husband, in which she understood one simple fact: that he had loved her to the extent of his ability. He'd done the best he could. Waking, remembering the dream, she changed her attitude, and in that moment their relationship was healed. So that dream realized a total change.

I know another woman who had a dream in which she felt she met her soul, was bonded in the deepest love, and when she woke she knew she had been given the intimate secret gift of her own self. All day the sensation remained with her, like the overtones of a musical note floating in the air. Her heart soaked itself in memory, even as the images died out. She thought the dream would have a permanent effect, permit her to approach all problems differently. Yet in a few months she had reverted to her former ways. It was only a wisp of a dream. So these manufactured means of altering states of consciousness, while they "work," may not have the same power as the raptures of God, in the sense that they do not accomplish the basic requirement of the spiritual awakening—a complete and permanent personality change.

And yet, I would not say it could not. Later on, I tell of several dreams of the Virgin Mary or the Mother which had permanent effects on those to whom they came.

The Monroe Institute claims that children live in theta more than adults. Children are close to little animals. Do animals then have mystical experiences? Do dolphins or the higher apes? We just don't know. Mainstream psychology may be more tolerant of the spiritual than it was in the 1970s, when an ecstatic rapture was counted as regression, escape from reality, or merely the bizarre expression of a disturbed personality. It is true that Viktor Frankl took such moments seriously, and Abraham Maslow considered a "peak experience" as a true reality, available after all other needs—food, shelter, sex, security—have been provided.

But more common was the attitude of Dr. Asa P. Ruskin, director of the department of rehabilitation medicine at Kingsbrook Jewish Medical Center in Brooklyn, who in February 1975 wrote to *The New York Times Magazine* attacking the article by Andrew Greeley and William McCready. Most such experiences, he said, are normal forms of consciousness, representing a temporary dominance by the right hemisphere of the brain. Noting that transcendence can be brought on by contemplative exercises, drugs, sensory deprivation, by repeating "non-sense syllables" (this is untrue), or by continual repetitive movements of the body, Dr. Ruskin dismissed not only the entire event but its implications as well.

> Recognition of the normal physiological mechanisms involved should expel any consideration of the supernatural or "religious" from our consideration.[4]

And that was the commonly held view at the time of my revelation.

The fact remains that no substantial research on mystical experiences exists.

We know nothing.

Nor is it likely that we ever shall. Dr. Elmer Green, father of biofeedback, director emeritus at the Center for Applied Psychophysiology at the Menninger Clinic in Kansas, who has spent decades researching the paranormal, says that although we can study the *samadhi* and trances of yogis, we can never hope to understand what happens during the mystical experience, because these raptures come without warning and cannot be captured by our present technology.

At this point my personal story loses chronology. Events no longer fell one after another in strict order, but chaotically, showings and knowings all ajumble as it were: a word here, a vision there, the sense of a Presence walking suddenly at my side, or a helping hand, a dream, a miraculous accident falling in my way. As the years have passed I have come to trust these Comings. I know how to draw them to me by prayer and gratitude, through an emptying of the mind, a lack of expectation. They are no longer mysteries, though always my soul lifts up with joy when one arrives. "You're back!" she sings.

In previous chapters we have spoken of mystical raptures that deliver peace, warmth, joy, light, beauty, radiant ecstasy, absolute intuitive knowledge, and love. Now let me describe the more tangible visions of spiritual beings that often accompany these transports. Some seem to overlap with incidences recounted in earlier chapters, but those told here widen our field of perception to include visions of angels as well as further stories of Christ or his Mother. Such apparitions are seen with the spiritual eye, or with the heart, but they are as real to those who see them as the book you hold in your hand.

Bear with me; be tolerant of my need to digress from my own story for a time and tell these others. I love the stories. I cannot get enough of the stories. Rain on parched earth. First they remind me of what I've seen myself, and second they validate, even if anecdotally, my own ecstasies: other people have had raptures similar to mine, and their reactions conform precisely to my own. What I speak of now wasn't known to me twenty years ago, but has been acquired over time, learned bit by bit. Still, the soul knows what it's seen.

What are angels? They are messengers of God. The very word in Greek, *angelos,* means "messenger." They come as voices, dreams, visions, nudgings, or as intuitions—that touch on the shoulder that says, Go here, not there. We have all heard these whispers. "I *knew* I shouldn't have gone down that alley," we say, "and I didn't *listen.*" I have received hundreds of letters from people, recounting their experiences with disembodied beings of radiant warmth and beauty and light. Some are the spirits of departed loved ones, come back to say they are all right or to ask forgiveness or effect a miracle, or to express in dreams or by telepathy their unbounded love. Some are distant, ancient forms, known from earliest Scripture, such as the Angel Gabriel or Prophet Elijah.

Angels come as accidents and strange coincidences. They come as animals—I have heard several stories of angels appearing in the form of dogs. They come as human beings. A total stranger will walk up to you and give you just the words you need, the answer to your prayers. Or perhaps while sitting on the bus you'll over-hear two people talking. Sometimes you will act as an angel to someone else, perhaps without even knowing it. One day someone comes to you and says, "You saved my life." You look at her astonished, trying to remember when you even saw the person before, the meeting meant so little to you at the time. "Don't you remember? I was standing on the bridge, staring at the water, and you passed and said, 'Good morning.' "

Sometimes the angels come in their own radiant and refulgent form, rippling with colors or gleaming with the whitest of light. They come either with or without wings, as male or female, or as neither, androgynous. They may be little cherubs or as big as jumbo jets. They may be balls of energy, without a humanlike form. But there are three marks to an angel, and everyone who sees an angel agrees with these.

First, they come with warmth, color, light, beauty. This is different from a ghost, which is a spirit of the dead and which is marked by cold. When a ghost walks past or through you, you feel an icy chill. A ghost is a troubled spirit, still caught in this dimension, unable to go home. It may not harm but it conveys none of the brilliance and radiance of an angel when it comes.

Second, the angels always say the same thing. They always say, "Don't be afraid." They never say, "Boy, are you ever in trouble; look what you've done now!" No, but always gently, "Hush. We're here. We'll do this work."

Third, you are always a little bit different after seeing one. You cannot forget.

These spiritual beings are often seen during near-death experiences, and as medical technology saves more and more lives, we hear these stories more frequently: of dead people who show no vital signs, no pulse, no heart-beat, no brain waves, dead for minutes or even for two or three hours, who suddenly return to life. The people later report on the luminous Other Side and the beauty of the radiant beings whom they saw.

Angels have been reported in every culture, in every age, in every religion—Christian, Jewish, Zoroastrian, Muslim, Hindu, Buddhist—wherever people live we find the vision of angels. One Stone Age tribe of the Philippines has a myth of the Sky People who come down to save them in times of famine or trouble.[5] We are familiar with the Judeo-Christian archangels—Michael, Raphael, Gabriel, Uriel.

Here is the vision that led to the enlightenment of the famous twelfth-century Iranian philosopher Yahya Suhrawardi, founder of the Ishraqi school:

Suddenly I was wrapped in gentleness; there was a blinding flash, then a diaphanous light in the likeness of a human being. I watched attentively and there he was. . . . He came towards me, greeting me so kindly that my bewilderment faded and my alarm gave way to a feeling of familiarity. And then I began to complain to him of the trouble I had with this problem of knowledge.

"Awaken to yourself," he said to me, "and your problem will be solved."[6]

Suhrawardi, as a Sufi, had the advantage of having systematically studied the mystic path. In the West, such visions often hit us more unexpectedly, with surprising and awe-full results.

A few years ago Genevieve W. Foster published her book, *The World Was Flooded with Light,* about a mystical experience that lasted an extraordinary *five days.* She was teaching English at Bryn Mawr at the time, and after a long struggle she came to a confrontation with her shadow side, the Self, the Other. Here I have divided her one long paragraph into smaller ones, to make the account easier to read.

The climactic event, the real turning point, came . . . I believe in the spring of 1945, and it came in a visitation that all my upbringing and education told me was simply an impossibility—unless of course one was psychotic. . . . I was at home on a Monday afternoon and the children were not around. I lay down for a nap on the living room sofa. I will tell the preliminaries as well as I can after thirty-odd years, since I think they are interesting. I had a dream of levitation; I seemed to be suspended above the sofa. But my good Jungian training had emphasized the importance of "keeping my feet on the ground," so, still in the dream, I said to myself, "This will never do," and I managed to pull myself back down to the sofa. There was a further fragment of a dream, something about the beating of wings above and around me.

Then I woke up. . . . In the technical language of mysticism (and I use the word in its strictest sense, not in the popular sense of some sort of fuzzy pleasurable contact with the unconscious) it is what is called "intellectual vision." (The Jungian reader must not confuse this medieval use of the word *intellectual*, meaning in the mind, not perceived by the outward senses, with our contemporary use of the word as referring to the thinking function.) That is, I saw nothing unusual with my outward eye, but I nevertheless knew that there was someone else in the room with me.

A few feet in front of me and a little to the left stood a numinous figure, and between us was an interchange, a flood, flowing both ways, of love. There were no words, no sound. There was light everywhere. It was the end of March, and everywhere outdoors shrubs were in flower, and indoors and out, the world was flooded with light, the supernal light that so many of the mystics describe and a few of the poets.

The vision lasted five days; sometime on

Saturday afternoon I had a sense of fatigue, and could sustain it no longer, and it faded.[7]

Like most of us, Foster told no one. Indeed it took her thirty years to write her book. "I knew I was in a precarious situation," she writes, "that if my ego could manage to annex or engulf the experience I might well be tilted toward psychosis. Yet the experience was so over-whelmingly good that I couldn't mistrust it."

She continues: "The thing that I did to help me understand the experience was to get Evelyn Underhill's *Mysticism*, the classic text on the subject . . . and to read the relevant portions over and over for the next year. I re-alized that some of the medieval poems I had been so in-nocently handling were written to invoke just such as an experience as I had had."

Did it change her? Outwardly, she says, in the practi-cal sense, her relations with her family were unaffected. She performed all her usual activities, entertained her mother-in-law, went to the movies. She spoke no differ-ently. But she saw her family, her students, all the people she dealt with, the house, the flowering world with differ-ent eyes, and this never left her. "I knew that I was 'com-panioned' and that the Companion was numinous. . . . That numinous figure is still there, I know, and it is the deficiency of my vision that prevents me from seeing it."[8]

This word *numinous* is interesting. Derived from the Latin *numen*, meaning "divinity," it refers to the feeling of attraction and awe that characterizes a sense of com-munion with Spirit.

Any work that Genevieve Foster did thereafter was done not as a personal achievement, she writes, but as an offering to that Other whom she now recognized. She no longer felt that *she* did this or that, but rather that life, in Jung's phrase, lived itself through her.

Saint Francis called himself God's troubadour and also "the donkey of God." Ignatius of Loyola called himself "Our Lady's knight"; Thérèse of Lisieux said she was "a ball in the hands of the child Jesus"; and Mother Teresa refers to herself as "a pencil in God's hands." I myself am God's dog, and I imagine a good black Lab that lies down disconsolately, but obediently, his head on his paws, when his master is out and he's been told to "stay." Or who leaps to his feet, turning in circles and holding the leash in his jaws when it's time to take a walk. God's dog. Going at heel.

True mystics live much of the time in the state of grace that Genevieve Foster described, but most of us move in and out of it. For most of us this passage into Joy smashes over us almost accidentally, by surprise, by grace, as happened to Dennis Kyte of Washington, Connecticut—whose vision, like Foster's, included the sound of "fluttering" before he was subsumed in the angel's peace.

A few years ago I had a dream (or so I thought). I was asleep, lying on my back, when I opened my eyes . . . and there was a beautiful orange-red male figure hovering about two inches above me—nose to nose, looking into my eyes and mirroring me all the way down to my toes. I heard a fluttering sound. As I gasped in amazement the figure dropped *into* me and then there was no sound but a feeling of incredible warmth and peace.[9]

Or we find this story from Angelina Smith of New Jersey, who heard the laughter of angel children and saw a spirit sprite.

A couple of years ago, I was home with my two children. One was six months and the other a bit more than one year old. They were in their bedroom taking a nap, when I kept hearing children laughing and giggling. I went into the kitchen to get a sandwich. I had a very small kitchen, nothing fancy. I was making my sandwich when I saw part of the room grow really bright. Then a beautiful little girl appeared. She was about six or seven years old, wore a white dress, and had a flower halo. She was so beautiful—the love she gave off. Her aura was a golden color. For a split second she was there, then she just disappeared. . . . It was such a peaceful sound to hear children having fun.[10]

We have no explanation for such apparitions, which are always accompanied by this sweet peace. Sometimes the encounter involves saving the person from danger,

but there are many books now that tell about these marvelous experiences, and I won't repeat more here. We
could talk all night telling one tale after another, all true.
If we've had the experience ourselves, we feel our souls
open up in love and adoration, remembering. And if
we've never had one, we go away pondering, and then
perhaps in a dream or just at the moment of falling
into sleep we recall when we too heard that siren music
in our ears.

Once I met a man who'd seen Jesus Christ. I was just
a girl, maybe sixteen or seventeen years old, driving into
town with my younger brother to buy some groceries for
our mother. Up ahead we saw an old man walking by the
side of the road, or rather we saw his back. In each hand
he carried an empty shopping bag. It was a good five
miles to town. This was a country road, without even a
yellow line painted down the middle. We drove past
without stopping, alert to our mother's warning never to
pick up strangers. We ran our errands and were returning home, when for the second time we overtook the old
man, this time plodding away from town, his arms and
shoulders pulled down by the load of the groceries in
his bags.

We picked him up. He set the groceries down on the
floor of the car, hauled himself heavily into the backseat,
and told us where he lived. I couldn't place his house by
his directions (no road, no mailbox), but drove him past
our own turnoff, toward a bridge that he said lay three
or four miles farther on. He said he lived a mile's walk

farther in the woods, in a hut without electricity or telephone. He was a kind of hermit. He liked to be alone, he said. Then, out of the blue, he announced: "I saw Jesus Christ."

It startled me. "You did?"

"In the trees. His face hung in the trees. He was looking right at me. His face caught in the trees."

"What did he look like?"

"He was beautiful. He just looked at me. He was beautiful."

We let him off at the bridge—a culvert, really—that crossed a little silver run, and watched him disappear down the fragile trace of a footpath that wound beside the thin stream into the thick green woods. He didn't look back. After that I looked for him every time we drove to town, hoping to give him another lift. I never saw him again.

Aldous Huxley, who had many mystical experiences both with drugs and without, wrote pessimistically that "the firsthand experiences of those who are not saints—not even better-than-average human beings—may be startling and exciting enough on their own psychic level; but they will certainly not be genuine experiences of ultimate Reality, or God."[11]

I disagree. I think that we all have these swift mysterious lapses, and they *are* genuine. We know because the moment leaves a trail of glory, evidenced afterward in the subtle shift of attitude noted by Genevieve Foster or in the effect you have on others—as the hermit had on me.

Sometimes, for a moment you experience what the Buddhists call "emptiness," or luminosity of mind. This is the state in which you hear music as if the notes were falling stars. Then everything and everyone around you is seen as holy, and nothing exists except the holiness, the sacred ground. Nothing is dirty anymore, or despicable. You are Adam before the Fall, Eve in the Garden of Innocence, watching with wonderment and awe, since all is as it should be and "wrong" has taken on no meaning yet. There is no judgment, and in everything paces God.

Here is the story of Franklin A. Robinson of Benedict, Maryland, who in a dream saw God, or Christ, face-to-face, and who is too modest to make much of it.

I believe that God manifests himself to people in whatever form they will most likely accept Him, hence Muslims, Buddhists, Christians, and so on. For me, God has manifested himself through Jesus Christ, and one of the most revealing passages Jesus spoke is John 13:34–35: "A new commandment I give unto you, that ye love one another; even as I have loved you, that ye also love one another. . . ."

I frequently have the privilege to be covered with what I term the Holy Spirit. I can be sitting at the typewriter, in the car, anywhere, and suddenly a feeling of comfort, love, and peace will wash over me. It is a most wondrous thing, and all worries and troubles become insignificant.

A few years ago I remember dreaming that I was walking over a rolling landscape, specifically my grandparents' farm, and all over the ground were small dead animals, squirrels, chipmunks. . . . All of a sudden I looked up and there was a great gray cloud covering the land. I fell to the ground as I was enveloped by the cloud. My face was then lifted to look into what I felt was the face of God. His eyes shone like two white-hot points of light, and he was without a bodily form but had a beard and mustache and in facial appearance favored artists' renderings of Christ.

This is as close as I can come to describing it. I remember thinking I had died. But I awoke, and to this day I have a hard time deciphering what it was all about. I remember feeling very humbled and unworthy.

The next day was Sunday and I distinctly remember that during church service the phrase was quoted, "Blessed are the pure in heart, for they shall see God." Now I don't even begin to think that I am that pure in heart, but I have yet to fathom what the encounter should mean to me. Maybe that I am never to forget my humanity, that all things come from God, not man. I just don't know.[12]

By far the greater number of experiences, though, seem to come in the form of angels. Or perhaps people now have permission to tell these stories openly, after the flood of books, TV shows, and films that has made such confessions acceptable. It is interesting that most of those written to me come from women—whether because more women than men read books, or more women than men write letters, or because women have the experiences more than men. The following vision of angels and God, however, like the one above, came likewise in a dream and to a man, Deane McGinnis of North Carolina.

I had a mystical experience once. It was on August 8, 1984, a Wednesday night, about seven P.M. My wife, Donna, and I had just finished supper at our home. We lay down for a nap. The weather was calm, but hot. I was asleep, but suddenly found myself up in Heaven. Heaven is immense, loftier and higher than the whole Universe. The floor was clear as crystal glass—sort of a transparent gold—very smooth, infinite in distance.

And I heard the "voices." I looked over in one direction and saw what must have been the Heavenly Choir. The Angels were tall, and they stood in vast rows, one row behind another row. And could they ever sing! Not using words as we do, but "vowels," going from one octave up to the next one, and when they reached the "highest octave," their sound literally filled me like light! So much joy, so much love, so much peace, so much *power*!

And then, I heard a Voice speak to me. It said

(and I literally quote): "My dearly beloved son, I have seen all that you have done to preserve my creation, and I am well pleased." And then He said: "This is God the Creator speaking." After that, I kind of "floated back down" to where I was sleeping and woke up. The time was seven-thirty P.M.

I don't know why it happened, unless it's because I pick up (rescue) turtles off the road, and love to see eagles and hawks soar. All life is sacred to God. I heard His Voice, but could not see His Face for all the "bright light" that was around Him.[13]

I come now to two more matters I want to comment on before we leave this subject. The first concerns visions of the holy Mother, the Goddess, the feminine in God, White Buffalo Woman.

Appearances of Mary are so common that we hardly turn to look anymore: she appears in Lourdes, in Medjugorje (in what used to be Yugoslavia), in Mexico, in Texas, Maryland, California, North Carolina. And to individuals both in waking visions and in dreams. Here are two mystical visitations of the Mother. It is true that they do not count as "ecstasies" or "raptures" in the rigid sense that I've been talking about so far, but each one came accompanied by that brilliant light, and each engendered in the recipient a kind of overpowering collapse, and carried him or her to further footsteps on the

Way. It is interesting that in both cases the recipient of the vision had had no prior experience with the Mother or a female Force.

The first comes from Andrew Ramer, of Jewish descent but reared as an atheist. He had heard voices for much of his childhood and grew up thinking he was crazy. In addition he was dealing with an anti-Semitic environment when the following occurred, totally beyond the realm of his experience.

In 1977 I was sitting on the edge of my bed, when a shimmer of light began to wash in and out of the top of my head. That shimmer then turned into a vast golden sea of light, infinite and eternal. There was a voice in the pulsing waves, a female voice that I both knew and did not know. Trembling, in awe, I asked, "Who are you?" Each time the voice answered, "You know who I am." Finally the truth dawned on me, and I asked Her what to call Her. Voice thundering, golden, She said, "Call me anything you like."

For weeks I was bathed in that light, filled with Her voice and Her love. I called her by many different names and knew that all of them were One. Until that day, it never occurred to me that God might be female. All this happened in Brooklyn, New York—not a place most of us would think of as the ground for spiritual experiences. But Brooklyn is holy to me.[14]

Later, he had visions of a masculine God, as well, each event leading always to higher illuminations.

The second story happened to "Gwen," and what she saw was not the Virgin Mary, but rather the angel sent by the Mother, and the light was so great it threatened to blind her. At the time Gwen was in deep despair.

> I was at a point of true decision, lying in the dark in my bedroom in Atlanta. Suddenly an incredibly *bright* light, about the size of a pea, came before my closed eyes. It spoke to me: "Keep your eyes closed for it is true that we can blind you."
>
> It moved closer and the Light was unbelievable. Even with my eyes closed as tightly as I could, I wanted extra lids because the light *hurt* my eyes. Finally it wrapped its wings around me in its embrace. I felt absolute peace, love, and protection. I could "see" my angel through closed eyes now. It was neither male nor female. It had wings. It told me the Mother had sent it to let me know I am watched over. I felt so badly because I was raised Episcopalian and we didn't spend much prayer or interest on the Mother. She guided me out of the dark and into my new life, and since then many new spiritual doors have opened to me.[15]

These experiences don't preclude life's trials, but somehow they give strength and peace. I know of another woman who, sleeping in the desert one night, awoke, looked up at the luminous stars, and saw the Mother and Child looking down on her. She gazed up at them with quiet pleasure and surprise. That can't be for me, she thought, at the same time memorizing the constellation, so that later she would always be able to find the image of the holy Virgin and her babe in the stars. For a long time the Mother remained, loving her on the Earth far below. Then feeling tired, my friend closed her eyes, she says, and when she looked up next, she could see the stars that had formed the headdress of the Virgin—but no face gazed down at her.

Are these raptures and visions real, or figments of our imagination? In George Bernard Shaw's play *Saint Joan*, one nobleman dismisses the voices of the Maid of Orleans. "They come from your imagination," he sneers.

"Of course," she answers simply. "That's how the messages of God come to us."

They come in other ways as well: in sorrow, in memory, in joy, in longings. And sometimes we feel the shiver that accompanies a rapture. Sometimes goosebumps lift the hair on our arms, as we perceive the proof.

A mystical experience does not always come as a vision of light or an ecstasy or sense of union. Sometimes it is marked by the most fragile "knowing," like a ripple on the surface of a lake. The use of the word *knowing* was coined by the English mystic Julian of Norwich. Here is a story of a "knowing" and a miracle, combined with the signature of an invisible Presence. It is instructive that the experience began with constant prayer, and that a healing confirmed its reality.

In 1992, Angel Bailey, a young Iranian woman living in Washington, D.C., fell ill. No one knew what was wrong.

One morning Angel felt the presence of a "being" beside her bed. She heard its message telepathically: that the next day the doctors "will come and tell you you have cancer. They are going to tell you to go to Georgetown Hospital to remove your voice box. Do not listen to them. Go to Johns Hopkins Hospital, where a Far Eastern doctor will heal you." The presence disappeared.

All happened as predicted. The disease was diagnosed as adenoid cystic carcinoma of the larynx, a rare form of throat cancer, and the doctors scheduled surgery to remove her voice box.

Immediately, Angel began the search for the Johns Hopkins specialist. After many calls she found a Dr. Haskins Kashima, at Hopkins, an expert in this field, but when she telephoned, she could get no appointment for a month.

> When I got home I was feeling very ill. The next day, since I could not go to Johns Hopkins for a month, I decided to go to George Washington University Hospital for a second opinion. Ten doctors saw me. I felt weird being examined under this strange apparatus by these male and female doctors. They all agreed I needed surgery to remove the voice box.[16]

Now doubt raised its head. She began to question. Was the "knowing" about Dr. Kashima real? How could she be sure? She began to pray, asking God to send one more message so clear that she would know whether to wait for Dr. Kashima or not.

The next day she went with a real estate agent to look at a house she'd agreed to buy. She sat on the deck in the warm sunshine. A small blond man—the gardener, she thought—was working in the garden. After a time he approached the deck and said, "You've had a tracheotomy. Why?"

"Cancer."

"I know about your disease," he said. "It's rare, not treatable with radiation or chemotherapy. And you're so young."

Surprised, she discovered he was the owner of the house, and a doctor who specialized in that disease.

"You must not go to any doctor," he said, "except Dr. Kashima at Johns Hopkins." He wrote a note to Dr. Kashima for Angel, who was given an appointment for the following day.

Ultimately the young woman was completely cured. When she went back to Johns Hopkins for a follow-up sonogram, no cancer could be found.

Do we make up the visions that we see, or is there a spiritual reality independent of our minds and imaginations, working miracles in our lives? If there's a Force is there Fate? Each person must answer for herself, and the response may change or shift, depending on one's circumstances.

During the twenty years that have passed since my ecstasy on Machu Picchu I have learned ways to converse with what I'm satisfied are beings of great spiritual beauty and delight. I ask them questions and they answer with deep wisdom and delight.

Once we were talking about this and that. I asked a question, and the answer came back: *Pray.*

I thought about that for a moment. "Why should I pray?" I asked. "You already know what I want. What's the point?"

Instantly the answer came back telepathically in three parts, but seen as a whole, the way you see a painting in its totality and only afterward analyze its brush strokes and colors and lines.

The first answer was, *So we will know what you want, in order that we may give you what you need.*

The second reason was, *Because when you pray, for a few moments you surrender—it may only be fifteen seconds out of fifteen minutes of attempted prayer. But in that moment of surrender, you open a window through which we can enter to execute the desires of your heart.*

The third reason I would never have been able to make up in my wildest imaginings. *Because your prayers give us the energy to do our work.*

With our thoughts we give or drain their energy. Our doubts, despair, and fear serve as hindrances for these spiritual creatures, who must expend energy combatting our anxiety before being able to do their work. It was only then that I understood that we stand in relationship to angels, to the spiritual beings that surrounds us. They need us as we need them. Their task is to serve and help us, and they need our help to do their work.

CHAPTER 12

THE SECOND JOURNEY

Perfection is not in exhibitions of miraculous powers, but perfection is to sit among people, sell and buy, marry and have children; and yet never leave the presence of God even for one moment.
—IMAM RABBANI, QUOTING SAYYID AL-KHARRAZ

The miracle is not to walk on water. The miracle is to walk on land.
—THICH NHAT HANH

Dress me, good mother, in a glorious robe of
*   many colors,*
and at dawn lead me to my toil.
My land is wrapped in light as in a prayer shawl.
The houses stand forth like frontlets;
and the rocks paved by hand, stream down like
*   phylactery straps.*
Here the lovely city says the morning prayer to
*   its creator. . . .*
—*AVODAH*, TRANSLATED BY T. CARMI

We are now approaching the close of this effort to describe some of the mysteries we have seen on the spiritual path. The subject is so vast we cannot hope to do more than stand on the bluff, point out a distant landscape, and even then the colors change: passion and celibacy, God, Goddess, heartbreak, ecstasy, joy, loneliness, the Second Journey of our lives. It is a fact that all things change, including our own narratives. The past ripples behind us in a continual revision, and we find there is no single truth, but a constant evolving of the sense of who we are.

I didn't marry my dear English friend. That was a surprise. I have never married again. That has also been a surprise. It didn't occur to me after my divorce that I would remain single for long. According to the story told when I was growing up, a successful woman is a married one. The princess marries the prince and they live happily ever after. It didn't occur to me that there were other tales to tell, or that later I would fall in love with other men. For that matter, when I lived in bliss, immediately after the revelation on Machu Picchu, it didn't occur to me that life would just roll on, full of loss and heartbreak, that I would wake up in the mornings with my pillow already drenched with tears shed during sleep.

There is a horrible sentence by the Greek playwright Aeschylus in his *Oresteia*:

Even in our sleep, pain that we cannot forget falls drop by drop upon the heart, and in our own despair, against our will, comes wisdom to us by the awful grace of God.[1]

Was I paying back a karmic debt? Paying for the pain I'd inflicted on my husband and my girls? Was each hurt given, as some people insist, to teach me something I needed to know? Or is life simply so rich, so inexorable, so full of passion that when you love deeply you open yourself to being hurt? Throughout this book we have been speaking especially of the ecstasies and raptures, the balloons and party favors that encourage us on the Way. But the spiritual pilgrimage is also marked by the hurts. Somehow I thought (wrongly: don't make the same mistake) that if I hurt, then surely the fault was mine, that I must be doing something wrong. But life—love— our dreams—are nestled in pain, and when we're alive there'll be moments when we hurt.

It didn't occur to me that God could use illicit love to heal. I make no pretense of understanding any of this. I joined a twelve-step program, and found in those meetings more spirituality and loving-kindness than I found in many churches. But what do I know? Today the littlest child will speak and teach me what I've forgotten or never thought about before.

How vast is love, how convoluted and chaotic. The whole question of spiritual and sexual love bothered me. The two are so inextricably intertwined that I wrote an entire novel, *Revelations,* in an attempt to come to grips with this conjunction of sexual and spiritual love—the fact that when you love spiritually you cannot help but love physically. (It doesn't work the other way round; the sexual does not transport us into spiritual love.) Well, God's laws are not the same as man's. God comes to us in a thousand different forms, each one perfectly adapted to the individual. Had I known more at the time, I might have comforted myself that love affairs are also love affairs with God.

The sages of ancient India, spiritual giants, thought a lot about love. It was a celibate, ascetic priest, Vatsyayana, who wrote the Kama Sutra, a love manual that is still read to this day. It's more famous as an erotic tract than it is for its philosophical parts; but the sages concluded that there are five degrees of love, by which a worshiper grows in the service and knowledge of his God, and the highest is passionate, illicit, and unobtainable love.

Joseph Campbell wrote about this in *Myths to Live By*. "The seizure of passionate love," he says, "can be . . . only illicit, breaking in upon the order of one's dutiful life in virtue as a devastating storm."[2]

Surely that was what had happened to me. Plutarch calls love a "frenzy" and says that "those who are in love must be forgiven as though ill." The Native Americans are also said to have considered it a madness, a sickness of some sort. It is a sledgehammer. It cracks us open. It breaks the locks on our hearts, exposing us to joy and also self-discovery.

Andrew Greeley reported that by far the majority of the respondents in his survey found the trigger for mystical experience in prayer, music, quiet reflection, or through observing the beauties of nature, but that for 18 percent the trigger was "sexual lovemaking."[3]

Indeed there is a long tradition of a sexual love being transformed into a mystical, sacred one. In 1201, we find the Sufi saint Muid ad-Din ibn al-Arabi deep in prayer while circumambulating the sacred Kabah in Mecca, when he lifted his eyes and was blinded by the sight of the young girl, Nizam. He saw her surrounded by a heavenly aura and in a flash he recognized her as Sophia, the incarnation of Divine Wisdom. Moreover, al-Arabi understood that all women represent this most powerful embodiment, for women awaken love in men and love is always directed to God. "We cannot see God himself," he wrote, "but we can see him as he has chosen to reveal himself, in [those] who inspire love in our hearts."[4]

At that time most seekers, including Christian monks (some of them surely terrified of their own passions and of the women who aroused them), sought God's love in the age-old path of austerities and chastity—the silent keeping to oneself. But in 1274 Dante Alighieri saw the young Beatrice on the Ponte Vecchio and felt his spirit so tremble before her beauty that it cried, "Behold a god more powerful than I who comes to rule over me."[5] It is Beatrice in *The Divine Comedy* who leads his soul to God, for she "spreads a light that makes the angels smile."

It seems God may be found both in sexual and illicit union and also in chaste vows. I think there is no space where God is not—mysterious and invisible, silent as a breath of wind. Why wouldn't we see God in those we love? Every mother sees divinity in the baby at her breast. Our loving is itself an expression of the Source.

But what do I know? All I can do is describe what I have seen on this mysterious journey: the sacred found in everything. Sometimes I think of God (this appalling word), the Source, as a Lake of the Fire of Love. It is immense. Bigger than the dome of sky at night. Out of this lake leap sparks and flames, flickering as on a log in the fireplace—blue, red, orange. The flames lick and leap about, flare up, die down. Who dares say that the orange part is fire and the blue is not? Out of the lake are born all living forms—an angel created, witnessed, gone; a dog, a horse, a tree, an old man or a little child, births and deaths, creation and dissolution, the rivers and the ocean beds, Christ and Krishna, volcanos and earthquakes, an absence and a fullness, saints and devils. All are composed of the fire of love. God taking form. And God flaming up also in the most intimate and private, personal ways, for this Lake is also the caring Father or Mother, wife or husband, knowing when the smallest sparrow's feather falls.

Or God is like an ocean. The water at the deepest part is black and cold and swept by underground rivers, while at the surface the waves sparkle with light, lift into spume, and billow on. Yet all of it is water. If you remove a drop of the ocean, the drop is still made of water. And if you divide it into smaller and smaller drops, they are each composed of water, though the droplet may be so small you need a microscope to see it finally. And if you take one drop and slide it next to another, it runs into that other drop, and then into the next, until you cannot single out one from another or find the original drop. It has grown into a puddle, a pool, a pond. It is all water, and you cannot find a space in that expanse that is not water, nor a space between the drops that form the puddle or lake or sea. It's all one single water from the ocean of God's holy love.

But even using a metaphor of ocean or fire does no justice to that Light. It places limits on the limitless and unnameable. In a way, even to speak of a path is wrong, for so long as we live, we are on the path: we can't fall off! That's the cosmic joke. The question is only whether we know we're traveling.

Jan van Ruysbroeck wrote of how when love has carried us into the Divine, there is no separation between ourselves and God. In the Divine Dark we are wrought and transformed and penetrated as air is penetrated by the sun.

"A tremor seizes our limbs," wrote the Jewish philosopher and mystic Abraham Heschel, "our nerves are struck, quiver like strings; our whole being bursts into shudders. But then a cry, wrested from our very core, fills the world around us, as if a mountain were suddenly about to place itself in front of us. It is one word: GOD. . . . we cannot comprehend it. We only know it means infinitely more than we are able to echo."[6]

All the spiritual masters agree that the value of a mystical experience depends not on the violence of the incident, but rather on its fruits—and that the test is whether the fruits conform to Scripture and the teachings of the masters.

Yet God is also shocking, violent. "I came not to send peace, but a sword," said Christ, as he violated established doctrine, "set a man at variance against his father, and the daughter against her mother, and the daughter in law against her mother in law," and made the religious Jews of his time so angry they rose up to dispose of him. It happens time and again. Sri Ramakrishna, a nineteenth-century Hindu saint, was the priest at a temple of Kali, the Divine Mother. One day the authorities discovered to their horror that he was allowing a cat to eat the holy offerings of food and milk placed on the altar for the goddess. He defended himself:

> The Divine Mother revealed to me that . . . it was she who had become everything . . . that everything was full of consciousness. The image was consciousness, the altar was consciousness . . . the door-sills were consciousness. . . . I found everything in the room soaked as it were in bliss—the bliss of God. . . . That was why I fed a cat with the food that was to be offered to the Divine Mother. I clearly perceived that all this *was* the Divine Mother—even the cat.[7]

Ramakrishna, suffused with Love, seeing only with the eyes of Love—blissed-out, as the hippies called it—saw even the darkness as love and light.

Which brings me back to my English friend, who not only cracked my shell but pointed out to me the Way. Frost called it the road less traveled, though it's a well-enough-worn track. It carries you step by step to recognition of who you really are and the work you are supposed to do, even if that opposes what society and parental voices tell you is correct. "To be nobody but yourself," wrote e.e. cummings, "in a world that is doing its best night and day to make you everybody else means to fight the hardest battle any human being ever fights and never stop fighting." It is a crusade. It is a spiritual pilgrimage. It's called the Second Journey.

The *Dictionary of Christian Spirituality* defines the Second Journey as a distinct period in a person's life when you set out in a new direction. The Second Journey is not to be confused with midlife crisis, although it often coincides with that period and often arises out of crisis. Midlife crisis shows itself generally as a frightened clutching at lost youth, old dreams: you divorce your wife and marry a girl young enough to be your child, or you buy a motorcycle, or you leave your husband, get a face-lift, new wardrobe, new job, perhaps a younger lover.

The Second Journey comes instead as a call to end one life and strike out on a new way. It does not necessarily coincide with conversion, but—as with conversion—you experience the anguish of loneliness and extreme dislocation, alienation from everything that had rooted you before. It is common among writers, artists, and

musicians. Joseph Conrad went through it; so did Rud-
yard Kipling, Leo Tolstoy, Thomas Hardy, John Bunyan.
You see the sharp change in their work. The journey is
exemplified classically by Aeneas and Odysseus—and in
real life by Dante, Ignatius of Loyola, John Wesley. The
catalyst can take the form of exile, illness, major disap-
pointment, despair at the grip of addiction, or just simple
boredom. It involves a search for new meanings, fresh
values.

On the Second Journey you either change careers—
begin a different life—or else pursue your work in a different way, to an inner siren song. A monk or nun may
leave the order, strike out into the world. A successful
businessman may sell his company—go off to repair fur-
niture, drive locomotives, study for the priesthood, trek
in Nepal.

Another word for this crisis is the Greek *metanoia*,
denoting a life-changing period, when you fully change
your course, and when even as you pull the tiller over
hard you feel lost, cast adrift, not knowing where you
are heading, but unable to continue as you were.

Susan Howatch, author of sixteen books, including
the six delicious Starbridge novels, speaks of her gentle
mystical experience in the mid-1980s. Hers did not begin
in cataclysmic revelation, as mine, but as "a sort of
driven, wordless groping for a new beginning and a more
authentic existence."

She was a successful novelist, then in her midforties
and living in England. Her work had come to a dead end.

She felt she was not allowed to move on. What was the purpose of her writing? she asked herself. To make her publishers rich?

Her conversion began consciously, she says, in 1983, when she moved to Salisbury, England, to an apartment right in the shadow of the magnificent medieval Salisbury Cathedral. But it had started deep in her unconscious long before. She was agnostic at the time, divorced and living alone. Then, choosing the very words I've used about myself, she added, "I felt myself stripped of everything important!"

Is this humbling required for the Second Journey?

"The cathedral came out to encircle me," she says. Today she sees how she began cautiously, first taking walks around the perimeter of the building, then in ever smaller, tighter circles, moving inexorably and symbolically toward the center of her Christian faith. She had been taught religion at school. She believed in God, but the concept seemed remote. In other words, she had a Christian but not a churchgoing background. By 1989 she was a regular churchgoer, although she had found the church-ish part hard at first to take.

"It is very important for a mystic to have a framework to keep herself in order," she adds. "It's a discipline, like jogging." She acquired a spiritual director, an "old boy, a religious," now in his eighties, with whom she corresponded in long letters. Gradually, her spiritual awakening took form.

It is hard to perceive how God's call works out. You

can be a complete failure in worldly terms, yet triumph spiritually, or you can have material success with no spiritual understanding or point of view.

Susan, walking round and round the cathedral, found that "God was drawing me out of unhappiness into something else." At first she didn't recognize it as God. She didn't think of God the personal Father, but simply of God the abstract force, Paul Tillich's "Ground of Being." She only knew that in order to write the series of novels that began to interest her, she had to study church history, Christianity, the formal aspects of the spiritual life, until she was herself reeled in, good fish. One day in 1994, she found herself delivering a lecture from the center of the "radiant, ravishing" cathedral that her apartment overlooked. She stood at the point where the main nave and the transepts cross, at the center of the symbol of Christ; and she marveled to find herself there, reeled in by God so gradually she'd hardly known it was happening.[8]

Quite different was the Second Journey for Jane McDonald of Gloucester, Massachusetts, whose journey was trumpeted with a disconcertingly loud blast. She was just over fifty at the time and recently divorced. She was scared and also angry, crisscrossing the country, wandering. She flew around the world. She lived in Paris for a while. Finally she settled in Massachusetts, near one of her daughters. One May morning, just as she was waking up, she heard a voice. "You must change the direction of your life," it said.

She didn't know what to make of it; she did nothing.

Five months later, she was hit by ecstasy. It was twelve-thirty or one o'clock in the afternoon. She was strolling out of doors, waiting for her daughter and admiring the beauty of the October colors, the oranges and reds. She lifted her head to see to the very top of a particular glorious tree, when: "I felt surrounded by unbounded Love. Everything I looked at, everything was *connected*. My heart went *ping!* and opened. I could feel it. It heated up. Now I can love Lynn, I thought, meaning my older daughter, who had given me lots of trouble."

Enraptured, she could only weep.

Her daughter came out. "Mom, what's happened?"

She remained in that ecstatic state for two hours and slowly came back to normal, but from that moment on she was transformed.

Where before she had been withdrawn, without confidence, Jane was now "radiant," as total strangers did not hesitate to remark. She opened an art gallery, began to do community theater, and so vital was her personality that she attracted friends and compliments. "Your presence lit up the whole stage," they said. How different from the shy and diffident, insecure woman she had been before.[9]

So began her Second Journey to her spiritual core. Or perhaps it began earlier, in that period of distress before the ecstasy—who can say? The catalyst is always something that happens to break up the even tenor of one's life. Often an outer journey symbolizes the inner movements of the soul.

We don't think of rabbis, priests, and ministers as

requiring a Second Journey. After all, they are already attached to a church, consciously following a spiritual path. Many, however, feel spiritually bereft. My friend and spiritual director, a former canon at the Washington National Cathedral, admitted that when she had her own ecstatic experience in a far-off land, she was experientially unprepared. She had the testament and stories of others retrieved from books, but no companions with whom to talk about it. She felt lost in time and space, without landmarks. There was lots of support, she says, but no one can bring real understanding without having had the experience itself. At that time she had no idea how to deal with what happens afterward.

Even those in the highest church positions feel spiritually lost at times or personally frail. For many years the Most Reverend Edmond L. Browning was presiding bishop of the Episcopal Church in the United States; that is the equivalent of a Roman Catholic cardinal. In England or Canada his position is called archbishop. Bishop Browning is a modest, simple man, with warm eyes and an open smile. He graciously agreed to an interview, candidly sharing his own spiritual search. His Second Journey began only a few years ago, in 1995, when he was in his sixties, and it started not with ecstasy or through a quiet long conversion, for he already held deep faith. The way opened to him through the doorway of failure and distress.

He'd had earlier experiences. Ten years prior, for example, when he learned he would be elected primate bishop, he'd had a dream. Browning was raised the eldest of three children in an alcoholic family, with all that that implies of dysfunction and abandonment. His father died of cirrhosis of the liver. Now Browning was to be elevated to the highest rank in his church.

"In my dream my father came to me. It was very clear he was there. 'I am well,' he said, 'I'm whole. Tell your mother to save a seat beside her—that I'll be there to watch your ordination.' "

That his absent father had come in a dream meant a great deal to this humble man. That the spirit of his now-healed father was proudly watching his ordination filled him with pleasure. He never doubted that his father watched. "I believe God can come in all kinds of ways," he says, "and everyone finds a place at the Table."

The dream marked a healing, but his Second Journey did not start until ten years later when Browning had what he calls the most difficult year of his ministries.

That year the church treasurer embezzled $2.2 million, one bishop committed suicide, and Bishop Browning was forced to preside at the trial of a second bishop for heresy.

"It really hit me. I was almost immobilized. People were calling for my resignation." For the first time in his life he sought out a spiritual director, an Episcopal monk of the Society of St. John the Evangelist in Boston.

"This man did more for me than anyone, in terms of identifying who I am, and assessing me and my place on the spiritual journey, and the balance we need between the spiritual and physical worlds. I have sat and cried with this man for hours."

Does he call this spiritual direction a mystical

experience? "Yes. All of those things." For Bishop Browning had never done anything like this before. "This guy is very gentle, very knowledgeable in Scripture. He has a loving, affirmative manner—and that's the sign of the spiritually rich."

What happens in his sessions? First they will read a psalm or scriptural passage, and together the two men sit and reflect on it. Then they talk about where Browning stands emotionally and spiritually that day. Finally he receives certain tasks. "Now I am really taking seriously the directions of my spiritual director," he said.

"Like what?"

"To be positive every day. That's God's gift. To work that day in that positive knowledge, knowing there will be bumps along the way. Second, to do something for myself every day—a cappuccino, a walk, a weekend off, a good book, more time in prayer. It must be something creative, fun, renewing."

In addition he has prayers. "He made me write out, forgive my language, a shit-list. I'd never done anything like this before. I have to name all the people who have given me a hard time. Then I take them to God in prayer, telling Him how I feel about them. But then I leave them there. I don't tell Him what to do about it.

"My spiritual director has made me put aside time for prayer and daily readings in the morning before work, and occasionally at evening prayer."

And what has he come to realize from all this?

"You realize how dependent you are on the grace of

God. If you are vulnerable and know about your own brokenness, you become more compassionate toward others—society, community, the individual spirit. Their brokenness, you say to yourself, is my brokenness."[10]

I am reminded of the words of the Dalai Lama. He would not talk in our interview of his own mystical experiences, though he allowed, eyes crinkling with good humor, that on the basis of a dream, he knew he'd been a particular great Indian master in a former life. He admitted to having "certain effects from my practice—more compassion, less greed, less anger, less attachment, less pride. I consider that these are the purpose of my spiritual practice."[11]

Many years have passed since those moments on Machu Picchu, and since then other visions and experiences have come to me, raptures and knowings, illuminations, insights. They don't seem important anymore, but come as little kisses, reminders of this spiritual medium—these angels, these Presences, that are working for us, walking at our side. Listen, it's a fabulous journey. The ecstasies, of course, don't last. You always come back down, and then you pick up your pack and continue doing just what you were doing before, one foot in front of the other, one day at a time. Except that nothing looks the same. For one thing, you see that God is found in the *dailyness* of life, in the details, in the squabbling children and the irritation with your husband or your wife, and in anxiety about your boss at work. You see that life is a feast, all right there spread out for us to enjoy.

Today I look back with bemused detachment on the wild, roller-coaster ride of those first eight or ten years, for now I have come around full circle and think I didn't need to look for God; He was staring me in the face. "If it were a snake," my mother used to say, "it would bite you." I was looking everywhere but in the right place. The face of God. It swims in the heat of a summer day. It glistens in the icy rainbows glittering off the frozen limbs of winter trees. In the rain. In the sky. In a clod of dirt, bursting with bacteria. In the hum of tires on macadam roads. In our well-intentioned, fumbling—often failing—efforts to reach out to one another, or to clasp a floating spar as we're swept out to sea.

Or perhaps there is no external creator God.

The sacred surrounds us in this physical world, but it begins inside. "When a man goes out of himself to find or fetch God," wrote Meister Eckhart in a sermon, "he is wrong. I do not find God outside myself nor conceive him excepting as my own and in me. A man ought not to work for any why, not for God nor for his glory nor for anything at all that is outside him, but only for that which is his being, his very life within him."[12]

Wasn't this what Dante was describing when he asked to see God and was met by his own image? Or Sister Katrei, crying in such inchoate and un-Christian language—indeed in the ecstasy of the Sufi—"I am God"?

What miracles abound in this fragile world of loss and suffering and joy! The miracle of a tulip. What makes it bloom? The miracle of water. The miracle of a bumblebee that can fly in spite of all the laws of aerodynamics. Everywhere lie miracles.

Sometimes I go through dry periods, when I feel no union at all with my Beloved. I cannot meditate. Then I stamp my metaphorical feet in annoyance at all things spiritual. I speak angrily to myself and God. Sometimes I run away and hide, disgusted with the spiritual journey—it's all dry dust! These periods can last for hours or even days. At such times I can hardly remember the mystical insights, and instead I wallow in irritation, and then discover that a spiritual quiet is already permeating my hunger, need, and brokenness.

Each time I get discouraged, each time my doubting mind intervenes to cast its rueful judgments, some little miracle occurs, and I am once more suffused with the laughter of the spheres. Not long ago at the checkout counter in the supermarket a little booklet on prayer caught my eye. Oh, how wonderful, I thought, I need to know how to pray. I opened it at random, and found it quoting *me*![13] What could I do but laugh? And buy the little monograph, of course.

Both Saint Catherine of Siena and Julian of Norwich discovered we must laugh at the devil when he comes, for doubt and the demons cannot stand that happy confidence.

Sometimes I feel a Companion walking at my side, and I have the impression that if I turned quickly enough, I would catch it out of the corner of my eye, in all its rippling, radiant colors. But when I turn . . . it does, too, still laughing behind me in its game of blindman's bluff. It's like the lines in T. S. Eliot's *The Waste Land*.

> Who is the third who walks always beside you?
> When I count, there are only you and I together
> But when I look ahead up the white road
> There is always another one walking beside you
> Gliding wrapt in a brown mantle, hooded
> I do not know whether a man or a woman
> —But who is that on the other side of you?[14]

So what do we know as we approach the end of this book? Less, perhaps, than when we started, for all paths seem to lead to God. We know there is a journey to discover who we are. It begins in despair. It carries us to unimaginable heights. The raptures cease, and slowly, like a balloon deflating, we are let down. Now comes a long hard period. This is the time when we need a teacher, someone who has gone before, and when we also need one another's help and that of all mystical tradition. It may take years to integrate what we've been shown. Afterward, we just walk on for all the rest of our days. We may see no more angels, hear no voices, receive no mystical ecstasies. Saint Teresa of Avila had no visions for the last twenty years of her life. That's the way of things. The *Tao Te Ching* describes the proper way to live. I used to read it over and over, wonderingly. But what it's describing is *hesychia*, the quiet calm stillness of a pool of water reflecting back the sun.

Yield and overcome;
Bend and be straight;
Empty and be full.

. . . .

Therefore wise men embrace the one
And set an example to all.
Not putting on a display,
They shine forth.
Not justifying themselves,
They are distinguished.
Not boasting,
They receive recognition.
Not bragging,
They do not falter.

. . . .

Therefore the ancients say,
"Yield and overcome."

. . . .

Be really whole,
And all things will come to you.[15]

My teacher once gave me the metaphor of the search for God being like a great wheel, the spokes of which all converge at the center; each spoke is a separate religion, tying us to God. But we must choose one path only, for if we spend our time dodging a few feet down one spoke, and then, discouraged, turning back to race around the perimeter of the rim before plunging down another route, we shall die before we ever reach the center of the wheel.

We can choose the path of action and service, or that of retiring into meditation, or my path, that of *bhakti* or devotion—love and constant gratitude. God comes one on one, and heart to heart. Afterward, after the dramatic ecstasies, another, gentler wisdom insinuates itself: to live as if each moment were a great privilege. To awake!

Once long ago, before any of the stories told here, I dreamt I'd died. Usually we dream that we are about to die. We're falling off a cliff—and wake up before we land. In this case I was quite dead. I was a spark of light, an atom, a will-o'-the-wisp, more fragile than smoke, and although I could see everyone around me, my family could not see or hear me.

I saw my older daughter, Sarah, then only eight or ten years old. She was sitting in a bathtub with my mother, who at the time was still alive, and I could see Sarah's lovely new clear naked skin and, by contrast, her grandmother's beautiful, battle-scarred, wrinkled body, each wound of which revealed a chapter in her life. Seeing them together, I was happy. It meant that my mother would take care of her.

I hovered at the cheek of my younger daughter, Molly.

"You should get into the bathtub, too, Molly," I whispered to her—I, a whirl of atoms, invisible.

"NO!" She stamped her foot. I laughed, it was so like her to answer in that way. Then I cajoled her into the safety of the tub, loving my daughters beyond compare.

The scene changed.

I was sitting on a green slat-backed bench in a park. There were tall conical trees and many strange statues.

(Only on waking did I recognize it as a cemetery.) My husband sat beside me on the bench, and though I had no form I could feel the weight of his arm on my shoulder. I was filled with urgency. It was time to go.

"Now I want you to remarry," I was saying, "but not some floozy I won't like."

I woke up. My pillow was drenched with tears, and I ran downstairs and hugged my husband and children, for as a spirit I'd had no arms with which to embrace my children, no tongue with which to taste good food, no eyes with which to absorb the beauties of this world. I'd had no *physical body*! All week I went around *touching* things—people, countertops, silverware, textiles, trees, stones, water, grass, all the materials of this beautiful miracle of Earth.

A psychologist might say the dream concerned the approaching death of my marriage—except that the dream came years before that fateful trip to Peru. Moreover, on awakening I understood its message: what a privilege it is to be a human. Rilke knew.

What will you do, God, when I die?
When I, your pitcher, broken, lie?
When I, your drink, go stale or dry?
I am your garb, the trade you ply,
you lose your meaning, losing me.
Homeless without me, you will be
robbed of your welcome, warm and sweet.

. . . .

What will you do, God? I am afraid.[16]

I know people who want never to hurt again, and seek enlightenment for that. But light casts a shadow, and as there can be no shadow without the light, so there can be no love without its sister, loss. I think the angels envy us our arms, our lips, the touch of skin, the sheer physicality, the pleasures and pains with which God manifests Himself as us.

You will say I am romantic and that life is not like this, but rather a howl of empty loneliness, violence, and demonic hurt. I do not know. Certainly I, too, am subject to the dark emotions. Then I lift my chin and strain a little on my leash, God's dog, remembering how sometimes I have seen this shining Earth, with its people haloed, gleaming with inner light.

But what do I know?

Less than the spaces between the letters on this page.

What I know cannot be said, yet reaches to the very rim of space. Better to rest. Better to listen to the silence of the ringing heart.

CHRISTIAN MEDITATION

Be still and know that I am God.

—PSALMS 46:10

For the past five hundred years Christian meditation—
or contemplation, as it was called—has largely been
lost. Today we find a renewal of this tradition. Monaster-
ies offer retreats for a week or a month, and spiritual
communities provide space where people, hungry for silence, may slow down and look inward toward the soul.

Dom Laurence Freeman, a Benedictine monk at the
Monastery of Christ the King in London and director of
the World Community for Christian Meditation, teaches
these ancient disciplines around the world; and since earlier we described a Buddhist path, it seems appropriate to
lay out a Christian meditation here, as practiced by the
Desert Fathers in the centuries after the death of Christ,
and taught by Dom Freeman today.

In part the practice was lost because of its secrecy.
"The uninitiated are not permitted to behold these
things," wrote Basil the Great, bishop of Caesarea from
370 to 379. "Their meaning is not to be divulged by
writing it down."

The idea behind an exclusive, even silent doctrine
was not to shut people out, but rather to underscore, as
Zen Buddhism also does, the holiness of the practice and
the idea that some truths cannot be expressed logically.[1]
They are known with the heart alone and are deeply
personal. By the Middle Ages spiritual pilgrims had developed strict methods of contemplation, their pathway
winding through the stony sweeps of *lectio* (reading of
Scripture), *meditatio* (pondering), *oratio* (aspiring to the
love of God), and *contemplatio* (resting in God's love).

Ironically, these paths, unbeknownst to the Inquisitors, were heavily influenced by the Jewish Kabbalah, and the Jewish texts were influenced in turn by Islamic practices, the seepage having occurred during one window of religious toleration that opened for two hundred years when the Moors controlled Spain. This period of tolerance ended in 1492, when King Ferdinand and Queen Isabella took the last Moorish stronghold of Granada and expelled all Muslims and Jews. Then the Inquisition began systematically to exterminate as heresy every deviant thought or hint of competing religions, Judaism or Islam. Christian meditation still flourished in the fifteenth century, began to fade in the 1600s, and by the Age of Enlightenment, except in isolated enclaves, was all but forgotten.

Dom Freeman's mentor, John Main, was born in London in 1926, and was introduced to meditation by an Indian monk. At the time such silent prayer was rare, having been replaced by "mental" or spoken prayer and by ritual. In 1958 Main became a Benedictine monk, and in 1969 he rediscovered the Christian tradition of "pure prayer," taught to Saint Benedict in the fourth century by Saint John Cassian. Main devoted the rest of his life to spreading this lost art to laypeople, in order to deepen their spiritual life. He recommended two periods—one in the morning, another in the evening—which could be integrated with other prayer.

How do you meditate? Dom Freeman's Benedictine practice is simply to be mindful—completely present in each activity of your day. Cutting vegetables or cooking soup becomes an act of devotion, a form of prayer. But the practice begins by carefully training the mind to concentrate.

THE TIME:

It is important to meditate every day. Most people find it best to meditate as soon as they get up in the morning, before the mind has started to churn with the duties of the day. Others choose to end the day with meditation, and some do both. But knowledgeable people advise you to choose the same time every day, to reinforce the habit and make it strong.

Set aside ten to twenty minutes. At first you may want to set a kitchen timer or an alarm, so that you won't keep worrying or glancing at a clock. Go to your place, sit, close your eyes, begin.

THE PLACE:

Set aside one place for meditation, one spot used only for this purpose. It may be as small as one corner of a room, but that corner is used only for prayer and meditation, so that soon it absorbs a quality of quiet. It becomes your holy sanctuary. Make it pretty. Build an altar. If you have a little table, place fresh flowers there, and on it whatever holy objects appeal to you—or none. A plain white cloth, a single lovely flower will suffice. This sacred space is yours, designed according to your wish.

Some people keep a little God-box there. On scraps of paper they write their worries, prayers, concerns, put them in the box and leave them there. Every few months they take out their prayers and see which have been answered. Other people use a mental God-box, and when they begin to meditate, they sweep all cares into their imaginary bin and set it outside the doors of their mind. Now you withdraw into your closet, the closèd heart, and enter holy space.

If you like incense and candles, then use these too. As you begin, create a little ritual: set the timer, light a candle, ring a delicate bell to call your mind into its holy space.

HOW TO SIT:

Every morning (or in the evening, if you desire), sit quietly either in a chair or on the floor. It does not matter which, so long as you are comfortable and so long as your back is straight. Scan your body. Your back should trace a straight line from the buttocks to the top of your head, and the top of your head should be parallel to the ceiling—your chin tilted neither up or down.

Some people sit easily on the floor, legs crossed. Others find it difficult. If you want to sit on the floor but find it hard, sit on two cushions and cross your legs, so that buttocks and knees form a strong triangle on the floor. But a chair will do as well. The important thing is to be comfortable. Relaxed.

Check yourself. This soon becomes so habitual that it requires no more than one quick sweep of an inner eye. But at first it may seem tedious. Is your chin too far forward, jutting out? Or is your head floating backward, so that you feel a downward pressure on the back of your neck? If so, adjust your head. Are your shoulders hunched? Let them drop. You should feel easy, fluid, without strain. Now make a prayer of gratitude and devotion and begin.

THE BREATH:

First, place your attention on your breathing, for the breath is the only thing we know for certain to be real. Our thoughts and emotions are changing constantly, and much of what we see as real is no more than a projection of our likes and dislikes, or of our ambitions, or of interpretations drawn from past experiences. Our breath alone is true.

Put your attention on your belly. Take three breaths from the diaphragm. Watch your belly rise and fall. Each exhalation is longer than the intake. Watch, as each breath slows. Are you guiding the breath? Pushing? Holding in? Trying to control? Observe.

Is there a pause between breaths? Don't try to force a pause. Just watch. Is the breath fragile? Heavy? Slow? Quick? Steady or uncertain? Simply watch.

Most people find it less disturbing to meditate with their eyes closed. Allow the eyeballs to float upward beneath closed lids.

THE WORD:

After a few breaths, turn to the word. Silently repeat the oldest Christian mantra known, the Aramaic syllables *Ma ra na tha.* "Come to me, Lord." The word has passed down from the first century after Christ and inspired the Desert Fathers: *Maranatha.*

You could use the Pilgrims' Prayer as well: "Lord Jesus Christ, have mercy on me." Or the longer version: "Lord Jesus Christ, Son of God, have mercy on me, a poor sinner." But the very fact that the Aramaic syllables convey no meaning in English makes them, as a meditation, the more powerful.

You concentrate totally on the sound: *Ma ra na tha.* As a violinist practices her scales three hours a day, listening to each note, recognizing that each progression is unique, so you train yourself to listen for fifteen or twenty minutes to the special word or syllables—utterly present. It is not easy. The stallions of the mind lunge first one way, then the next, leap into the past, rush into a fantasy future, make plans, fight and jerk at the reins that hold them in. They want to be anywhere but here, right now, concentrating on one sound.

Ma ra na tha.

You will find at first that you go "in" and "out." It does not matter. Each time you notice that you were unable to hold concentration, simply return your attention to the sound: *Maranatha.* There is nothing wrong with the mind leaping off. But when you notice you've been following the hounds of your thoughts, as they hunt through the underbrush, just say, "Oh," and return to the chant. "Lord, come to me now." *Ma ra na tha.*

———

Gradually, as you practice, the horses will calm down as soon as you begin; the dogs will lope home to their kennel. They learn by your dedication that this is the feeding time for prayer. Soon they come to love the restful silence, the wash of the light of God. At first five minutes may feel like an eternity. Later you are surprised to discover how quickly it passes. Soon you will no longer need the kitchen timer or the alarm to tell you when the time is up. Your body knows. In twenty or thirty minutes you pull out.

But in the early stage your timer marks the end. When the bell rings, take a moment to come slowly out of concentration. Draw a final watchful breath. Allow yourself to consider what happened. Take a few moments to give thanks: "Thank you, God, for permitting me this time to learn . . . for permitting this time with you." If you keep a journal you may want to jot down notes of what you saw or understood, or of what happened or did not.

Then go about your day mindfully, and don't think about what's happening until it's time to meditate again.

Father Freeman presents a map of the meditating mind:

On the surface we find the everyday mind, what the Tibetans call *sem*. This is the place of worries, doubts, fears, thoughts, anxieties, dreams, sex, food, memories, and plans. This is the stuff we thrust into the God-box as we begin. It is the world of troubles and judgments, critical analysis, resentments, jealousy, fears, and hurts. Here also lie happiness, pleasure, boredom, physical irritation, the desire for a cup of tea. It is the world of dualities, of good/bad, yes/no, either/or, virtue/evil, of jagged eruptions that look like this:

But if you continue meditating, you drop down into a deeper mind-state of l o n g s l o w w a v e s. . . . This is the ocean of archetypes, of kings and queens, gods and myths, the world of the unconscious or subconscious, of repressed memories and psychological storms, which rise to the surface like bubbles in a lake. The deeper level looks like this:

Sometimes you ride the breath.

Other times you feel, not that you are breathing, but that you are being breathed by the earth, the universe—by God.

Still, you continue, repeating the prayer. *Ma ra na tha.* "Lord, come to me." If you were Muslim, you would say the same thought in Arabic: *"La ilaha ill-Allah."* If Buddhist, *"Om mani padme hum."* If Hindu, *"Om Ram Om."* If Catholic, "Lord Jesus Christ, have mercy on me." Or you would say the rosary, which is also a kind of meditation, hour after hour absorbing the images of God.

After a while you drop still deeper into meditation, and now you hit a brick wall of naked awareness of the self. This is the ego with its puffed-up fears and pride.

Here lie existential sorrows, loneliness, and separation even in close relationships. Here lies the uninhibited wail of the breaking heart. You cannot stop weeping. I could cry for a thousand years, you think.

You want to flee this place that carries you to such torment. But the only way around this wall is through. You stay. Repeating the syllables, *Ma ra na tha*. Without expectations you listen, poor in spirit, poor in arrogance, waiting humbly. One day a brick falls out of the wall, and then another, and a third, until the entire wall crumbles before your patient demand.

Was this what Christ meant when he said that we should pray like the importunate woman pleading her case before the judge? Beseeching God's ear with the longings of our heart?

The wall collapses and you expand outward without boundaries, beyond images. Now ego serves instead of controls us, and trembles at the fragile edge of the tragedies of life.

It's foolish to describe what's on the Other Side, for it is different for each person and different with each meditation. Perhaps you see yourself inside a golden vessel, or perhaps you are the golden interior of the vessel. Or perhaps the golden light enfolds you within the shield of an invisible vessel. You no longer exist. You are not even aware of light or peace, joy, dark serenity, or the silent raptures covering you, for awareness requires words and words require thought, and thought has been annihilated, too, in this sweet love . . . until your mind heaves slowly under you, and the mind swells outward in the faintest movement. *Light,* it notices, and falls back into the bliss of the abyss. You know you are thinking when a word or sentence forms, and now you shift back into the mind as it slowly shrugs its shoulders in a stronger wave and overthrows sweet love, starting already to name and analyze what you felt, to fix the moment into images and space.

Perhaps your meditation was difficult, full of anger and anxiety. Or perhaps it brought a vision or the answer to a problem. Or perhaps it brought only sweet quietude and rest.

The bell rings. The meditation is done. Take another breath and slowly begin to climb back to the surface of your mind. Consider what you saw.

Give thanks.

Tomorrow you will return and something different will happen on that day.

THE DARK SIDE AND THE WAY OUT

"Oh the devil, the devil" we say when we might be saying, "God! God!"... I am quite sure I am more afraid of people who are themselves terri-fied of the devil than I am afraid of the devil himself.

—ST. TERESA OF AVILA, *LIFE*, CH. 25

Our discussion would not be complete without an acknowledgment of the dark side of mystical affairs. The path is often likened to a razor's edge, so fine and sharp that we can easily fall off. This is why everyone agrees we should not set out on the ecstatic journey without a proper guide. I do not care to spend much energy describing those unfortunates whose mystical ecstasies resulted from mental disturbances, or those others whose experiences were later distorted into satanic or destructive cults. It is possible to tell the difference. One of the curious marks of the true mystical encounter is that the recipient feels utterly humbled and utterly blessed and yet often moves away from any formal church. She prefers the intimate, interior communion with a personal God, unmediated by a hierophant. At the same time she becomes *more tolerant of all religions*. Any place of worship serves, for she is praying continuously in her heart, and no place is to be found where God is not.

A cult, on the other hand, demands one's loyalty sometimes even to the point of death. If such loyalty is not given, the retribution can be cruel. The cult closes its doors against the outside world. Often it rules by terror, and this is the furthest possible remove from the joyous, singing freedom of the mystic's life.

We humans are alike all over the world. We all want to be happy, safe. To varying degrees we all want peace of mind and also a little excitement in our lives. We want to love someone and also we want to be loved. We all harbor within us the possibilities for both good and bad. I spoke earlier of how the mystic during union makes no

288

distinction between opposites, not even good and evil. Yet we live on a physical plane, and when she returns from raptures the mystic subjects herself again to everyday judgments. Every moment of our lives we are choosing, good over less good. It's not an easy task. To grow into the fullest expression of ourselves takes constant attention and courageous introspection, especially because, as Carl Jung pointed out, as we grow toward enlightenment, so, too, does our dark side grow.

But although we are alike, we also differ in our tendencies. What appeals to one person may be poison to another. Spiritual experiences come to most people, I believe, mysteriously and magically. Some people as a consequence grow gentler, more vulnerable, radiant, life-affirming, yielding up their selfish desires, while others who may likewise have mystical experiences turn into monsters. They start cults, train followers. The difference defines, in a nutshell, whether the ecstatic experience was "real."

In March 1997, thirty-nine members of the California cult Heaven's Gate committed mass suicide by drinking a lethal cocktail. They were all dressed in the same black clothing, and they lay on their neat bunk beds, each with a purple cloth across his or her face. Beside each person's hand lay a five-dollar bill, and at the foot of each bed was a neatly packed suitcase. They were ready to be transported to the alien spaceship that was said to be trailing the comet Hale-Bopp. Thirty-eight of them calmly and methodically, with great discipline, followed their charismatic teacher, Marshall Applewhite, convinced that in three and a half days, like Christ, they would be resurrected. Years earlier, Applewhite had been fired from his position as music professor at Houston's University of St. Thomas, when a relationship with a male student came to light. Depressed, ashamed, guilty, and now hearing voices, Applewhite checked himself into a psychiatric hospital. Later, still fighting his homosexuality (and who knows what voices in his head), he castrated himself. What he wanted, and what his followers wanted, was to shift from the "human level to the heavenly kingdom." They wanted to remove themselves from the dirt and grind of the physical body and live entirely as spiritual beings of light. Their cult was not too far removed from some of what we've talked about earlier in this book. The members lived communally in celibacy. They shared their food and money, begging for meals from churches or students. They traveled as spiritual vagabonds. Each member renounced all worldly possessions in order to pursue the spiritual search. Is this much different from a monk? Most were in their forties. One was the daughter of a federal judge, another a postal worker who had left her children for the cult, a third was the son of a prominent businessman.

What happened? Why are some mystical encounters life-enhancing while others fall into madness? Applewhite's group committed voluntary suicide. Some cults go even further toward the edge of darkness, into murder. Are their charismatic leaders possessed, as some would claim, by demons or attaching spirits?

A few years ago in Switzerland the Templars of the

Sun killed first their own children, then themselves in a mass suicide reminiscent of nothing so much as another earlier cult and yet another mass murder. In 1978 in the forests of Guyana the followers of James Warren Jones drank poisoned Kool-Aid. Women, children, men all lay dead on the ground, as the police closed in. In that tragic case many members had apparently tried vainly to escape—to flee into the jungle or leave Jones's group. They were brought back and forced to drink the poison with the rest.

Both the Templars and Jim Jones founded their secret sects on the basis of a spiritual search, and surely the leaders had experienced mystical ecstasies of some sort.

Likewise, in Japan in 1995, the charismatic Shoko Asahara must have had his own mystical encounters before he instructed the inner circle of his Aum Shinrikyo cult to pour lethal gas into the Tokyo subway, killing twelve people and injuring more than five thousand. He is charged with ordering the murders of twenty-five people—some of them kidnapped and their bodies microwaved in his basement into a dry powder that was later scattered along the rural roads.

By 1993 Japan had 231,019 registered religious sects, claiming a combined membership of 200 million— some 70 million more, in fact, than the population. Many people belonged to several organizations.

What is a cult? The word is often tossed around loosely. The early Christians were called a cult. In France the angry mayor of a nearby town called one internationally renowned gentle Buddhist community a cult. In general, a cult is a closed organization, often with secret rules and initiations. Typically a cult follows one authority or "perfect master" who demands total obedience. The cult requires you to give up the world and all ties of affection to your family of origin and past friends, thus isolating you. It forces you to "voluntarily" donate all your worldly goods to the community. At first it appears benign. Almost imperceptibly it tightens the noose of its demands until you are drawn in too deeply to withdraw.

In 1996, prompted by the horrors of the Templars, the French government issued a report on one hundred seventy-two cults and eight hundred "satellites" operating in France. It defined ten signs of a "cult," the first of which is a kind of self-righteous isolation from the surrounding world. The signs are, first, a mental destabilizing of the participants, exorbitant financial demands (including giving all one's money to the group), and a complete rupture with one's environment and family of origin; this stage is followed by the gradual undermining of one's physical well-being through extreme deprivation, threats, or even torture, and the roping-in of children (starvation and physical abuse are often involved). Now the participants are trapped and cannot or perhaps don't want to leave the cult and with increasing devotion come the demands for antisocial behavior. These may include embezzlement, deliberate sabotage of economic systems, or the infiltration of public authorities.

According to the French report, it is not the poor and

uneducated who find themselves most susceptible to cults, but rather the most intellectual and brilliant strata of society. The victims are primarily idealistic young people, ready to change the world. They are the college graduates, the scientists and engineers. Some are married couples, steady citizens attracted to a brilliant teacher and on a conscious spiritual journey. Others are drawn to the liberation promised by fundamentalism that provides clearly delineated boundaries of how to think and act.

All are drawn to the magical charisma of the self-appointed master. And he? Did he have mystical encounters himself, get partway on the journey, and fall victim to the shadow side? Some people would say he was tempted by Satan. Others that he let his ego intervene between himself and God—"My will not Thine be Done!" Others that he was seduced by the *siddhas*, the paranormal abilities that so often seem to accompany mystical experiences. Or perhaps he had already believed that he was God.

There are a dozen explanations, but given the pitfalls, the more practical question to ask is, How do we choose a good teacher?

If we have the discernment to avoid openly deranged gurus, how do we spot those who once were true visionaries and may now be falling from grace? Not all are as easy to see as Bhagavan Sri Rajneesh, who when kicked out of India in the 1970s established an ashram in Oregon, where he stockpiled Rolls-Royces as others collect glass figurines, while guards, armed to the teeth, patrolled the ranch, his holy ashram, protecting against his paranoid fears. More than one Hindu or Buddhist guru has become a woman-chasing alcoholic, seduced by the freedom of Americans and by the spiritual junkies who came to them for a holy fix. Over the last several years these tales of supposedly ascetic gurus betraying their wide-eyed disciples have become commonplace—almost as common as those about straying ministers or priests.

It's a serious problem.[1]

The Dalai Lama is said to be "particularly worried" and deeply concerned about the issue. He advises students to get close to a teacher and to "spy" on him or her for "at least three years," to see if the teachings conform to how the guru behaves. He counsels testing the teacher at every step.

Interviewing one Tibetan lama, Demmo Loche Rinpoche, I asked what you should do if you find your teacher has misused sexual practices, alcohol, or anger.

"If you have already accepted that teacher," he answered with surprising common sense, "then when you see the failing, do not take notice. It is natural that there are failings, because the teacher is a human being. Don't plant a thorn in your heart, because it will become an obstruction to your own growth." He also advised, however, that the student may gently approach the teacher, reprove his conduct, and lead him back on the Way, for are not the students also teachers to their guides?

Demmo Loche Rinpoche listed the qualities to look for in a teacher, first naming—his black eyes sparkling with laughter—what *not* to look for. You are not to be concerned with psychic powers. "If you think the teacher must attain levitation," he said, laughing, "then you may as well rely on a vulture. Vultures fly. Vultures see long distances. . . ."

The good teacher is completely at peace. He has more knowledge than you. In addition, he has

- High ethical and moral standards
- Stability of meditation
- Wisdom and gentleness
- Strong compassion—a feeling for the student's welfare
- Infinite patience, allowing the student to ask all questions, anything.

The true teacher gives more importance to spiritual practice than to worldly concerns and cares more for a future life than for this one. He shows more concern for others than himself. He feels responsible for the welfare of his student.

In my experience the good teacher is lighthearted and playful and also displays much common sense. There is a saying, "When the student is ready, the teacher will appear." At a certain point, having given yourself to God with utter abandon, having asked and prayed for a teacher, you simply wait. The teacher will appear. Then trust your intuition. The soul knows her own teacher, as the calf knows its mother. Moreover, the soul will also change teachers over time, for the task of a good teacher is to help his student graduate. The student adores the teaching, not the teacher.

How do you recognize the good teacher? The same way you know that a mystical vision is not illusion but from God.

"By its JOY!" my teacher said. "God does not give poison. God gives only Joy." So should the teaching, too.

But if the teacher falls from the path, you do not have to follow him.

We cannot finish better than by drawing on Saint Catherine of Siena, who for years battled her inner demons of temptation, doubt, and fear. Finally she laughed at the devils. They vanished instantly, for doubt and anguish cannot stand up against sheer joy. Saint Catherine explained the difference between things sent from the Devil and things sent from God, and whether or not we believe in a tangible Prince of Darkness, intent on disguising himself as light, creating false teachers and tempting us with mystical insights in order to lead us astray, still her definition metaphorically holds true. Those experiences sent by demons, she said, inspire first sweetness and then in the long run pain and nausea, while those sent by God inspire awe and fear in the beginning, but are followed only by sweetness and by good.

So let us apply the same test to choosing the teachers who will guide us on the Way. The teaching is sweet, is good, and it guides us slowly at a steady and suitable pace to glories we cannot imagine, to love beyond our wildest dreams, to knowledge that we cannot die, and to mountain peaks so high, with views so clear that all we can do is to sink to our knees in rapture, reverence, and awe, weeping at the ecstatic journey we've been on.

NOTES

INTRODUCTION

1. John of the Cross, "Rimes after an Ecstasy of Profound Contemplation," in *The Poems of St. John of the Cross*, English versions rev. and rewritten by John Frederick Nims (New York: Grove Press, 1959; 1968).

2. Daniello Bartoli, *Vie de Saint Ignace de Loyola*, trans. P. L. Michel (Brüges, 1893), i: 34–36, as quoted in William James, *The Varieties of Religious Experience* (New York: Penguin Books, 1982), 410.

3. Teresa of Avila, *Life*, as quoted in James, *Varieties*, 411.

1. ROWING TOWARD GOD

1. Anne Sexton, "Rowing," from *The Awful Rowing Toward God*, in *The Complete Poems* (Boston: Houghton Mifflin, 1981).

2. His Holiness the Dalai Lama XIV, interview with author, 13 February 1996.

3. Thich Nhat Hanh, *Peace Is Every Step* (New York: Bantam Books, 1991; 1992), 10.

4. Teresa of Avila, *Life,* as quoted in Carol Lee Flinders, *Enduring Grace* (San Francisco: HarperSanFranciso, 1993), 177.

2. ECSTATIC VISIONS: FAIRY TALES

1. Aldous Huxley, *The Perennial Philosophy* (New York: Harper & Row, 1970), xi.

2. Song of Sol. 1–3.

3. John of the Cross, *The Poems of St. John of the Cross,* English versions rev. and rewritten by John Frederick Nims (New York: Grove Press, 1959; 1968), 19.

4. *The Song of God: Bhagavad-Gita,* trans. Swami Prabhavananda and Christopher Isherwood (New York: New American Library, 1972), 11:11.

5. Ibid., 11:28.

6. Ibid., 11:45.

7. Qur'an 96:1, as quoted in Karen Armstrong, *Muhammad* (San Francisco: HarperSanFrancisco, 1992), 83. From the translation of Arthur J. Arberry, *The Koran Interpreted* (Oxford, 1964).

8. Legend has it that Muhammad was illiterate. This is probably not so. As a merchant he could read and write the language of trade, but not the kind of poetry that became the Qur'an.

9. In Karen Armstrong, *A History of God* (New York: Knopf, 1993), 139; quotation from Maxim Rodinson, *Mohammad,* trans. Anne Carter (London, 1971).

10. *Shiur Qomah,* in *The Penguin Book of Hebrew Verse,* ed. and trans. T. Carmi (London, 1981), 199; as quoted in Karen Armstrong, *History of God,* 216.

3. DRUNKS AND BUMS AND SAINTS

1. Bill Wilson, quoted by Wesley Miller in letter to *The New York Times Magazine* (23 February 1975): 6.

2. Bill Wilson, *Alcoholics Anonymous,* 3rd ed. (New York: Alcoholics Anonymous World Services, 1976), 14.

3. Ibid., 56.

4. His Holiness the Dalai Lama XIV, interview with the author, 13 February 1996.

5. Dalai Lama XIV, *The Good Heart* (Boston: Wisdom Publications, 1996), 91.

6. Ibid.

7. Hildegard of Bingen, *Scivias,* in *Hildegard of Bingen: Mystical Writings,* ed. Fiona Bowie and Oliver Davies (New York: Crossroad, 1990), 68.

8. Ibid.

9. Catherine of Siena, as quoted in Carol Lee Flinders, *Enduring Grace* (San Francisco: HarperSanFrancisco, 1993), 117.

10. Catherine of Genoa, as quoted in Flinders, *Enduring Grace,* 138, 141–142.

11. Catherine of Genoa, *Purgation and Purgatory,* trans. Serge Hughes (New York: Paulist Press, 1979), 79–80; as quoted in Flinders, *Enduring Grace,* 142.

12. Catherine of Siena, *The Dialogue,* trans. Suzanne Noffke (New York: Paulist Press, 1980), 48; as quoted in Flinders, *Enduring Grace,* 103.

13. Teresa of Avila, *The Way of Perfection,* as quoted in Flinders, *Enduring Grace,* 184; and note a similar passage in Teresa's *The Interior Castle:* "Consider our soul to be like a castle made entirely out of a diamond or of very clear crystal, in which there are many rooms" (in Flinders, 1985). From *The Collected Works,* trans. Kieran Kavanaugh and Otilio Rodriguez (Washington, D.C.: Institute of Carmelite Studies, 1980).

5. LIGHT AND HEAT: BURNING WITH THE FIRE OF LOVE

1. Richard Maurice Bucke, *Cosmic Consciousness* (Philadelphia, 1901), 2, as quoted in William James, *The Varieties of Religious Experience* (New York: Penguin Books, 1982), 398.

2. In chapter 9 we take up another survey, by Andrew Greeley, who found the same preponderance of men.

3. Bucke, *Cosmic Consciousness*, as quoted in James, *Varieties*, 399. I have chosen to take James's version, which "follows the privately printed pamphlet that preceded Dr. Bucke's larger work and differs verbally a little from the text of the latter." The full passage may be found in Richard Maurice Bucke, *Cosmic Consciousness* (New York: Dutton, 1969), 9–10.

4. Bucke, *Cosmic Consciousness*, 3, as quoted in James, *Varieties*, 398.

5. Gerard Manley Hopkins, "God's Grandeur," in *The New Golden Treasury of English Verse*, chosen by Edward Leeson (London: Macmillan London, 1980).

6. See Hélène Renard, *Des Prodiges et des Hommes* (France: Lebaude, 1989), 43, n. 3. All translations from Renard's French are mine.

7. See Renard, *Des Prodiges*, 43, n. 1.

8. See Renard, *Des Prodiges*, 51.

9. His Holiness the Dalai Lama XIV, interview with the author, 13 February 1996.

10. For a long time I misunderstood this Buddhist concept of non-attachment. I thought it referred to some passionless isolation or nonfeeling. This is wrong. It does not mean that the enlightened one does not *care*, for he forms the deepest attachments to his family, children, students, and friends. But he

THE ECSTATIC JOURNEY

loves without motive or agenda; he is not controlling those around him, does not lose himself in the dramas, but remains steadily in a state of liquid joyful centeredness. And when someone whom he loves dies, then tears of grief may come, as the enlightened Lord Marpa, guru to Milarepa, wept at the death of his son. As Jesus is known to have wept.

11. Isabelle Robinet, *La Méditation Taoïste* (Dervy Livres, 1979), quoted in Renard, *Des Prodiges,* 47.

12. Mark 4:21–22; Luke 11:33; Matt. 5:15.

13. Richard Rolle, *The Fire of Love,* as quoted in Karen Armstrong, *Visions of God: Four Medieval Mystics and Their Writings* (New York: Bantam Books, 1994), 10.

14. The word *sufi* comes from the coarse woolen garments—"SWF," in Arabic—supposedly favored by the Prophet and worn by these ascetics. The Sufis appeared in the eighth or ninth century in opposition to the luxury and wealth of the court, the abandonment of the earlier simplicity of Islam. Social justice remained crucial to their piety.

15. Recently I told this story to a group of women, one of them from India, who said she had never heard of the Tibetan *g tumo* but *had* heard of Christian nuns who become so heated during prayer that a circle of snow melts around them. As a Christian, I had never heard about that, and we laughed together, marveling that we should each be familiar with the foreign culture and unversed in our own religion's lore. But in truth I don't know what order these nuns might belong to, or where they might be praying in the snow. It is interesting that the Japanese martial arts, teaching mastery over one's body, also instruct the practitioner in how to control body heat.

16. Herbert Benson, et al., "Body Temperature Changes

302

during the Practice of g Tum-mo Yoga," in *Nature* 295 (1982): 234–236.

17. Herbert Benson, with Marg Stark, *Timeless Healing: The Power and Biology of Belief* (New York: Simon & Schuster/Fireside, 1997).

18. Rainer Maria Rilke, untitled, in *Poems from the Book of Hours*, trans. Babette Deutsch (Norfolk, Conn.: New Directions, 1941).

19. A young Chinese girl, Xiong Zaidung, who had fallen sick with a fever that rose to 107.6° F, ate no solid food from 1978 to 1988, but survived only on glucose injections. If food hit her esophagus she was wracked by such violent spasms that she threw it up. But others, considered saints, have gone for longer periods and eaten less. Marie-Madeleine de Pazzi, who died in 1602, ate only dry bread. Louise Lateau (1850–1883) went seven years without eating anything except the Communion host. Anne-Catherine Emmende, who died in 1826, went five months drinking only water; Therese Neuman, fourteen years; Angela de Foligna, twelve years; Nicolas de Flue, twenty-nine years; Saint Ludwine, twenty-eight years. Catherine of Siena's eight-year fast has already been mentioned. The record is probably held by the late Martha Robin, who was known to have subsisted only on the Eucharist for fifty-eight years, from 1923 until her death in February 1981.

20. A *mala* is a string of beads similar to a rosary and used for prayer.

21. Sophy Burnham, *A Book of Angels* (New York: Ballantine, 1990), 215–219.

6. COMING DOWN, GOING OFF

1. Teresa of Avila, *Life,* chapter 18, as quoted in Evelyn Underhill, *Mysticism* (New York: Doubleday Image Books, 1990), 357.

2. Malaval, *Théologie Mystique,* as quoted in Underhill, *Mysticism,* 361.

3. Kabir, *The Kabir Book: Forty-four of the Ecstatic Poems of Kabir: Versions by Robert Bly* (Boston: Beacon Press, 1977), 3.

4. Ibid., 2.

5. William James, *The Varieties of Religious Experience* (New York: Penguin Books, 1982), 337.

6. The Sufi tradition carried the love of God to a point of danger easily misunderstood. In the tenth century, al-Hallaj, the "wool carder," roamed Iraq preaching the establishment of a new social order and crying in his ecstasy, "I am the Truth!" just as mystics everywhere have tried to explain their annihilation in God. Imprisoned for his blasphemy and refusing to recant, al-Hallaj was crucified like his hero, Jesus Christ.

7. George Fox, as quoted in James, *Varieties,* 292.

8. Interview with the author, 9 April 1997.

9. Sogyal Rinpoche, *The Tibetan Book of Living and Dying* (San Francisco: HarperSanFrancisco, 1992), 56.

10. Saint Augustine of Hippo, *Confessions* (New York: Penguin Books, 1961; 1983), 170–178.

11. Ibid., 197–198.

12. George Foreman, interviewed on *60 Minutes,* CBS Corporation, 16 April 1995.

13. Jakob Böhme, as quoted in James, *Varieties*, 410–411, n. 2.

14. Ibid.

15. Jean Houston, *A Mythic Life: Learning to Live Our Greater Story* (San Francisco: HarperSanFrancisco, 1996), 65–66.

16. Ibid.

7. THE SWEETNESS OF THE PAIN OF LOVE

1. William Blake, "Eternity," in *The Norton Anthology of Poetry*, 3rd ed. (New York: Norton, 1983), 508.

2. Letter to author, name of correspondent withheld by request.

3. Arthur Koestler, *The Invisible Writing* (New York: Macmillan, 1954), 352, as quoted in W. T. Stace, *Mysticism and Philosophy* (Los Angeles: Tarcher, 1960), 120–124.

4. Mrs. Jonathan Edwards, as quoted in William James, *The Varieties of Religious Experience* (New York: Penguin Books, 1982), 276–278.

5. Aryeh Faltz, letter to author.

6. Ibid.

8. HOLY CRAZINESS, CRAZY HOLINESS

1. Stephen Mitchell, *Dropping Ashes on the Buddha* (New York: Grove, 1976), 52–54.

2. Rick Fields, "Who Was Buddha?" in *Tricycle: The Buddhist Review* (Spring 1997): 46.

3. Karen Armstrong, *A History of God* (New York: Knopf, 1993), 213.

4. E. D. Starbuck, *The Psychology of Religion*, as quoted

in William James, *The Varieties of Religious Experience* (New York: Penguin Books, 1982), 353–354, n. 1.

5. Leo Tolstoy, as quoted in James, *Varieties*, 185.

6. As quoted in Tom and Dorothy Hopkinson, *Much Silence: Meher Baba, His Life and Work* (New York: Dodd, Mead, 1975), 27.

9. CHAOS AND DISINTEGRATION

1. William Wordsworth, "Ode to Duty," in *The Oxford Book of English Verse, 1250–1918,* chosen and ed. by Arthur T. Quiller-Couch (Oxford: Clarendon Press, 1900; new ed. 1939; 1957), 622.

2. Andrew M. Greeley and William C. McCready, "Are We a Nation of Mystics?" *The New York Times Magazine* (26 January 1975): 6.

3. *Alex Haley's Queen,* CBS miniseries written by David Stevens, produced by Mark M. Wolper, Burlington, 14 February 1993. According to this TV series, four people in ten in the United States have had a mystical experience; in England, five in ten.

4. Andrew M. Greeley, *The Sociology of the Paranormal: A Reconnaissance,* Sage Research Papers in the Social Sciences, vol. 3, no. 90-023 (Beverly Hills and London: 1975), 61.

5. Debbie Matthews, letter to the author.

6. Patanjali, as quoted in J. M. Cohen and J. F. Phipps, *The Common Experience* (Los Angeles: Tarcher, 1979), 117. From G. Costa, *Yoga and Western Psychology.*

7. *Confessions of al-Ghazali,* as quoted in Cohen and Phipps, *Common Experience,* 118.

8. See Cohen and Phipps, *Common Experience,* 90. From M. Lasky, *Ecstasy.*

9. Meister Eckhart, as quoted in Cohen and Phipps, *Common Experience,* 110. I have modernized the language. The original translates Eckhart's words as: "All joy be thine, an thou remainest God."

10. William James, *The Varieties of Religious Experience* (New York: Penguin Books, 1982), 18, 267–268, 272–274.

11. *The Mirror of Simple Souls,* as quoted in Evelyn Underhill, *Mysticism* (New York: Doubleday Image Books, 1990), 427. Underhill, writing in 1911, could not know that in 1946 the *Mirror* would be found to be the mystical work of Margareta Porete, a Beguine whose book was condemned in 1306 and who was herself burned at the stake for heresy around 1310.

1 0. THE HIDDEN MYSTICS

1. Catherine Brown, letter to the author.

2. Elinor Fuchs, *Waking Up,* unpublished memoir.

3. Howard Thurman, as quoted in Hal Bridges, *American Mysticism: From William James to Zen* (New York: Harper & Row, 1970), 54.

4. Andrew M. Greeley and William C. McCready, "Are We a Nation of Mystics?" *The New York Times Magazine* (26 January 1975): 6.

5. Joan Borysenko, interview with the author.

6. Thomas Merton, *The Seven Storey Mountain* (New York: Harcourt, Brace, 1948; Signet Books, 1952), 278–279. Also quoted in Bridges, *American Mysticism,* 67.

7. Thomas Merton, *The Asian Journal of Thomas Merton* (New York: New Directions, 1973), 236.

8. Nellie Lauth, letter to the author.

9. Quoted in William James, *The Varieties of Religious Experience* (New York: Penguin Books, 1982), 288–289. From Claparède and Goty, *Deux Héroines de la Foi* (Paris, 1880).

10. James, *Varieties,* 388.

11. Ram Dass tells about his meeting with his guru, Neem Karoli Baba, in India. The guru appeared to be expecting him, and when he arrived, said, "Do you have something for me?" Ram Dass, then still Richard Alpert, gave him enough acid to fell a steer. The guru popped the pills in his mouth and swallowed them without any effect at all. It was then that Alpert decided there might be more interesting paths to transcendence than through drugs and LSD.

12. A. J. Symonds, as quoted in James, *Varieties,* 391.

13. "Lily," interview with the author; name changed by request.

14. Aldous Huxley, *The Doors of Perception* (New York: Harper & Row, 1954), 55.

15. See W. T. Stace, *Mysticism and Philosophy* (Los Angeles: Tarcher, 1960), 71.

1 1. ANGELS AND VISITATIONS

1. Five have since been published: three nonfiction, *A Book of Angels, Angel Letters,* and *For Writers Only;* and two novels, *Revelations* and *The President's Angel.*

2. William James, *The Varieties of Religious Experience* (New York: Penguin Books, 1982), 13.

3. James, *Varieties*, 14.

4. Asa P. Ruskin, letter to *The New York Times Magazine* (23 February 1975): 6.

5. This was told to me by a Christian missionary who lived with these people for a number of years. Unfortunately I have lost my notes of our conversation and cannot give the name of the tribe or its location.

6. Yahya Suhrawardi, *Hiqmat al-Ishraq,* as quoted in Karen Armstrong, *A History of God* (New York: Knopf, 1993), 232. From Henri Corbin, *Spiritual Body and Celestial Earth* (London, 1990).

7. Genevieve W. Foster, *The World Was Flooded with Light* (Pittsburgh: University of Pittsburgh Press, 1985), 42–43.

8. Foster, *World Was Flooded*, 48.

9. Dennis Kyte, letter to the author.

10. Angelina Smith, letter to the author.

11. Aldous Huxley, *Huxley and God: Essays,* ed. Jacqueline Hazard Bridgeman (San Francisco: HarperSanFrancisco, 1992), 237.

12. Franklin A. Robinson, letter to the author.

13. Deane McGinnis, letter to the author.

14. Andrew Ramer, letter to the author.

15. "Gwen," letter to the author; name changed by request.

16. Angel Bailey, letter to the author.

12. THE SECOND JOURNEY

1. From Aeschylus, *Agamemnon*, as translated in Edith Hamilton, *The Greek Way* (New York: W. W. Norton, 1958), 257.

2. Joseph Campbell, *Myths to Live By*, as quoted in Graham Barbera, "The Future of Love," *Utne Reader* (November–December 1996): 48.

3. Andrew Greeley, *The Sociology of the Paranormal: A Reconnaissance*, Sage Research Papers in the Social Services, vol. 3, no. 90-023 (Beverly Hills and London, 1975), 64.

4. Ibn al-Arabi, as quoted in Karen Armstrong, *A History of God* (New York: Knopf, 1993), 235.

5. Dante Alighieri, as quoted in Armstrong, *History of God*, 235.

6. Abraham Joshua Heschel, *Man Is Not Alone* (New York: Farrar, Straus & Young, 1951), 78.

7. W. T. Stace, *Mysticism and Philosophy* (Los Angeles: Tarcher, 1960), 76–77.

8. Susan Howatch, interview with the author, London, Spring 1996.

9. Jane MacDonald, letter to the author.

10. Bishop Edmond Browning, interview with the author, 23 October 1996.

11. His Holiness the Dalai Lama XIV, interview with the author, 13 February 1996.

12. Meister Eckhart, as quoted in J. M. Cohen and J. F. Phipps, *The Common Experience* (Los Angeles: Tarcher, 1979), 112.

13. Sophy Burnham, *A Book of Angels* (New York: Ballantine, 1990), 221–226.

14. T. S. Eliot, "The Waste Land," in *The New Golden Treasury of English Verse*, chosen by Edward Leeson (London: Macmillan, 1980), 439.

15. Lao-tzu, *Tao Te Ching,* trans. Gia-fu Feng and Jane English (New York: Knopf, 1972), no. 22.

16. Rainer Maria Rilke, untitled, in *Poems from the Book of Hours,* trans. Babette Deutsch (Norfolk, Conn.: New Directions, 1941).

APPENDIX A: CHRISTIAN MEDITATION

1. In Judaism, in Islam, and in Greek and Russian Orthodox Christianity and other Eastern religions, the Holy of Holies, the inner sanctum of the church, is always hidden by a screen from sight. In some places it is too holy even for the priests to visit, lest they soil it with their feet; they enter it only after careful cleansing rites.

APPENDIX B: THE DARK SIDE AND THE WAY OUT

1. For more on this important subject, I recommend Anne A. Simpkinson, "Soul Betrayal: Spiritual Leaders and the Abuse of Power," *Common Boundary* 14, no. 6 (November–December 1996): 24–37. On cults, see *Le Monde,* "Societé" (11 January 1996): 8–9.

BIBLIOGRAPHY

It is my observation that bibliographies and reading lists are largely fruitless undertakings, since after having admired their length and the author's picky-minded attention to conventional format (executed with enormous effort), I, the reader, simply close the book, ignoring all suggestions in favor of personally browsing in a bookstore—new or second-hand. Nonetheless, here presented are some of my personal favorites, offered knowing that the list leaves out more than it provides and suggesting that you go hunting for yourself. There are too many historical giants to try to cull a list to any manageable size.

Armstrong, Karen. *A History of God*. New York: Knopf, 1993.

Armstrong, Karen. *Muhammad: A Biography of the Prophet*. San Francisco: HarperSanFrancisco, 1992.

Armstrong, Karen. *Visions of God: Four Medieval Mystics and Their Writings*. New York: Bantam Books, 1994.

Augustine of Hippo, Saint. *Confessions*. Translated by R. S. Pine-Coffin. New York: Penguin Books, 1961; 1983.

Baba, Meher. *God Speaks: The Theme of Creation and Its Purpose*. New York: Dodd, Mead, 1955.

Bancroft, Anne. *Modern Mystics and Sages*. New York: Granada Publishing, 1978.

Benson, Herbert, with Marg Stark. *Timeless Healing: The*

Power and Biology of Belief. New York: Simon & Schuster/Fireside, 1997.

Bridges, Hal. *American Mysticism: From William James to Zen*. New York: Harper & Row, 1970.

Bucke, Richard Maurice. *Cosmic Consciousness*. [1901] New York: Dutton, 1969.

Cohen, J. M., and J. F. Phipps. *The Common Experience*. Los Angeles: Tarcher, 1979.

Dalai Lama XIV. *The Good Heart: A Buddhist Perspective on the Teachings of Jesus*. Boston: Wisdom Publications, 1996.

David-Neel, Alexandra. *Magic and Mystery in Tibet*. [1933] New York: Dover, 1971.

Edelman, Marian Wright. *The Measure of Our Success: A Letter to My Children and Yours*. Boston: Beacon, 1992.

Field, Reshad. *The Last Barrier*. New York: Harper & Row, 1976.

Flinders, Carol Lee. *Enduring Grace: Living Portraits of Seven Women Mystics*. San Francisco: HarperSanFrancisco, 1993.

Flinders, Carol Lee, ed. *A Little Book of Women Mystics*. San Francisco: HarperSanFrancisco, 1995.

Foster, Genevieve W. *The World Was Flooded with Light: Mystical Experience Remembered*. Pittsburgh: University of Pittsburgh Press, 1985.

Futehally, Shama, trans. *In the Dark of the Heart: The Songs of Meera*. New York: HarperCollins, 1994.

Graham, Barbara. "The Future of Love," *Utne Reader* (November–December 1996), 47.

Greeley, Andrew M. *The Sociology of the Paranormal: A Reconnaissance*. Sage Research Papers in the Social Sciences, vol. 3, series no. 90-023. Studies in Religion and Ethnicity, sponsored by Center for the Study of American Pluralism—National Opinion Research Center. Beverly Hills and London, 1975.

Greeley, Andrew, and William C. McCready. "Are We a Nation of Mystics?" *The New York Times Magazine* (26 January 1975): 6, 12, 15, 16, 18, 20, 21, 22, 24, 25.

Hafiz. *The Subject Tonight Is Love: 60 Wild and Sweet Poems of Hafiz.* Edited by Daniel Landinsky. North Myrtle Beach, S.C.: Pumpkin House Press, 1996.

Hampl, Patricia, ed. *Burning Bright: An Anthology of Sacred Poetry.* New York: Ballantine Books, 1995.

Hays, Edward. *In Pursuit of the Great White Rabbit: Reflections on a Practical Spirituality.* Leavenworth, Kans.: Forest of Peace, 1990.

Heschel, Abraham Joshua. *Man Is Not Alone: A Philosophy of Religion.* New York: Farrar, Straus & Young, 1951.

Hildegard of Bingen, Saint. *Hildegard of Bingen: Mystical Writings.* Edited by Fiona Bowie and Oliver Davies. New York: Crossroad, 1990.

Hopkinson, Tom, and Dorothy Hopkinson. *Much Silence: Meher Baba, His Life and Work.* London: Gallancy, 1974.

Houston, Jean. *A Mythic Life: Learning to Live Our Greater Story.* San Francisco: HarperSanFrancisco, 1996.

Hsu-yun. *Empty Cloud: The Autobiography of the Chinese Zen Master Xu-Yun.* Translated by Charles Luk. Revised and edited by Richard Hunn. Longmead, Shaftesbury, Dorset: Element Books, 1988.

Huxley, Aldous. *The Doors of Perception.* New York: Harper & Row, 1954.

Huxley, Aldous. *Huxley and God: Essays.* Edited by Jacqueline Hazard Bridgeman. San Francisco: HarperSanFrancisco, 1992.

Jalel al-Din Rumi, Maulana. *The Essential Rumi.* Translated by Coleman Barks. San Francisco: HarperSanFrancisco, 1995.

James, William. *The Varieties of Religious Experience: A Study in Human Nature.* [1902] New York: Penguin Books, 1982.

John of the Cross, Saint. *The Collected Works of St. John of the Cross.* rev ed. Translated by Kieran Kavanaugh and Otilio Rodriguez. Washington, D.C.: ICS Publications, 1991.

John of the Cross, Saint. *Dark Night of the Soul.* Translated and edited by E. Allison Peers. Garden City, N.Y.: Doubleday Image, 1959.

John of the Cross, Saint. *The Poems of St. John of the Cross.* English versions revised and rewritten by John Frederick Nims. New York: Grove Press, 1959; rev. 1968.

Kabbani, Shaykh Muhammad Hisham. *The Naqshbandi Sufi Way: History and Guidebook of the Saints of the Golden Chain.* Chicago: Kazi Publications, 1995.

Kabir. *The Kabir Book: Forty-four of the Ecstatic Poems of Kabir: Versions by Robert Bly.* Boston: Beacon Press, 1977.

King, Godfre Ray. *The Magic Presence.* [1935] Schaumburg, Ill.: St. Germain, 1963.

Koestler, Arthur. *The Invisible Writing.* New York: Macmillan, 1954.

Lao-tzu. *Tao Te Ching.* Translated by Gia-fu Feng and Jane English. New York: Knopf, 1972.

McLuhan, T. C. *Cathedrals of the Spirit: The Message of Sacred Places.* New York: HarperPerennial, 1996.

Mayne, Michael. *This Sunrise of Wonder: Letters for the Journey.* London: Fount, 1995.

Meera, Mother. *Answers.* Ithaca, N.Y.: Meeramma, 1991.

Merton, Thomas. *The Asian Journal of Thomas Merton*. New York: New Directions, 1973.

Merton, Thomas. *Mystics and Zen Masters*. New York: Farrar, Strauss & Giroux, 1967.

Merton, Thomas. *New Seeds of Contemplation*. New York: New Directions, 1961.

Merton, Thomas. *The Seven Storey Mountain*. New York: Harcourt, Brace, 1948; Signet Books, 1952.

Mitchell, Stephen, ed. *The Enlightened Heart: An Anthology of Sacred Poetry*. New York: HarperCollins, 1989.

Nhat Hanh, Thich. *Peace Is Every Step*. New York: Bantam Books, 1991; 1992.

Porete, Marguerite. *A Mirror for Simple Souls: The Mystical Work of Marguerite Porete*. Translated and edited by Charles Crawford. New York: Crossroad, 1990.

Prabhavananda, Swami, and Christopher Isherwood, trans. *The Song of God: Bhagavad-Gita*. [1954] New York: New American Library, 1972.

Puri, Lekh Raj. *Mysticism: The Spiritual Path*. vol. 2. India: Sondhi, 1964.

Renard, Hélène. *Des Prodiges et des Hommes*. France: Lebaud, 1989.

Rilke, Rainer Maria. *Poems from the Book of Hours: "Das Stunbeuch."* Translated by Babette Deutsche. Norfolk, Conn.: New Directions, 1941.

Rinpoche, Sogyal. *The Tibetan Book of Living and Dying*. San Francisco: HarperSanFrancisco, 1992.

Roy, Dilip Kumar, and Indira Devi. *Pilgrims of the Stars: Autobiography of Two Yogis*. Porthill, Idaho: Timeless Books, 1985.

St. Albans, Suzanne Marie Adele Beauclerk, Duchess of. *Magic of a Mystic: Stories of Padre Pio*. New York: Potter, 1983.

Scholem, Gershom G. *Major Trends in Jewish Mysticism.* New York: Schocken, 1946.

Seung San. *Dropping Ashes on the Buddha: The Teachings of Zen Master Seung San.* Compiled and edited by Stephen Mitchell. New York: Grove, 1976.

Shah, Idries. *Tales of the Dervishes: Teaching-Stories of the Sufi Masters Over the Past Thousand Years.* New York: Viking Penguin, 1993.

Spong, John Shelby. *Resurrection: Myth or Reality.* San Francisco: HarperSanFrancisco, 1994.

Staal, Frits. *Exploring Mysticism: A Methodological Essay.* Berkley: University of California Press, 1975.

Stace, W. T. *Mysticism and Philosophy.* Los Angeles: Tarcher, 1960.

Suzuki, D. T. *An Introduction to Zen Buddhism.* New York: Grove Press, 1964.

Suzuki, Shunryu. *Zen Mind, Beginner's Mind.* New York: Weatherhill, 1970.

Teresa of Avila, Saint. *The Life of Teresa of Jesus: The Autobiography of St. Teresa of Avila.* Translated and edited by E. Allison Peers. [1944] Garden City, N.Y.: Doubleday Image Books, 1960.

Underhill, Evelyn. *Mysticism: The Preeminent Study in the Nature and Development of Consciousness.* [1911] New York: Doubleday Image Books, 1990.

Wilson, Bill. *Alcoholics Anonymous.* 3rd ed. New York: Alcoholics Anonymous World Services, 1976.

Yogananda, Paramahansa. *Autobiography of a Yogi.* [1946] Los Angeles: Self Realization Fellowship, 1981.

SUGGESTED READING

Attar, Farid ad-Din. *The Conference of the Birds*. Boulder, Colo.: Shambala, 1971.

Bacovcin, Helen. *The Way of the Pilgrim and The Pilgrim Continues His Way*. Garden City, N.Y.: Doubleday Image Books, 1978.

Bloom, Anthony. *Beginning to Pray*. New York: Paulist Press, 1970.

Burtt, E. A., ed. *The Teachings of the Compassionate Buddha*. New York: New American Library, 1955; 1963.

Catherine of Siena, Saint. *Letters of Saint Catherine of Siena*. Translated and edited by Vida D. Scudder. New York: Dutton, 1911.

Foster, Richard J. *Prayer: Finding the Heart's True Home*. San Francisco, Calif.: HarperCollins, 1992.

Fox, Emmet. *The Sermon on the Mount*. New York: Harper & Row, 1934; 1938.

Lewis, C. S. *Letters to Malcolm: Chiefly on Prayer*. New York: Harcourt, Brace & World, 1964.

Merton, Thomas. *The Wisdom of the Desert*. New York: New Directions, 1970.

Nasrudin, Mulla. *The Pleasantries of the Incredible*. New York: Viking Penguin, 1993.

Needleman, Jacob. *Lost Christianity*. New York: Doubleday, 1980; Bantam, 1982.

Nhat Hanh, Thich. *Cultivating the Mind of Love: The Practice of Looking Deeply in the Mahayana Buddhist Tradition*. Berkeley, Calif.: Parallax Press, 1996.

Nhat Hanh, Thich. *Touching Peace: Practicing the Art of Mindful Living*. Berkeley, Calif.: Parallax Press, 1992.

Pearce, Joseph Chilton. *The Crack in the Cosmic Egg: Challenging Constructs of Mind and Reality*. New York: Julian Press, 1971; 1988.

Sanford, John A. *The Kingdom Within: The Inner Meaning of Jesus' Sayings*. rev. ed. San Francisco: Harper & Row, 1987.

Shah, Idries. *Reflections*. New York: Penguin, 1972.

Teresa of Avila, Saint. *The Collected Works of St. Theresa of Avila,* translated by Kieran Kavanaugh, o.c.d., and Otilio Rodriguez, o.c.d. Institute of Carmelite Studies, Washington, D.C., 1985. Consisting of: –v. 1 *The Book of Her Life. Spiritual Testimonies,* and *Soliloquies;* –v. 2. *The Way of Perfection, Meditations on the Song of Songs. The Interior Castle.* –v. 3. *The Book of Her Foundations. Minor Works and Poetry*

Teresa, Mother. *A Simple Path*. New York: Ballantine Books, 1995.

Thomas à Kempis. *The Imitation of Christ*. Edited by Paul Simpson McElroy. New York: Peter Pauper Press, 1965.

Watts, Alan. *The Book on the Taboo Against Knowing Who You Are*. [1966] New York: Vintage, 1972.

INDEX

© Michael Davis

ABOUT THE AUTHOR

SOPHY BURNHAM, mother of two grown daughters, is the award-winning author of ten books, including two *New York Times* bestsellers—*The Art Crowd* and *A Book of Angels*. She is best known for her speaking and writing on angels and the spiritual dimension. She has written prize-winning works for both children and adults—novels, plays, films, articles, essays, and investigative journalism. Her work has been translated into twenty languages.